OFF THE BEATEN PATH® SERIES

ELEVENTH EDITION

ALABAMA

OFF THE BEATEN PATH®

DISCOVER YOUR FUN

JACKIE SHECKLER FINCH

Globe
Pequot
Guilford, Connecticut

All the information in this guidebook is subject to change. We recommend that you call ahead to obtain current information before traveling.

Globe Pequot

An imprint of The Rowman & Littlefield Publishing Group, Inc.
4501 Forbes Blvd., Ste. 200
Lanham, MD 20706
www.rowman.com

Distributed by NATIONAL BOOK NETWORK

British Library Cataloguing in Publication Information available

Library of Congress Cataloging-in-Publication Data available

ISBN 978-1-4930-4269-2 (paperback)
ISBN 978-1-4930-4270-8 (e-book)

∞™ The paper used in this publication meets the minimum requirements of American National Standard for Information Sciences—Permanence of Paper for Printed Library Materials, ANSI/NISO Z39.48-1992

Printed in the United States of America

My gratitude to my family for their encouragement:
Kelly Rose; Sean Rose; Stefanie, Will,
Trey, and Arianna Scott; and Logan Peters.
And a special remembrance to my husband, Bill Finch,
who taught me how to value every day on this Earth.

—Jackie Sheckler Finch

Florence

Huntsville

NORTHWEST
ALABAMA

NORTHEAST
ALABAMA

Birmingham

CENTRAL ALABAMA

★ Montgomery

SOUTHWEST
ALABAMA

SOUTHEAST
ALABAMA

Mobile

Contents

Acknowledgments

As I crisscrossed Alabama while researching this book, many people offered suggestions and provided information. I want to thank everyone who helped me with the birthing of the previous editions as well as this one. My appreciation to Verna Gates, Dawn Hathcock, Michael Hicks, Andrea Horton, Meg Lewis, and the excellent team of public relations officials who promote the awesome aspects of Alabama, as well as to the residents, volunteers, and business owners who took the time to share what makes Alabama special. Gratitude to Sarah Parke, Amy Lyons, and the friendly and professional staff at Globe Pequot Press for allowing me the pleasure of revising this book.

Introduction

As a vacation destination, Alabama surprises most first-time visitors. With its varied and splendid geography, moderate climate, and Southern hospitality, the state makes an ideal year-round getaway. From its craggy Appalachian bluffs to sugar-sand beaches on the Gulf of Mexico, Alabama's wealth of natural beauty offers a happy (and uncrowded) vacation choice for everyone.

Alabama's link with sports is legend—think Bear Bryant, Joe Namath, Bo Jackson, Pat Sullivan, John Hannah, Hank Aaron, Joe Louis, Willie Mays, Jesse Owens, LeRoy "Satchel" Paige, Bobby Allison—and the list goes on. Although racing fans throng Talladega's speedway and Birmingham's Alabama Sports Hall of Fame represents diversity, visitors soon discover that football reigns supreme here. The first Alabama–Auburn clash dates to February 22, 1893, and loyalty lines continue to divide families, friends, and lovers. The stirring words "Roll Tide" and "War Eagle" enter the typical childhood vocabulary early on.

Designed by Robert Trent Jones, the largest golf course construction project ever attempted winds its way through Alabama. The world-famous golf architect, who died in 2000, called this project the greatest achievement of his career; the *New York Times* calls it "some of the best public golf on Earth." Unless you agree with Mark Twain that golf is a good walk ruined, you can't pass up the **Robert Trent Jones Golf Trail**, which tests the skills of all golfers from scratch handicappers to hopeless duffers. Beginning in the mountains and lakes of the Appalachian foothills and continuing southward to the white sands and wetlands of the Gulf Coast, this group of PGA tour–quality courses, ranging from 36 to 54 holes each, provides superb golfing and splendid scenery.

The Trail continues to shine, and the two top public golf courses in the US await you here, according to *Golf World* readers, who recently ranked Opelika's Grand National site #1 and Prattville's Capitol Hill #2. Also, out of roughly 13,500 public-access courses, Mobile earned #32. "With rankings like this one and being named the top golf value destination in the country by *Golf Digest*," said Dr. David Bronner, "we hope to introduce even more people to golf in Alabama." Conceived by Bronner and funded by the Retirement Systems of Alabama (RSA), the Trail has transformed Alabama into a golfing mecca. So come on down and play.

To learn more about all 11 locations on the RTJ Golf Trail or to settle into one of the nearby upscale resorts along the way, call (800) 949-4444 or visit rtjgolf.com or pchresorts.com.

And while you're at it, check out the **RTJ Spa Trail**, part of the Robert Trent Jones Golf Trail's Resort Collection at Four-Diamond-rated properties in

Point Clear, Mobile, Montgomery, Birmingham, and Florence. After all, who doesn't need a little pampering, particularly in these trying times?

Speaking of trails, anglers will want to follow their bliss on the **Alabama Bass Trail**. Developed by the state Department of Conservation and Natural Resources and the first of its kind in the country, this trail consists of 13 premier bass fishing lakes across the state with plenty of outstanding bass tournaments on the agenda. And that's not all. *Audubon* magazine named the **Alabama Coastal Birding Trail**, which stretches through Baldwin and Mobile Counties, one of the country's best viewing sites. Birders will find directional and interpretive signs all along the way.

alabamatrivia

Alabama's Robert Trent Jones Golf Trail is the world's largest golf-course construction project.

Stars still fall on Alabama, and visitors can dip into a rich musical heritage throughout the state. Depending on your own particular penchant, you may catch a classical music concert at the Birmingham Civic Center or a swinging jazz session during Florence's yearly tribute in July to the "Father of the Blues," W. C. Handy. The **Alabama Music Hall of Fame**. near Tuscumbia, features memorabilia of Nat King Cole, Hank Williams, Sonny James, Lionel Richie, the Commodores, Emmylou Harris, Dinah Washington, the Temptations, and many other musicians with Alabama connections.

This guide book spotlights some of the state's special places—not only major sites such as the United States Space & Rocket Center in Huntsville but also small towns frozen in time and tucked-away treasures occasionally overlooked by the natives. In the state's northern section, Huntsville makes a handy launching pad from which travelers can easily loop both east and west to take in north Alabama's unique attractions. Heading south, the Birmingham area serves as a convenient base from which to branch out into the state's central section. From there you can sweep farther south to Montgomery to see the state capital area and southeastern section, which includes the historic Chattahoochee Trace. This account concludes with the beaches of Gulf Shores and one of the state's most beautiful cities, Mobile. In his book *A Walk across America*, Peter Jenkins describes being captivated by Mobile, calling it a fantasy city. "Even more than by the psychedelic azaleas," he said, "I was moved by the great-grandfather live-oak trees."

Alabama's surprises start as soon as you cross the border, and the following sneak preview will give you an idea of what to expect. Huntsville, while playing a strategic role in the nation's space program, also preserves its past at

EarlyWorks and at *Alabama Constitution Village*, a living-history museum. Delegates drafted Alabama's first constitution here in 1819, and when you enter the village, you may smell bread baking and see aproned guides dipping beeswax candles or carding cotton—quite a contrast to the future-focused Space & Rocket Center. By the way, if you've harbored a secret yen to taste the astronaut's life but always thought Space Camp was just for kids, you're in for another surprise: The Space & Rocket Center offers programs for all who dare to delve into space technology, from fourth graders to grandparents. You might even participate in a simulated space-shuttle mission. If you're not ready for such a challenge, you can still stop by the gift shop and sample some freeze-dried astronaut ice cream.

Heading east gets you to Scottsboro, home of the "First Monday" market, one of the South's oldest and largest "trade days." Also known for its many caves, this area attracts spelunkers from around the world. Russell Cave, located at Jackson County's northeastern tip, could be called Alabama's first welcome center. Some 9,000 years ago bands of Native Americans began occupying the large cave; archaeologists, using carbon dating, have determined it to be the oldest known site of human occupancy in the southeastern US.

At DeSoto State Park, also in the northeast region, visitors can view Little River Canyon National Preserve, the largest and one of the deepest gorges east of the Mississippi River. Near the charming mountain hamlet of Mentone, Cloudmont Resort features a dude ranch and ski slopes (albeit with Mother Nature getting some assistance from snow machines).

Lakes Guntersville, Wheeler, and Wilson make northern Alabama a haven for water sports enthusiasts. Lake Guntersville State Park hosts *Eagle Awareness Weekends* in January through the second weekend in February, a good time of the year to spot bald eagles. Many visitors report being surprised by Alabama's state parks, which offer a sampling of some of the state's most spectacular vistas, such as the awe-inspiring *Cathedral Caverns*, plus a host of recreation options—and at bargain prices.

At Cullman, visitors can take a Lilliputian world tour at Ave Maria Grotto, a unique garden filled with more than 125 miniature reproductions of famous buildings. The reproductions were made by a gifted Benedictine monk named Brother Joseph Zoettl. And nearby Hanceville has become a mecca for pilgrims who want to visit the Shrine of the Most Blessed Sacrament of Our Lady of the Angels Monastery.

In Blount County you can see three of the state's covered bridges. Master-and-slave team John Godwin and Horace King built a number of Alabama's early bridges. After gaining his freedom, King joined Godwin as a business partner, later erecting a monument in "lasting remembrance of the love and gratitude he felt for his lost friend and former master." The monument can be seen at a Phenix City cemetery.

Each summer visitors can witness the reenactment of a miracle in northwest Alabama at Ivy Green, home of America's courageous **Helen Keller**.

As Alabama's major metropolis, Birmingham's paths are well trampled. Still, the Magic City offers some not-to-be-missed treats, such as the historic Five Points South area with its boutiques and outdoor eateries and the 740-acre **Barber Motorsports Park** near Irondale. On the somber side, the Birmingham Civil Rights Institute and nearby complex re-creates a journey through the darkness of segregation.

Farther south you'll find Montgomery, a backdrop for sweeping drama since Jefferson Davis telegraphed his "Fire on Fort Sumter" order from here and the Civil War proceeded to rip the country apart. Less than a century later, the Civil Rights Movement gained momentum in this town, paving the way for overdue national reform. The interpretative Rosa Parks Library and Museum offers an in-depth look at the Montgomery bus boycott and pays tribute to the "Mother of the Civil Rights Movement." Also located here, the **Alabama Shakespeare Festival** provides top dramatic entertainment.

Don't miss Selma, a quintessential Southern city, but one that preserves its drama-filled past—from Civil War to civil rights. Spring Pilgrimage events include home tours, a reenactment of the Battle of Selma, and a grand ball on Sturdivant Hall's lovely lawn. Selma also stages an annual Tale Tellin' Festival honoring Alabama's first lady of folk legends and ghost stories, Kathryn Tucker Windham, who died in June 2011.

Traveling down to Monroeville, the Literary Capital of Alabama, you'll see the courthouse and surrounding square where **Truman Capote** and **Harper Lee**, author of *To Kill a Mockingbird*, roamed as childhood friends.

Still farther south, the Gulf Shores and Orange Beach area, with glistening white beaches, sea oats, and sand dunes, lures many visitors. The coastal area also offers historic forts, grand mansions, a multi-rooted (French, British, and Spanish) heritage, and superb cuisine.

On Mobile Bay's eastern shore, a strange spectacle known as "Jubilee" sometimes surprises visitors. Spurred by unknown forces, shrimp, flounder, crab, and other marine creatures suddenly crowd the shoreline, usually several times a summer. When the cry of "Jubilee!" rings along the beach, people rush to the water's edge to fill containers with fresh seafood.

Alabama's colorful celebrations run the gamut from Mobile's Mardi Gras (which preceded New Orleans's extravaganza) and Gulf Shores' National

Shrimp Festival to Opp's Rattlesnake Rodeo, Dothan's National Peanut Festival, and Decatur's hot-air balloon gala called the "Alabama Jubilee."

When making travel plans, call ahead because dates, rates, and hours of operation change from time to time. Unless otherwise stated in this guide, all museums and attractions with admission prices of $5 or less per adult are labeled modest. A restaurant meal (entree without beverage) classified as economical costs less than $10; moderate prices range between $10 and $25; and entrees $25 and above are designated expensive. As for accommodations, those that cost less than $85 per day are described as standard; an overnight price between $85 and $150 is called moderate; and lodging costing more than $150 is designated deluxe.

Director of tourism Lee Sentell and the Alabama Bureau of Tourism & Travel encouraged everyone to eat their way around the state by creating the coveted brochure *100 Dishes to Eat in Alabama before You Die*. "This is the largest brochure we have ever printed and it's full of exciting places to discover and experience," Sentell said.

General Alabama Trivia

In 1540 Hernando de Soto traveled through much of what is now Alabama.

On December 14, 1819, Alabama became the 22nd state in the Union.

Alabama seceded from the Union on January 11, 1861, and rejoined on June 25, 1868.

Montgomery has served as the state capital since 1846. Former capitals included St. Stephens, Huntsville, Cahaba, and Tuscaloosa.

In 1959 the camellia became Alabama's state flower, replacing the goldenrod, which held that honor from 1927.

The tarpon was designated as Alabama's official saltwater fish in 1955.

Red iron ore, scientifically known as hematite, is the state mineral.

Distinguished educator and humanitarian Julia Tutwiler wrote the words for "Alabama," the state song.

Alabama comprises 67 counties.

Mobile's RSA Battle House Tower is the state's tallest structure.

Alabama has fifty-three miles of coastline and 240 species of commercially harvested freshwater fish, marine fish, and shellfish.

Alabama is a place where the waitresses (not servers, please) may call you darlin'. But don't take it personally—they call everybody that. As for food, many of us agree with a quote by Linda Vice, who represents Alabama's Black Belt in the state's southwestern section: "We can cook like Grandma did, or we can cook fancy. We draw from a number of food traditions. Food is one of our religions, and we worship at every shrine we pass!"

For travel information, maps, and brochures, stop by one of the eight Alabama Welcome Centers; call (334) 242-4169 or (800) 252-2262 or visit Alabama.travel. To preview the state parks, log onto alapark.com. You can make reservations at any Alabama state park by dialing (800) 252-7275. So pack your bags, head for the unforgettable Heart of Dixie, anticipate some surprises, and watch out for falling stars.

Fast Facts about Alabama
Climate Overview

Alabama's climate falls in the temperate range, becoming mostly subtropical near the Gulf Coast. Spring's first flowers appear early, often in February. By April, average statewide temperatures reach the 60s. Summer days often fall in the hot and humid category. Fall brings changing foliage and refreshing cooler weather. Snow is such a rarity in most parts of the state that when the weather person predicts it, everyone gets excited and makes a mad dash to the grocery stores for bread and milk—even if they're curbing their carbs and are lactose intolerant.

Famous Alabamians

Some famous Alabamians include Condoleezza Rice, Helen Keller, Harper Lee, Winston Groom, Fannie Flagg, Lionel Richie, Channing Tatum, Hank Williams Sr. and Jr., Rosa Parks, Kenny Stabler, Hank Aaron, Willie Mays, Jim Nabors, Joe Louis, Jesse Owens, Lionel Hampton, Emmy Lou Harris, and Octavia Spencer.

Newspapers

The state's major newspapers include the *Huntsville Times*, the *Birmingham News*, the *Montgomery Advertiser*, and the *Mobile Press Register*. Since printed papers started in the state around 1806, according to Bill Keller, former executive director of the Alabama Press Association, Alabamians have demonstrated a long-standing appreciation for newspapers. Every county in Alabama produces a newspaper.

Northeast Alabama

Space Capital

Traveling through this area of Alabama, with its wooded glens, rugged mountain vistas, and sparkling lakes, is almost like moving through a calendar of splendid landscapes. Keep your camera handy because you'll discover some spectacular scenery.

Entering at the state's northern border, you'll drive through the rolling Tennessee Valley to reach **Huntsville**, a handy hub whether you're heading east or west to explore north Alabama's numerous attractions.

The birthplace of America's space program, Huntsville also served as an early capital of Alabama and later grew into a cotton mill town. After Dr. Wernher von Braun and his crew of German scientists arrived in the 1950s to pioneer the space program at Redstone Arsenal, Huntsville traded its title as World Watercress Capital for World Space Capital. The decade from 1950 to 1960 saw the population in Rocket City, USA, mushroom from 15,000 to 72,000. Even today, ongoing road construction cannot keep pace with the burgeoning population and traffic.

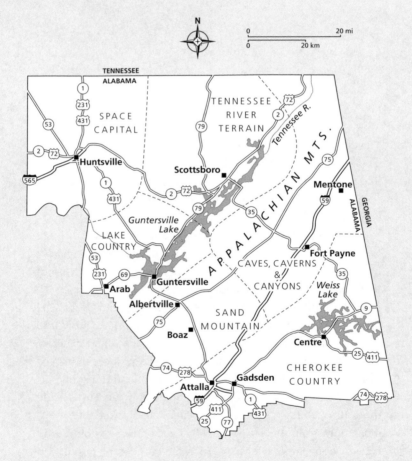

As for the green scene, Huntsvillians recognize the importance of protecting local and global environments and preserving natural resources. In *The Green Guides* in 2013, Huntsville was listed among The Top 10 Green Cities in the U.S. for environmental excellence.

If you want to pretend you're in Venice, you can take a gondola ride at **Bridge Street Centre** in the heart of Huntsville's Cummings Research Park. Or enjoy a brisk walk or leisurely stroll through this European-style plaza that features upscale shops, restaurants, and lodging. Only a stone's throw away (depending on how far you can hurl) from the city's famed Space & Rocket Center, the complex features entertainment from multiple movies and a full-size carousel to a 10-acre lake with pedal boats and gondolas. Pavement performers entertain on evenings and weekends. Visit bridgestreethuntsville.com.

Only two miles from Bridge Street Town Centre is the lovely **Huntsville Botanical Garden** (256-830-4447; hsvbg.org), home of the nation's largest open-air butterfly house. Stroll through the aquatic garden, nature trails, many specialty gardens, children's garden, and plant collections. With a motto of "There's Always Something Growing On at Huntsville Botanical Garden," the 112-acre attraction offers five festivals each year—Beaks & Barks, Huntsville Blooms, Summer Butterfly House, Fall Scarecrow Trail, and Holiday Galaxy of Lights.

A good place to start a local tour is the **Huntsville Depot & Museum** (256-564-8100) at 320 Church Street. Take time to tour the authentically restored depot, a big yellow building where a robotic telegrapher, stationmaster, and engineer welcome visitors and describe railroad life in 1912. During the Civil War the depot served as a prison, and upstairs you'll see some interesting

Watercress Capital of the World

Huntsville acquired the title "Watercress Capital of the World" because in earlier days it produced and shipped a large volume of watercress throughout the eastern half of the country. A member of the mustard family, watercress thrives in limestone spring water and once grew prolifically in the Tennessee Valley's many limestone springs.

Huntsville's old **Russell Erskine Hotel** was noted for its watercress salad, and several local cookbooks feature this specialty, sometimes known simply as "cress." The *Huntsville Heritage Cookbook* contains a section devoted to watercress including the Frozen Cheese and Cress Salad, a tasty recipe, once served at a White House state banquet. Long a local favorite, this book is again in print, thanks to the Huntsville Junior League. Look for it at gift shops and bookstores throughout Huntsville, and while browsing, pick up a copy of the Junior League's award-winning *Sweet Home Alabama*, a handsome volume featuring "Food for Family and Friends from the Heart of the South."

graffiti such as a rather unflattering drawing of Union officer Major Strout and an inscription that reads happy new years to all in the year of our lord 1864. The depot's hours are 10 a.m. to 3 p.m. Wed through Sat. Admission: $10 per person. Visit earlyworks.com/Huntsville-depot-museum.

Huntsville Depot & Museum became the new home for Santa's Village in 2018 from November 19 to December 21. Previously the popular event had been at Alabama Constitution Village. Visitors can see a live reindeer, create a holiday craft, navigate the Icicle Maze, and visit Santa's Workshop.

As you drive around the area, check out the ***Von Braun Center*** (256-533-1953; vonbrauncenter.com) at 700 Monroe Street. This large multipurpose complex may well be hosting a concert, sporting event, or play you'd like to take in while in town. A major expansion set for completion in 2019 will add a 1,200-capacity Von Braun Center music venue with a new ballroom, outdoor terrace, meeting space, concourse, full-service kitchen, food and beverage venue, and extended parking facilities.

Continue your self-driving tour through Huntsville's ***Historic Twickenham District*** with more than 65 antebellum houses and churches. Architectural styles represented include federal, Greek revival, Italianate, Palladian, Gothic revival, and others. For a fine example of federal architecture, tour the ***Weeden House Museum*** (256-536-7718; weedenhousemuseum.com) at 300 Gates Avenue. Built in 1819, the home contains period antiques and features the work of Huntsville artist and poet Maria Howard Weeden, who lived here until her death in 1905. Her impressive body of work includes book illustrations, whimsical drawings, fascinating character studies, and portraits. History tours are offered from 10:30 a.m. to 11:45 a.m. Wed through Sat, with tours available at other times by appointment. Admission: adults $5; children (ages 12 and under) $3. No debit or credit cards accepted.

On the square in downtown Huntsville, stop by ***Harrison Brothers Hardware Store*** (256-536-3631 or 866-533-3631; harrisonbrothershardware. com), located at 124 South Side Square. Here you can purchase marbles by the scoop, old-fashioned stick candy, cast-iron cookware, vintage mix-and-match silverplate flatware, and other merchandise that speaks of yesteryear. The store also features regional and locally handcrafted gifts. Historic Huntsville Foundation volunteers ring up sales on a 1907 cash register. The interior, with pot-bellied stove, ceiling fans, rolling ladders, barrels, tools, and antique safe, looks much as it did in 1879 when the store opened for business a few blocks away before moving to its permanent home on the square. Hours are 9:30 a.m. to 5 p.m. Mon through Sat.

Don't miss ***Alabama Constitution Village*** (256-564-8100; earlyworks. com/alabama-constitution-village) just around the corner at 109 Gates Avenue.

BEST ATTRACTIONS IN NORTHEAST ALABAMA

Alabama Constitution Village, Huntsville

Buck's Pocket State Park, Grove Oak

Burritt on the Mountain, Huntsville

Cathedral Caverns, Grant

DeSoto State Park, Fort Payne

EarlyWorks, Huntsville

Huntsville Museum of Art, Huntsville

Lake Guntersville State Park, Guntersville

Little River Canyon National Preserve, Fort Payne

Noccalula Falls and Park, Gadsden

Sequoyah Caverns & Ellis Homestead, Valley Head

Town of Mentone

US Space & Rocket Center, Huntsville

Entering at Franklin Street and Gates Avenue takes you back to 1819, when delegates met here to draft Alabama's first constitution. Afterward, on a tour of the complex, you'll see costumed guides going about their seasonal business of preserving summer's fruits or making candles at hog-killing time.

Stop by the gift shop, with such unique items as "ugly jugs," once used as containers for harmful substances. Hours are 10 a.m. to 4 p.m. Mon through Sat year-round. Admission: adults $12; seniors and youth $10; toddlers $5.

Kids—both young and old—love traveling back in time to the nineteenth century and exploring *EarlyWorks Children's History Museum*, a hands-on history museum (256-564-8100; earlyworks.com/earlyworks-childrens-museum) at 404 Madison Street, where new adventures await around every corner. Special exhibits include an amazing 16-foot-tall tale-telling tree, giant-size musical instruments, and a 46-foot keelboat. Youngsters can dress up in vintage clothing and practice tasks that children in the "olden days" performed, and toddlers can milk a "pretend" cow and gather garden vegetables. Except for major holidays, hours run from 9 a.m. to 5 p.m. Mon through Sat. Special prices are available for combination tours of EarlyWorks with the historic Huntsville Depot and Alabama Constitution Village. Metered parking is available throughout the downtown area with handicapped parking on the Gates Avenue side. Learn more about this hands-on facility at earlyworks.com. Admission: adults $12; seniors and youth $10; toddlers (ages 1 to 3) $5.

Don't miss *Monte Sano Mountain*, which offers sweeping views of Huntsville and the surrounding Tennessee River valley. *Burritt on the Mountain*, a living-history museum (256-536-2882), at 3101 Burritt Drive, just off Monte Sano Boulevard, features 167 wooded acres with walking trails and picnicking facilities. At this living-history site, you'll find a blacksmith shop, smokehouse, church, barnyard with live animals, and some log houses depicting rural life between 1850 and 1900. An X-shaped house, built in 1937 by Dr. William Henry Burritt, serves as the park's focal point. Both a physician and gifted inventor who held 20 patents during his life, Burritt combined classical and Art Deco elements when he designed this unusual home.

Inside you'll see archaeological and restoration exhibits, clothing, toys, and displays on Huntsville's history. One room features the paintings of local artists. Special events include Spring Farm Days, International Heritage Festival, fall festivals, and Candlelight Christmas. Admission prices are slightly higher for special events. The museum is open Tues through Sat, from 10 a.m. to 4 p.m. and Sun noon to 4 p.m. Nov through Mar. Summer hours are Tues through Sat, 9 a.m. to 5 p.m. and Sun noon to 5 p.m. Admission: adults $10; seniors $9; children (ages 3–18) $8. Visit burrittonthemountain.com.

Dogwood Manor (256-859-3946) at 707 Chase Road makes a lovely base for exploring the Huntsville area. Valerie and Patrick Jones own this restored federal-style home, set on a sweeping lawn with century-old trees. The home's builder once operated a thriving nursery here and shipped his plants all over the country. Patrick, an attorney, shares history about the home and the Chase community with interested guests.

The couple reserves four charming rooms—appropriately named Dogwood, Magnolia, Azalea, and Rose—for overnight visitors and serves afternoon tea on request. The Devon Cottage offers two bedrooms, full kitchen, dining area, patio, garage, and much more. Valerie, a school counselor, prepares gourmet breakfasts, complemented by her own homemade breads and muffins. She often makes apple French toast, crumpets, and English scones. Moderate rates. Visit Dogwood Manor's website at dogwoodmanorbandb.com.

Across from Dogwood Manor's driveway stands the ***North Alabama Railroad Museum*** (256-851-6276) at 694 Chase Road. The restored green-and-yellow Chase Depot houses a waiting room, freight room, and agent office filled with exhibits. Home of the Mercury and Chase Railroad and the country's smallest union station, the facility now features a walk-through passenger train and more than 30 pieces of major railroading stock. The museum can be visited from 9 a.m. to 4 p.m. daily, and a staff member is available each Wed and Sat from 8:30 a.m. to 2 p.m. The facility offers guided tours and excursion train rides. Children enjoy watching for the concrete animals staged along the track. In addition to regular trips, a Peter Cottontail Express, Pumpkin' Pickin' Train, and Santa Trail Special are also scheduled. Call for more information on schedules, fares, and reservations, or visit the website at northalabamarailroadmuseum.com for current happenings.

A Tribute to Everybody's Favorite Aunt

For more than half a century, Eunice Merrell served what many considered the best country ham and homemade biscuits in the world. Former governor Fob James declared her biscuits "the best in Alabama," and his proclamation made them the official state biscuit.

Although Eunice (better known to her customers as "Aunt" Eunice) described her diner as "just a little greasy spoon," the fame of her homemade biscuits made the *Congressional Record* in a tribute introduced by US Senator Howell Heflin, who represented Alabama.

At **Eunice's Country Kitchen**, you often had to wait a bit for a table or share one with someone else. Some people even kept their own favorite brand of jelly or preserves in Eunice's refrigerator, retrieving it when the hot biscuits arrived, but most folks dipped into the honey or Sand Mountain sorghum on every table.

In this small cafe that did a booming business with no advertising, it was customary to warm up your neighbors' coffee if you got up to pour yourself a refill. In fact, when prospective candidates for office visited (this was a popular stop on political campaigns), Aunt Eunice expected them to follow protocol and wait on her customers; otherwise, they did not deserve the office to which they aspired—and she told them so.

Look for an authentically replicated Eunice's Country Kitchen at the Historic Huntsville Depot. You'll see the cafe's famous "Liars' Table," with its suspended wooden sign reserving it for politicians and preachers. (During a meal, Eunice sometimes presented customers with an official "Liar's License," permitting them to prevaricate "at any time or place without notice.") Other memorabilia include favorite quotes and an extensive collection of autographed photos from governors, congressmen, actors, astronauts, sports figures, and even a president.

Aunt Eunice, we miss you.

For a lovely view and peaceful visit, head to **Burritt on the Mountain** at 3101 Burritt Drive Southeast. Overlooking the city of Huntsville, Burritt is situated on 167 acres atop Round Top Mountain. Burritt showcases area ecology and the lives of 1800s farmers. Interpreters in period dress give tours, answer questions, and demonstrate old-time farm life. Donated by Dr. William Henry Burritt, the site and his 1938 mansion tell the story of Dr. Burritt's love of goat's milk and homeopathic medicine. The mansion is considered one of Huntsville's most unique and eccentric homes. Burritt's nature trails are popular with geocachers who travel from around the

alabamatrivia

During its territorial and statehood days, Alabama had five capitals.

world to explore Round Top Mountain and find interesting caches. Burritt on the Mountain is open Tues through Sat. 9 a.m. to 5 p.m.; Sun, noon to 5 p.m. Admission is $10 for adults, $9 for seniors, $8 for students and children (ages 3 and up). For more information, call (256) 536-2882 or visit burrittonthemountain.com.

Tennessee River Terrain

From Huntsville take US 72 east to **Scottsboro**, home of **First Monday**, one of the South's oldest and largest "trade days." This outdoor market might feature anything from cast-iron skillets, church pews, and butter churns to gingham-checked sunbonnets and pocketknives—all displayed around the Jackson County Courthouse Square. Lasting from morning till dark, the event dates to the mid-1800s, when people met at the courthouse square on the day Circuit Court opened to visit as well as to trade horses, mules, and other livestock. The merry mix of folks who still come to browse, banter, and barter carry on a Southern tradition, and many have honed their trading techniques to a high level of skill. Although this event takes place on the first Monday of every month (plus the Saturday and Sunday preceding it), the Fourth of July and Labor Day weekends typically prove most popular.

If you miss Scottsboro's First Monday, you can console yourself by dipping into a chocolate milk shake, ice-cream soda, or banana split at **Payne's** (256-574-2140), located at 101 East Laurel on the town square's north side. This eatery occupies the site of a former drugstore dating from 1869. The interior, complete with old-fashioned soda fountain, features a black-and-white color scheme with red accents. You can perch on a bar stool, order a fountain Coke that's mixed on the spot and served in a traditional Coca-Cola glass, and munch on a hot dog with red slaw straight from the original drugstore menu. Other options include Payne's popular chicken salad and a variety of sandwiches. Hours are 10 a.m. to 4 p.m. Mon through Wed; 10 a.m. to 6 p.m. Thurs through Sat. To learn about the area's history, visit the **Scottsboro-Jackson Heritage Center** (256-259-2122; sjhc.us), located at 208 South Houston Street. This neoclassical–style structure, built in 1881, houses some interesting exhibits, including Native American artifacts found on land later flooded by the Tennessee Valley Authority (TVA) and rare photographic displays depicting the early days of Skyline, a unique community north of Scottsboro.

Behind the big house stands the small 1868 Jackson County Courthouse. Nearby, a pioneer village called Sage Town features a collection of authentic log structures that includes a cabin, schoolhouse, barn, and blacksmith shop, all filled with vintage items.

The museum offers a wealth of genealogical materials, says Judi Weaver, who promotes archaeological awareness in her role as director. The facility focuses on the area's history from the Paleo-Indian era through the 1930s. Special events include heritage festivals and art exhibitions. Hours are 9 a.m. to 4 p.m. Mon through Fri, or by appointment. Arranged tours are offered Tues through Fri from 9 a.m. to 11 a.m. or by appointment. Donations are welcomed.

If, after a plane trip, you've ever discovered yourself divorced from your bags and wondered about their final destination, it's entirely possible that your lost luggage wound up at ***Scottsboro's Unclaimed Baggage Center*** (256-259-1525), located at 509 West Willow Street (although your bags may have traveled instead to nearby Unclaimed Baggage in Boaz). At this unique outlet you can find such items as cameras, caviar, clothing, hammocks, hair dryers, jewelry, scuba gear, and ski equipment. The ever-changing merchandise from around the world also features baby strollers, books, briefcases, luggage, personal electronic devices, and high-tech equipment. Over one million items pass through the 40,000-square-foot store annually with about 60 percent being clothing.

"We have to stay on top of technology to know what's coming in here," says a company executive. The diverse inventory of lost, found, and unclaimed items comes from various airlines to be sorted and offered for sale at reduced rates—20 to 80 percent or more off retail prices. In this shopping mecca, which now covers more than a city block, you can enjoy a mug of brewed Starbucks coffee, freshly-baked cookies, Barry's Backcountry BBQ, or some Dippin Dots at the facility's in-house cafe, called Cups Cafe.

Business boomed here—even before Oprah spread the word on her TV show. The parking lot gets especially crowded on weekends, and car tags reveal shoppers from many states. Recent visitors also came from Ontario, Bavaria, New Zealand, South America, France, and England. Hours Mon through Fri, 9 a.m. to 6 p.m.; Sat 8 a.m. to 7 p.m. Closed on Sun. The website is unclaimedbaggage.com.

Be sure to stop by the ***Etc.*** store next to the main Unclaimed Baggage Center. With three floors of lost luggage for sale, Etc. offers surprise treasures as well, including a 4,000-square-foot area just for children and a popular Roll-Outs section where new finds arrive hourly.

After sightseeing in the Scottsboro area, you can easily head south on State Route 79 toward Guntersville to take in some Marshall County attractions, or you can continue your loop northeast to Stevenson. ***Goose Pond Colony Resort*** (256-912-0592), a peninsula surrounded by the Tennessee River, is located five miles south of Scottsboro on State Route 79 at 417 Ed Hembree Drive and offers vacation cottages, picnic facilities, camping sites, swimming pool, marina and launching ramp, two 18-hole championship golf courses, restaurant, and nature/walking trail. Popular with both geese and golfers, the golf courses are noted for their beauty and design. Opened in 1971, the George Cobb-designed Lake Course at Goose Pond Colony Resort is known for its natural layout and views of the Tennessee River from every hole. A four-star rated course, the Lake Course has been honored as one of the top places to play in Alabama and the No. 1 public golf course in North Alabama. Built in 1994, Plantation Golf Course at Goose Pond Colony Resort has undergone many renovations over the years, including new MiniVerde greens. The course features open fairways and plenty of hazards. Now a Tee It Forward golf course, the Plantation Course is a joy for golfers of any expertise. For more information visit goosepond.org.

The Docks Seafood and Steakhouse (256-574-3071), a restaurant on the grounds behind the swimming pool, offers a variety of seafood including Cajun fare with its signature shrimp and grits. The menu also features steak, Alaskan snow crab legs, and much more. You can dine on the deck with a fine view of the water. Some diners arrive by boat and tie up at the property's private pier. The restaurant is open Tues through Thurs, 5 to 9 p.m.; Fri and Sat, 5 to 10 p.m. The bar opens at 4 p.m. Prices range from moderate to expensive. The Docks is a smoke-free facility.

Before leaving this area, you may want to call the *Mountain Lakes Chamber of Commerce* (256-259-5500; mountainlakeschamberofcommerce. com) or stop by the headquarters at 407 East Willow Street to pick up brochures on various local and area attractions.

Although you might find the tiny town of Pisgah on your road map, you won't find *Gorham's Bluff* (256-451-VIEW [8439])—yet. This traditional neighborhood community (inspired by Florida's Seaside) offers travelers some stunning scenery, especially from the Overlook Pavilion, and accommodations at The Lodge. The property commands sweeping bluffside views of the Tennessee River. *Travel and Leisure* magazine chose Gorham's Bluff for inclusion in "The 30 Great US Inns," and *Southern Living* magazine voted the property "Most Romantic Spot in Alabama."

This lovely site remained undeveloped until Clara and Bill McGriff (a CPA still remembered by locals as a basketball star) started exploring their daughter Dawn's idea of creating a brand-new, arts-oriented Appalachian town—a walking town with a strong sense of community where residents stop for front-porch chats. With each new home and resident, the McGriffs watch the family vision being translated to reality.

"There is a peace that pervades this place," says Clara, a former English teacher. "We feel it, and guests feel it." The Lodge on Gorham's Bluff gives guests ample opportunity to sample this serenity and beauty.

Spacious suites, individually decorated by Clara (who also creates the beautiful floral arrangements), doublesided fireplaces, and whirlpool tubs make accommodations even more inviting. Gorham's Bluff also offers rental cottages.

Hiking, biking, birding, rocking, reflecting, reading, and listening to classical music all rank as popular pastimes here. Dawn frequently schedules special events such as concerts, the Alabama Ballet's summer residency, and storytelling.

Sometime during your stay, slip up to the observation deck for a panoramic overview. Many visitors want to linger at Gorham's Bluff forever. A quote from the guest book reads: "Forward our mail. We are not leaving."

Meals (enhanced by the property's own fresh herbs) feature traditional Appalachian food—served with flair. Dinners are served with candlelight and white tablecloths as a pianist plays old and new favorites by request on Friday and Saturday nights. By reservation only, the lodge's 30-seat dining room offers dinner for guests and the public nightly at 7 p.m. Dress is casual. Gorham's Bluff is located in a dry county. Diners are invited to bring their own beer, wine, or spirits. Servers will cork and serve the wine without a corkage fee.

From Pisgah, located on Jackson County Road 58, signs point the way to Gorham's Bluff. Call for hours and specific directions or write the staff at 101 Gorham Drive/Gorham's Bluff, Pisgah, AL 35765. Lodge rates range from moderate to deluxe. Make reservations for an evening or a weekend. You just may decide to become one of the town's new residents. For more background or a map, visit gorhamsbluff.com or e-mail reservations@gorhamsbluff.com.

To reach the ***Stevenson Railroad Depot Museum*** (256-437-3012), take US 72 and travel northwest. Near Stevenson turn at State Route 117 to go downtown. At 207 West Main Street, you'll see the museum positioned between two railroad tracks. Look carefully before crossing the tracks because the Iron Horse still whizzes by. This railroad junction played a strategic role during the Civil War, and the museum director showed me an assortment of uniform buttons, coins, and other military items brought in by a resident who had dug them up nearby. The Stevenson Depot also contains displays of Native American artifacts, period costumes, early farm tools, and railroading history information.

Each June the annual Stevenson Depot Days celebration commemorates the city's past with a variety of family activities that might include an ice-cream social, spelling bee, pioneer breakfast, wagon ride to the nearby Civil War fort, square dancing, tour of homes, parade, old-fashioned street dance, and fireworks. The museum is open year-round Mon through Fri from 8 a.m. to 3:30 p.m. Admission is free.

From Stevenson return to US 72 and continue to ***Bridgeport***, in Alabama's northeastern corner.

TOP ANNUAL EVENTS IN NORTHEAST ALABAMA

Siege of Bridgeport
Bridgeport, fourth weekend of March
(256) 437-8873 or (256) 495-1169
siegeatbridgeport.com

Art on the Lake
Guntersville, third weekend of April
(256) 571-7597
artonthelake-guntersville.com

Panoply Arts Festival
Big Spring International Park, Huntsville
Last full weekend of April
(256) 519-2787
artshuntsville.org

Rock the River
Gadsden, August
(256) 543-2787
culturalarts.com

Stevenson Depot Days
Stevenson, first full week of June
(256) 437-3012
stevensondepotdays.com

World's Longest Yard Sale
Gadsden, Alabama, to West Unity, Ohio
First Thursday through Sunday in August
(800) 327-3945 or (931) 879-9948
127sale.com

St. William's Seafood Festival
Guntersville, early September
(Labor Day weekend)
(256) 582-4245
stwilliamchurch.com

Depot Days Festival
Hartselle, September
(256) 773-4370 or (800) 294-0692
hartsellechamber.org

Harvest Festival
Boaz, early October
(256) 593-8154
boazareachamberofcommerce.com

Heritage Day
Attalla, October
(256) 538-9986
attallacity.org

Mentone Fall Colorfest
Mentone, third weekend of October
(256) 634-0704
mentonealabama.org

Christmas at the Falls
Noccalula Falls, Gadsden
Thanksgiving through December
(256) 549-4663
Noccalulafallspark.com

Galaxy of Lights
Huntsville/Madison County
Botanical Garden
Thanksgiving through New Year's Eve
(256) 830-4447
hsvbg.org

Caves, Caverns & Canyons

While exploring this region in June 1540, Spaniard Hernando de Soto and his crew chose this area for their entry into what is now Alabama. You might like to take a driving tour of Bridgeport, once called Jonesville but renamed in the 1850s for the railroad bridge that spans the Tennessee River.

Drive through Kilpatrick Row Residential District and up bluff-based Battery Hill, the site of several Civil War battles, to see the lovely historic homes of Victorian vintage with turrets, fish-scale shingles, and wraparound porches.

Russell Cave National Monument (256-495-2672), about eight miles west of Bridgeport, is located at 3729 Jackson County Road 98. Long before de Soto's visit, the large limestone cave served as an archaic hotel for Native Americans traveling through the area about 9,000 years ago.

The visitor center, in addition to housing a museum that displays weapons, tools, pottery, and other artifacts found in the cave, also offers several audio-visual presentations. After browsing through the museum, you can walk about 250 yards to the cave's big opening at the base of craggy bluffs. A ranger-led tour takes you to the cave, where you can learn about how the occupants fed, clothed, and protected themselves.

One of the century's most significant archaeological finds, the relic-filled cave remained pretty much a secret until 1953 when some members of the Tennessee Archaeological Society discovered the history-rich shelter and alerted Smithsonian Institution officials, who collaborated with the National Geographic Society to conduct extensive excavations here. The National Park Service carried out more excavations in 1962. Their joint research revealed Russell Cave to be one of the longest, most complete, and well-preserved arch-aeological records in the eastern US. Radioactive carbon from early campfires placed human arrival between 6500 and 6145 BC. Remains of animal bones, tools, weapons, and pottery all helped archaeologists fit together portions of this ancient jigsaw puzzle. The evidence implies seasonal occupation, suggesting that various groups of early people wintered in Russell Cave, then moved on to hunt and live off the land during warm-weather months. Be sure to ask a ranger about a living-history demonstration.

Except for Thanksgiving, Christmas, and New Year's Day, you can visit Russell Cave from 8 a.m. to 4:30 p.m. seven days a week, and there's no admis-sion charge. For more information, write to park personnel at 3729 County Road 98, Bridgeport, AL 35740. Explore the cave on the Internet by clicking on nps.gov/ruca.

One block off State Route 117 in the center of *Valley Head* stands *Winston Place* (256-635-6381 or 888-494-6786), a white-columned antebellum mansion owned by Leslie and Jim Bunch. Located two miles from Mentone, the property features a panoramic view of Lookout Mountain. Two levels of encircling porches with ferns, white wicker rocking chairs, and a nanny swing invite guests to relax and savor the setting. Built by William Overton Winston from Virginia, the circa-1831 home boasts a rich history. During the Civil War, Union officers occupied the home, and 30,000 soldiers camped on its grounds

Exploring Cathedral Caverns

Both Native Americans and Confederate soldiers used these caverns as a refuge, and Disney used them as a movie setting for *Tom and Huck*. Ensconced in Marshall County's northeastern corner near the town of Grant, Cathedral Caverns (256-728-8193) opened as a state park in August 2000.

You don't have to assume a crouching position to enter because the opening to these caverns measures 125 feet wide by 25 feet high. Meandering along the lighted walkway takes you past Goliath, a massive stalagmite that appears to be a floor-to-ceiling column, and what are believed to be the world's largest stalagmite forest and frozen waterfall. Besides stalagmites and stalactites, other cave features include drapery, soda straws (capillary tubes), all the common types of shields, and "just about any formation you can expect to find in a cave," said a guide.

The deeper you go into the cave's interior, the more wondrous the surroundings. Before the grand finale, you'll enter a magnificent chamber that soars to a height of 120 feet and presumably contains the largest flowstone wall in any commercial cave. Then, to top that off, the Cathedral Room features a staggering number of fanciful, stalagmitic formations. Beyond the portion open to the public lies a magnificent crystal room with stunning calcite configurations (or so they say).

Former owner Jay Gurley, who died in 1996, dedicated much of his life and fortune to making the caverns accessible so others might share their wonder. His active involvement in developing the park spanned the period from 1952 until 1974 when he sold the property. Although the caverns were open from time to time after Gurley's tenure, they closed in 1986, and the state bought the site in 1987. Inside the cave, a plaque acknowledges Gurley's contribution and serves as a monument, as does the Jay Gurley Memorial Bridge that transports visitors across Mystery River.

The river is aptly named because you can't see where the stream comes from or where it goes. Normally placid, the river can reach a depth of 40 feet during flooding conditions when the swirling water becomes chocolate-colored.

Bring a jacket (the temperature hovers at 57 to 60 degrees Fahrenheit) and jogging shoes. The 1.5-mile round-trip takes about an hour and 30 minutes. The 461-acre park includes hiking trails and camping facilities. Hours change seasonally. Call or check the schedule at alapark.com and follow the link to Cathedral Caverns. The park is open seven days a week from 9 a.m. to 5 p.m. Admission $18.50 for adults, $8 for children (ages 5 to 12 years).

before leaving to fight at Chickamauga. Leslie, who shares anecdotes about her family home and its fascinating background, has amassed a collection of books and articles detailing Winston Place's role in history.

Previously selected for inclusion in *National Geographic's Small Town Getaways*, Winston Place contains lovely period antiques and lends itself well to entertaining, just as its builder intended. Original outbuildings include servants' quarters, a slanted-wall corncrib, and a smokehouse with hand-painted murals depicting the area's history.

While immersing yourself in the home's ambience, take time to see the tucked-away media room with Jim's football awards—trophies, plaques, and photos. A former Alabama football All-American (whose mastery of the game took him to three Sugar Bowls and a Liberty Bowl), Jim played under legendary coach Bear Bryant.

The couple offers six elegant suites for guests and a full breakfast, served in the dining room. Rates range from moderate to deluxe. Visit the property at virtualcities.com/al/winstonplace.htm or search Winston Place on the Internet.

From Valley Head it's a short but scenic drive up to **Mentone**, a charming hamlet perched on the brow of Lookout Mountain at the intersection of State Route 117 and DeKalb County Route 89. Once a fashionable summer resort town that flourished through the 1890s, Mentone attracted visitors from all over the country with its cool mountain temperatures, especially appealing in the days before air-conditioning. Shops, rustic and quaint, line the single main street.

The name Mentone translates into "musical mountain spring," appropriate because the town once boasted two springs—Mineral Springs and Beauty Springs—which were reputed to possess "strengthening and curative properties." You might inquire about the dates of upcoming festivals because Mentone stages special events throughout the year.

Take a break at **The Wildflower Cafe** (256-634-0066), located at 60078 Alabama State Road 117. The eatery offers espresso, cappuccino, and other specialty coffees and a variety of food choices from soups, sandwiches, and vegetarian dishes to gourmet pizzas and a casual gourmet dinner on weekends. Lunch hours are 11 a.m. to 2 p.m., Mon through Wed; 11 a.m. to 3 p.m., Thurs through Sat. Brunch is served on Sun from 11 a.m. to 3 p.m. The Wildflower's Country Store sells a variety of items including pottery, jewelry, local artwork, jams and jellies, candles, and other items. The Country Store is open Mon through Wed from 10 a.m. to 3 p.m.; Thurs through Sat, 10 a.m. to 9 p.m.; and Sun from 10 a.m. to 4 p.m. Ask about the musical nights every Thurs through Sun. Standard to moderate.

Take time to see **St. Joseph's on the Mountain**, an unusually constructed Episcopal Church at 21145 Scenic Highway. Notice the log structure, dating to 1826, that serves as the central portion of this unusual church. North of the church on the mountain's brow, you'll find Eagle's Nest, a massive rock formation overlooking Valley Head.

After exploring the village, take a drive along the area's meandering roads. You'll see strategically placed destination markers nailed to trees and posts at junctions—these are quite helpful because the mountain terrain can prove confusing to newcomers.

Tucked away at 651 County Road 644 stands **Raven Haven** (256-634-4310), a bed-and-breakfast perched atop Lookout Mountain. Owners Eleanor and Tony Teverino welcome travelers to share their 10 acres of nature and theme rooms: Queen Anne, Nautical, Casablanca, and Prairie Room—each with private bath.

"Two things that drew us here were the beauty of the place and the people," said Eleanor, who was born in Northern Ireland. "When I came to Mentone, it was very much like going back home." The Teverinos hosted recent guests from Ireland, who compared some of Mentone's narrow, boulder-flanked curves with "driving on the roads right back at home."

Eleanor whisks warm and wonderful pastries from her oven and prepares a delightful breakfast daily, complete with homemade jams. Served buffet style, the menu always features a main dish, fruit, and vegetable to get your day off to a good healthy start. From Scotch eggs to fried green tomatoes to sticky buns, each morning's choices offer plenty of variety. A copy of *The Raven Haven Cookbook* makes a great souvenir. Afterward, you can trek through the woods and admire the wildflowers along the property's quarter-mile walking trail. Standard rates. For more information on this hideaway, pay a visit to ravenhavenbandb.info.

While driving through the area, you'll pass a number of summer camps for youngsters. In fact boyhood days spent at one such camp called Cloudmont inspired local landowner Jack Jones to pursue his unlikely dream of creating a ski resort in Alabama. After buying Cloudmont in 1947, he started developing the property as a resort and opened "the southernmost ski resort in the country" in 1970. **Cloudmont Ski and Golf Resort** (256-634-4344), about three miles from Mentone on DeKalb County Road 89, is marked by a large roadside sign on the left. To reach the information center, take a left onto County Road 614 for a half mile or so. Besides skiing (and, yes, Mother Nature does get help from snow machines), this unique family enterprise offers golfing, hiking, fishing, and swimming for guests. Jack's son Gary and his instructors have taught thousands of people to ski. Winter season at Cloudmont usually begins around mid-December and extends through March 15. It's a good idea to call ahead and check on slope conditions. Better yet, visit cloudmont.com for lodging packages, schedules, rates, and information on current activities, which include golfing, horseback riding, and more at both Cloudmont and **Shady Grove Dude Ranch**. You can write the resort at PO Box 435, Mentone, AL 35984.

While in this area, don't miss the **Sallie Howard Memorial Chapel**, on County Road 165 located 6.7 miles from

downtown Mentone and adjacent to DeSoto State Park. Dedicated in 1937, the chapel was built by Milford Howard as a tribute to his wife Sallie. A quote she reportedly wrote is written on one of the chapel's beams: "God Has All Ways Been As Good To Me As I Would Let Him Be." As he had requested, Milford Howard's ashes were placed inside the giant rock in 1938 after his death. A 20-foot-tall boulder serves as the rear wall of the small church, and stones from Little River form the pulpit. Visitors often attend worship services held here each Sunday at 10 a.m.

To more fully explore this area's magnificent terrain, consider headquartering at **DeSoto State Park** (256-845-5380 or 800-568-8840; alapark.com/desotoresort) on County Road 89 at 7104 DeSoto Parkway Northeast, about seven miles from Mentone. You'll find almost 5,000 acres of breathtaking beauty and glimpses of unspoiled nature at every turn. The gorgeous scenery around here makes it hard to concentrate on driving, but if you don't, you might bash into one of the big weathered boulders that partially jut into the road.

The park extends about forty miles along Little River, a unique waterway that runs its complete course on top of a mountain. Resort facilities include a stone lodge with large restaurant, chalets, cabins, nature trails, playgrounds, a store, and picnic areas. Miles of hiking trails, bordered by Queen Anne's lace, black-berry vines, honeysuckle, and black-eyed Susans, beckon you to explore the terrain. The park's wheelchair-accessible boardwalk attracts families and features a covered pavilion and waterfall view. Don't miss spectacular **DeSoto Falls** (about seven miles northeast of the park's information center), where water rushes over a dam to crash more than 100 feet before continuing its journey.

About ten miles away in the park's southern section, you'll find the beginning of **Little River Canyon National Preserve**, the largest and one of the deepest chasms east of the Mississippi River. Stretching about sixteen miles, the canyon drops to depths of some 700 feet. Skirting the western rim, a canyon road offers breathtaking views of rugged bluffs, waterfalls, and the rushing river.

Start your local exploration here at **Little River Canyon Center**, a great place to learn about the canyon's incredible geography as well as other area attractions. Located on State Route 35 at 4322 Little River Canyon Parkway, just a few hundred yards from the bridge across Little River Falls, this $7 million facility represents a major commitment to environmental sustainability.

Here, you can step out to the large rear deck for a sweeping view of the area, check out the multimedia exhibits about Little River Canyon, and stretch your legs on one of the short hiking trails. If buildings can multitask, this one gets an A+. More than a full-scale visitor center, the lodge-type facility is home base for Jacksonville State University's Little River Canyon Field School, an instrumental force in environmental education in northeast Alabama. Also, it serves as National Park Service ranger headquarters for Little River Canyon National Preserve.

Many recycled materials went into the construction of this interesting structure that relies on geothermal energy for heating and cooling. "It's probably the greenest building in the state," said Pete Conroy, Canyon Center director, who oversees JSU's Environmental Policy and Information Center and Field Schools. The Visitor Center is open daily from 8 a.m. to 4 p.m. For more information on the Canyon Center, call (256) 845-3548.

Don't miss **Fort Payne**, the stomping ground of award-collecting country music group Alabama and home to the redbrick **Fort Payne Opera House** at 510 North Gault Avenue. The building, which dates to 1889, has served as a vaudeville playhouse, a theater for silent movies, and an upholstery shop. The opera house is listed on the National Register of Historic Places and the National Register of Nineteenth-Century Theatres in America. Restored in 1969 the opera house now opens for special events and performances. Tours can be arranged by appointment. Call (256) 845-6888.

The building on the opera house's north side is home to the **DeKalb County Hosiery Museum** and the **Richard C. Hunt Reception Hall**. The hall's interesting mural, entitled *Harvest at Fort Payne*, dates back to the Great Depression when President Franklin D. Roosevelt initiated the Work Projects Administration (WPA) to aid the unemployed. Harwood Steiger, an out-of-work artist from New York, received a commission to paint murals for Southern post offices, and this is one of his creations. Before its placement here, the mural was housed in the old post office building and later the DeKalb County Courthouse. Visitors to the hosiery museum can see early mill machinery and other exhibits as well as a video providing background on the industry that played a major role in the area's history and economy. The Opera House and the Hosiery Museum are open Thurs through Sat from 10 a.m. to 3 p.m. or by appointment by calling (256) 845-6888. For more information about DeKalb, contact the **DeKalb County Tourist Association** at (256) 845-3957.

Visit Tigers for Tomorrow at Untamed Mountain

For a walk on the wild side, head to Untamed Mountain, home of more than 175 animals ranging from the barnyard variety to exotic big cats. Located in the state's northeastern corner about eight miles from Collinsville, this rescue preserve now serves as home base for Tigers for Tomorrow (TFT).

When you arrive, say hello to Tootles and Zack (the camel and zebra greeters), who will be on hand to welcome you. Then head to the barnyard contact area and meet the sheep, llamas, emus, pigs, goats, and other creatures. Kids will love their encounters with these animals, and so will you.

Nearby, you'll see the carnivore compound, where more than 40 big cats, wolves, and bears roam about 18 acres in the sanctuary. Timber wolves Bear and Lakota may howl a hello to you. Handlers and keepers provide visitors with spontaneous interactions and give talks throughout the day. "This is the closest you will get to the big cats in a natural setting," said Susan Steffens, TFT board treasurer.

And how did this area become a habitat for tigers, lions, leopards, cougars, and other exotic animals, you ask? After Hurricanes Frances and Jeanne battered their South Florida home, Benny the leopard and Tinkerbell the Bengal tiger along with other cohorts made the move north to this 140-acre refuge. Here, they joined 25 other animal residents at the former Bluegrass Farm Sanctuary. The two operations later merged to become Tigers for Tomorrow at Untamed Mountain. Many of these exotic animals were rescued from animal attractions or came from individuals who could not provide proper care for them.

When you visit TFT, consider packing a picnic to enjoy in the pavilion, and don't forget to bring bottled water. Also, slather yourself in sunscreen and wear closed-toe shoes or hiking boots—no sandals or flip-flops—because this adventure calls for lots of walking over hilly terrain with limited shade. When the weather heats up, the big cats become languid and prefer napping to prowling. So for the best viewing during hot months, plan your arrival early. No photos or cell phones are allowed. Photos are only allowed on private guided tours. A two-hour private tour costs $30 per person for a minimum of four people.

The park (256-524-4150) opens for public walk-abouts Sat and Sun from 9 a.m. to 4 p.m. Private tours, group tours, and school field trips are available by reservation. Hours are seasonal, so before you strike out, check tigersfortomorrow.org for current operating times, admission prices, and directions. You'll find Untamed Mountain at 708 County Road 345 in DeKalb County, just minutes from I-59. Watch for the signs. Also, check out the link to TFT's guardian angel program and consider adopting the care of an animal for one year. Admission: adults (ages 12 and up) $15; children (ages 3 to 11) $7.50.

Nearby, the Fort Payne Depot at 105 Fifth Street Northeast houses the **Fort Payne Depot Museum** (256-845-5714; fortpaynedepotmuseum.com). Completed in 1891, the handsome Romanesque depot of pink sandstone served as a passenger station until 1970. The museum's permanent collection includes artwork, early farm equipment, pottery, glassware, and a restored caboose containing railroad memorabilia. You'll also see beaded moccasins, Iroquois baskets made of birch bark trimmed with porcupine quills, and Mayan and pre-Columbian artifacts dating from AD 400 to 800. An area resident willed to the museum her Cherokee, Hopi, Pueblo, Apache, and Seminole artifacts. Be sure to notice the collection of dioramas that were once part of a traveling medicine show and an unusual bed that belonged to local resident Granny Dollar, whose lifetime spanned more than a century. The museum is open Wed through Fri 10 a.m. to 3 p.m. Sun hours are 2 to 4 p.m. Admission: adults (ages 19 and up) $3; students (ages 7 to 18) $1; children (ages 6 and under) free.

Before leaving the "Sock Capital of the World," stop by **Big Mill Antique Mall** (256-845-3380) and browse among yesteryear's treasures. Located at 151 Eighth Street Northeast, this 1889 structure, once home to Fort Payne's first hosiery mill, now houses antiques, collectibles, reproductions, a deli, and a bakery. Mall hours are 10 a.m. to 4 p.m. Mon through Sat.

While traveling through **Collinsville**, you might want to consider spending some time at **Trade Day**, an event that draws some 30,000 or so bargain hunters and browsers every Saturday. Spread over 65 acres near Collinsville on US 11 South, this weekly occasion has had a country carnival flavor since it first cranked up in 1950. Vendors start setting up their wares at the crack of dawn and stay until early afternoon. Sightseers can munch on snacks such as boiled peanuts and corn dogs while surveying displays of wares from antiques and crafts to fresh vegetables and houseplants. Swans, ducks, rabbits, geese, goats, peacocks, hunting dogs, game cocks, and other animals often find new owners here. Parking costs $1, but admission is free. Hours are 4 a.m. to 4 p.m. Overnight camper parking with electrical hookup is $6 per night. For more information call (256) 524-2127 or (866) 262-2127.

Cherokee Country

From Collinsville it's just a short jaunt to **Leesburg** and **The Secret Bed & Breakfast Lodge** (256-523-3825). Located at 2356 Highway 68 West on a mountaintop overlooking Weiss Lake, the lodge boasts a view that won't stop. Innkeepers Charlie and Kris Thomas own this property perched on the eastern brow of Lookout Mountain.

The view, the sunsets and sunrises, and the deer make The Secret a special place. Breakfast is served on a 10-foot-wide round table topped by a lazy Susan. Four guest rooms are located on the second floor above the Main Lodge: Tranquility, Serenity, Remembrance, and Enchantment. The Lodge also offers a lovely rooftop pool and suspended deck. Four cottages also are available for guests—the Treehouse with a tree trunk and ceiling of greenery; the 1850s Jail House with a wooden life-size gunslinger named Shakes; the Sugar Shack, a layered stone cottage; and the Nautical Cottage with its lighthouse motif. Movie buffs will find a video library containing more than 400 titles. Moderate to deluxe rates. Visit The Secret Bed & Breakfast Lodge at secretbedandbreakfastlodge.com.

Cherokee County, home of **Weiss Lake**, offers beautiful scenery. Add a chunk of Little River Canyon to this 30,200-acre lake bordered by 447 miles of shoreline, and you've got plenty of recreational options. Famous for its fine fishing, the Crappie Capital of the World also offers ample opportunities for catching bass and catfish. The water attracts large populations of wintering birds such as seagulls, wild ducks, and cranes.

While exploring Cherokee County's many scenic spots, don't overlook **Cornwall Furnace Park**, about three miles east of Cedar Bluff. To reach the park, take State Route 9 east and turn left onto Cherokee County Route 92. Then make another left onto a gravel road and follow the signs. A flight of steps leads down a steep bank (covered by lilies in spring) to the picturesque stone stack that stands about 5 feet tall—all that remains of a structure built to supply crude iron to be transformed into Confederate arms. General Sherman's forces destroyed the furnace works during the Civil War.

The well-kept grounds offer attractive picnicking facilities and a short nature trail. The park, which opens at daylight and closes at sundown, can be visited year-round. Running water is available, but there are no bathroom facilities. Admission is free.

Afterward take State Route 9 to **Centre**, about six miles away. Next to the courthouse stands the **Cherokee County Historical Museum** (256-927-7835), located at 101 East Main Street. This museum, formerly a department store, houses historical objects and memorabilia that characterize the area's past. You'll see a Pennsylvania Amish town buggy. Other exhibits include Bob Hope's first typewriter, Grand Ole Opry memorabilia, wagons, housewares, antique telephones, Civil War relics, early appliances, Native American artifacts, a printing press, a telephone switchboard, a doll collection, and a bale of cotton. The basement contains a blacksmith shop as well as old farm equipment such as plows, mowing machines, cotton planters, and tractors. The museum has a collection in excess of 15,000 items. Admission: $3 per person. The museum is open Tues through Fri 9 a.m. to 4 p.m.

Continue toward **Gadsden**, situated in Lookout Mountain's foothills. **Turkeytown**, named for Chief Little Turkey during the late 1700s, is a tiny community on the Coosa River's banks near Gadsden that once served as the capital of the Cherokee nation.

Although long known as one of the state's leading industrial centers with abundant deposits of iron, manganese, coal, and limestone, Gadsden is gaining recognition for its rich Cherokee legacy. **The Turkeytown Association of the Cherokee**, a nonprofit organization, works to preserve and promote the region's Native American heritage.

Downtown at Gadsden's Broad Street entrance to the Coosa River Bridge stands the statue of Emma Sansom, who, at age 16, helped Confederate troops find a place to ford Black Creek after Union forces crossed and burned the local bridge.

While in Gadsden, stop by the **Mary G. Hardin Center for Cultural Arts** (256-543-2787) on the corner of Fifth and Broad Streets at 501 Broad Street. The complex, with a bold gold-and-black exterior in a Mondrian-like design, offers plays, concerts, lectures, classes, and art exhibits. To see the current art shows, take the escalator to the second floor. Before returning downstairs, be sure to notice the model railroad layout depicting Gadsden during the 1940s and 1950s with trains traveling past miniature reproductions of more than 100 historical structures, including the Gulf States Steel complex. The complex also houses the Courtyard Cafe. Admission: $8 per person; free for children 2 and under. Call for information on current exhibits or visit the website at culturalarts.com. Open Mon through Sat 10 a.m. to 5 p.m.; Sun 1 to 5 p.m.

alabamatrivia

Alabama ranks among the top 10 states with conditions most favorable for starting a small business.

Adjacent to the Center for Cultural Arts, the historic Kyle Building now houses the **Imagination Place Children's Museum** (256-543-2787). Youngsters can play in a life-size tree house or a kid-size city complete with Grandma's House, a bank, grocery store, doctor's office, fire station, and other interesting sites. Hours are Mon through Sat 10 a.m. to 5 p.m.; Sun 1 to 5 p.m. Admission is $8 per person; free for kids 2 and under. An adult must accompany children at all times.

At **Noccalula Falls Park** (256-549-4663; noccalulafallspark.com), situated on Lookout Mountain Parkway (and easily reached from I-59), the bronze statue of a legendary Cherokee princess stands ready to leap to her destiny in a rushing stream 90 feet below. Legend says Noccalula loved a brave of her own tribe and chose to die rather than marry the wealthier suitor selected by her father.

Explore the park's botanical gardens, especially attractive in spring with masses of azaleas in bloom. You can either walk through the park or take a mini-train ride to see the Pioneer Homestead, a village of authentic log structures including a barn, blacksmith shop, gristmill, school, and cabins moved here from various sites in Appalachia. Also here you'll find the restored *Gilliland-Reese Covered Bridge* and a miniature golf course.

Nearby are campgrounds, hiking trails, picnic tables, play areas, and a pool. The park closes from Nov to Mar. Hours vary so check to be sure when the park is open. Admission: adults $6; seniors and children (ages 4 to 12) $4; children (age 3 and under) free. Admission includes unlimited train rides. The campground number is (256) 543-7412.

If you're in the area on a weekend, you may want to schedule a jaunt to *Mountain Top Flea Market*, which is open every Sunday year-round from 5 a.m. to about 3 or 4 p.m. You'll find this all-day market with some 1,500 dealers about six miles west of Attalla at 11301 US 278. For more information call (800) 535-2286 or visit the website at lesdeal.com.

Attalla, home of the world's first hydroelectric generator and birthplace of Alabama Power, lures antiques shoppers. Clustered in the downtown area are more than a dozen shops. *Emma Kate's Cottage Antique Mall & More* (256-504-7810) at 309 Fifth Avenue Northwest houses several shops inside the 1869 building. The mall is open Mon through Sat from 10 a.m. to 5 p.m. Call ahead before traveling because dealers keep their own hours, and these vary from shop to shop.

To reach Boaz, located on Sand Mountain, take US 431 north from Attalla.

Sand Mountain

A foothill of the Appalachians, Sand Mountain covers an area twenty-five miles wide by seventy-five miles long. Approximately 30,000 people descend on *Boaz*, population 9,710, for the annual Harvest Festival held the first full weekend in October. The weekend celebration features an antique car show, musical entertainment, an Indian powwow, and some 200 booths brimming with handcrafted items ranging from birdhouses, corn husk dolls, and crazy quilts to paintings, leather items, and furniture. Music runs the gamut from bluegrass, country, and gospel to jazz. For more information on the outlets or the festival, contact the Boaz Chamber of Commerce, 100 E. Bartlett St., Boaz, AL 35957; call (256) 593-8154; or visit the website at boazareachamberofcommerce.com.

After exploring Boaz, continue north on US 431 toward Albertville, watching for the Winery sign. To reach *Jules J. Berta Vineyards* (256-891-5115) at 1409

Strange as It Sounds

Buck's Pocket State Park (256-659-2000), a secluded expanse of rugged nature that spills into three counties—DeKalb, Jackson, and Marshall—is rich in botanical beauty and local lore. Covering more than 2,000 acres of craggy canyon scenery on the western side of Sand Mountain, the park is located near Grove Oak.

For a magnificent overview of the entire canyon, head first to Point Rock, the park's highest area and a wonderful place for picnicking and hiking. According to local legend, early Native Americans took advantage of the area's geography to help them acquire their food supply by driving deer over the edge at Point Rock right into the "pocket." Both spring, with its plentiful supply of wildflowers, and fall make great times to visit.

To reach the headquarters and campground, you'll descend from Point Rock about 800 feet via a curving road to the canyon's base. The bottom line on the park's wooden sign says: HAVEN FOR DEFEATED POLITICIANS. Buck's Pocket acquired its reputation as a refuge for election losers after "Big Jim" Folsom, a former Alabama governor, lost a senate bid and announced his intention to go to Buck's Pocket, get his thoughts together, and "lick his wounds." He invited other defeated candidates to join him at this favorite retreat.

In addition to trails for hiking and rocks for climbing, recreation options include swimming and fishing at South Sauty Creek. Also, nearby Morgan's Cove offers a fishing pier and boat launching ramps. Rappelers and rock climbers should first stop by headquarters for a permit, good for a year. Write to Buck's Pocket at 393 County Road 174, Grove Oak, AL 35975. For reservations call (800) 252-7275. Visit the website at alapark.com/buckspocket. Open daily 7 a.m. until sundown.

Darden Avenue, turn right and drive a short distance until you see a white fence on the left with vines growing beyond. Stop by to meet owners Jules Berta and his wife, Becky, learn about the challenges of growing grapes in Alabama, and sample a vintage or two in the tasting room.

"We have one-acre tracts of Chardonnay, Merlot, Cabernet Franc, and Sylvaner with small tracts of Blaufrankisch, Petit Syrah, Riesling, and Aurore grapes," said Jules. The vineyard has an elevation over 1,100 feet, the highest in the state. The Bertas also import muscadines from local farmers and recently planted Sauvignon Blanc, Petit Syrah, and a new varietal known as Red Chardonnay.

Jules's parents (his father was a freedom fighter in Hungary's 1956 Revolution) immigrated to America in 1959. His father's career as a materials engineer later brought him to Alabama, where he planted his first vines in 1987. "Those first plantings, a combination of vinifera and French-American hybrid grapes, evolved from a hobby into an obsession," said Jules, who joined his father in this venture in 1993, having previously served in the Gulf War and Special Forces with the Navy. Jules continued to develop the vineyard after his father's death in 2005. Although still in the experimental stage, the vines are doing well, and the family is com-

mitted to making quality wines. Future plans call for adding varietals more suitable to the state's climate. Despite the challenges of sandy soil and hot, humid weather, Jules finds it gratifying to carry on his father's "impossible dream—grape growing in Alabama." You can visit the grapes Mon through Thurs between 11 a.m. and 6 p.m.; Fri and Sat from 10 a.m. to 7 p.m. Check out julesjbertavineyards.com for a wine list and more information.

Afterward continue about five miles north to *Albertville*, the "Heart of Sand Mountain." For a look at some of the city's lovely historic homes, drive along East Main Street off US 431. At the street's end stands the 1891 *Albertville Depot*, which is listed on the National Register of Historic Places. The depot now houses a senior citizens center.

Albertville acquired its title as "Fire Hydrant Capital of the World" because the local Mueller Company turns liquefied steel into dome-topped fire hydrants and ships them to countries near and far. In front of the chamber of commerce building, you'll see a special nickel-plated version that marks Mueller's one-millionth locally manufactured fire hydrant.

When visiting a new place, some travelers like to search out a restaurant where the locals eat. Here it's *The Food Basket* (256-878-1261), located just off US 431 at 715 Sampson Circle. The Daniel family has been feeding folks in Albertville since 1959.

Noted for its country ham and homemade biscuits, the restaurant draws a big breakfast crowd. Lunch specialties include Sand Mountain fried chicken and home-style fresh vegetables. Economical to moderate. Hours are 5:30 a.m. to 2:15 p.m. seven days a week for breakfast and lunch.

Take time to drive along some of Marshall County's rural roads. Along the way you'll notice fertile rolling farmland and chicken houses. Broilers, eggs, and turkeys produced on the state's individual farms add up to a billion-dollar poultry industry. In broiler production, Alabama ranks second in the nation.

When your taste buds crave Cajun cuisine and you can't make it to Louisiana, then stop by *Papa Dubi's Cajun Kitchen* (256-894-7878; papadubis.com) on the Albertville-Guntersville line. Located at 3931 Brasher's Chapel Road, the eatery offers seafood gumbo, jambalaya, red beans and rice with sausage, Creole dishes, po'boys, and more.

While living in Germantown, Tennessee, Dan and Lisa Younghouse hit the road to celebrate their 25th wedding anniversary. After visiting the Shrine of the Most Blessed Sacrament of Our Lady of the Angels Monastery near Hanceville, they toured the surrounding area—never dreaming they would soon become Alabama residents. But that's exactly what happened when they fell in love with the area's beauty while staying at *Lake Guntersville State Park Lodge*.

Their restaurant takes its name from Lisa's grandfather, a Cajun descendant, who lived in Gulfport, Mississippi, and the recipes—including the one for tasty gumbo—came from her grandmother, Nanny Dubi. Parents of seven, the couple and various family members have some restaurant experience, but starting their own eatery represented a leap of faith. However, the locals kept them so busy they had to expand soon after opening. The kids pitch in to help with this family venture. Hours are Mon through Thurs 11 a.m. to 8:30 p.m.; Fri and Sat 11 a.m. to 9 p.m.; Sun 11 a.m. to 2 p.m. Economical to moderate.

Lake Country

The lodge at *Lake Guntersville State Park* (256-571-5440 or 800-548-4553) makes a handsome base while exploring this area. Perched atop Taylor Mountain with views nothing short of stunning, the lodge sits just off State Route 227 at 1155 Lodge Drive. Simply seeing the sunset from the sweeping rear deck overlooking Lake Guntersville makes the trip worth it.

The lodge's thirteen suites and ninety-nine hotel rooms contain refrigerators, microwave ovens, large TVs, DVD players, pillow-top mattresses, and more. (Be sure to request a bluffside view.) Other park accommodations include cabins and chalets. Moderate to deluxe. The lodge's Pinecrest Dining Room serves breakfast, lunch, and dinner. The Hickory Lounge offers drinks and daily food specials such as sandwiches, salads, chicken wings, nachos, quesadillas, and fried cheese curds.

Nature lovers will enjoy seeing the wildlife and exploring thirty-six miles of color-coded hiking trails with varying degrees of difficulty. The park's pastimes also include tennis, fishing, canoeing, golf, sailing, and water skiing. Fishing boats and pontoons can be rented during spring, summer, and fall.

The park features several miles of scenic drives, a helipad, and camping facilities. Campsites range from primitive to fully equipped with utility hookups, tables, grills, bathhouses, hot showers, and play areas. You'll also find a camp store and nature center. For more information about the park and special packages like Eagle Awareness weekends, see alapark.com/lakeguntersville.

Continue to nearby Guntersville Lake, a Tennessee Valley Authority (TVA) creation, where sailboats and fishing vessels dot shining expanses of open water.

"The most striking thing about Guntersville," a local resident said, "is that it's a country town with a lake all around it. Of the five approaches to Guntersville, four take you across water." With 69,100 acres of water, **Guntersville** bills itself as a vacationer's paradise. Truly a haven for water-sports enthusiasts, the area offers boating, swimming, skiing, and fishing. The Bass Anglers Sportsman Society calls Lake Guntersville "one of the finest sport fishing lakes in America," and the Alabama Bassmasters stage invitational tournaments here. *Field & Stream* magazine placed Guntersville in America's top 10 fishing towns. And *Where to Retire* magazine recently ranked the town one of the country's top choices for retirees, citing a variety of reasons including its heart, the lake.

Drive through the downtown area and stop by Lake Guntersville Chamber of Commerce and Welcome Center (256-582-3612; lakeguntersville.org), which is in a house with a beckoning front porch at 200 Gunter Avenue near the big river bridge. Here you can pick up brochures on area attractions and inquire about current happenings. For instance, the local theater group **The Whole Backstage** mounts a mix of productions throughout the year, so check on possible performances during your visit. For more information about The Whole Backstage, call (256) 582-7469 or visit the website at wholebackstage.com.

Atop a hill, **Lake Guntersville Bed and Breakfast** (256-505-0133) at 2204 Scott Street offers suites with private entrances and more lovely water views from its two levels of wraparound porches. The handsome circa-1910 white brick home is also known as the historic Hooper House because it was built by Alexander Hooper. Innkeepers Michelle Louze and Michael Snedden have made major upgrades and offer many extra amenities.

Formerly an attic, the third floor is now a "common space" with a game room featuring a pool table, media area, and gym. The second floor is a common area with a business center, refrigerator, and coffee/tea station. All seven guest rooms have their own baths—the Hooper, Lucinda, Lavender, Aerie, Fig, Alexander, and Fisherman. A bountiful breakfast is served in the dining room or on the veranda when weather permits.

A Happy Hour each evening from 5 to 6 p.m. serves complimentary beer, wine, or homemade sangria. Guests are welcome to use complimentary bikes, paddle boards, and kayaks. Special occasion packages include one-hour massages along with champagne and chocolates or a tea tray and pastries. A "Get Hitched" package is specially designed for "the couple that doesn't want the hassle of all the wedding details and expense." The package includes one night in the Lucinda honeymoon suite, a wedding officiant, flower bouquet and boutoniere, small wedding cake, champagne with two keepsake glasses, and photography with images on a CD. Visit Lake Guntersville B&B's website Lakeguntersvillebedandbreakfast.com. Standard to moderate rates.

Encounters with Eagles

Sipping hot apple cider or coffee, listening to Appalachian music, and basking in a fireplace's glow set the tone for eagle-watching adventures at Lake Guntersville State Park. Each year from the last weekend in January through the first weekend in February, birders can band together for stimulating interpretive programs, live birds, and guided field trips.

"As if seeing the eagles were not worth it, the educational programs are fantastic," said a previous participant from Boston. The weekend gathering starts on Friday evening with a social hour at the park's lodge. Attendees meet each other and get an overview of the scheduled birding activities. Everyone is encouraged to get a good night's sleep because the first eagle sighting takes place Saturday at dawn's early light. (And don't forget your goose down jacket.)

"There's just something about eagles," said former state park naturalist Linda Reynolds. "I see the birds every winter day, and I still get goose bumps." Eagles from the Great Lakes area start trickling in during October, but most arrive in November to make the park's wooded terrain and lake their winter resort until their exodus in February.

As the stars disappear in dawn's silvery light, watchers scrutinize the sky over a valley lacking summer's lush foliage but still beautiful in its starkness. The greenery of pines softens interlacing barren tree branches. With all eyes searching the sky, the waiting group listens intently for that first whispered announcement: "There goes one!" Watchers continue to study the horizon with their scopes, which range from binoculars to serious tripod versions. During an hour's watch, you might see a dozen or so bald eagles soar from their roosts and spiral toward the nearby lake.

After the birds depart, the group also heads to the lake for a chance to see the eagles dip down to the water, extend their talons, and grasp fish—their favorite breakfast. From the vantage point of a nearby bank, it's thrilling to see the great birds at close range. "Morning is feeding time, and afternoons are for play," said a staffer helping with Eagle Awareness programs. "Then it's home to the roost at dusk."

The group also gathers at twilight to watch the eagles return for the evening. Before retiring, the birds preen and strike regal poses as if compelled to perform for the audience training binoculars in their direction. Some watchers set up telescopes, inviting others to enjoy the view. You might find yourself sharing a scope with a pharmacist, truck driver, teacher, dentist, computer programmer, retiree, or student.

The group's mix confirms that you don't have to be an ornithologist to get excited by encounters with eagles. "We've noticed that everyone loves eagles even if they're not bird enthusiasts," Reynolds said. "I don't know if it's a spiritual thing or because the eagle is our national symbol. Historically, eagles symbolize that which is uplifting and inspirational."

After the morning sighting, you can head to the lodge for a bountiful breakfast. Later, you may want to take a daytime field trip with one of the designated guides. Depending on your individual interest, you can choose a park tour, a visit to the

Nature Center located near the campground, an outing to the water bird refuge, or opt for more eagle viewing at other observation points. Eagle watchers come not only from Alabama, but also from Tennessee, Georgia, North and South Carolina, Florida, Mississippi, Louisiana, and beyond, and repeaters make up about a third of each group.

Each weekend features a different program. At the birding seminar, which stars live raptors, you might see eagles, hawks, owls, falcons, and other previously injured birds that recovered with the help of individual volunteers and such groups as the Southeastern Raptor Rehabilitation Center and the Alabama Wildlife Rescue Service. The agenda also includes programs on various birds of prey and their mating, nesting, migration, and feeding habits.

In addition to bald eagles, many species of birds populate the area. This lovely wild region is also home to deer, weasels, raccoons, opossums, muskrats, beavers, bobcats, cougars, and foxes. Some of the park's hiking trails follow paths once traveled by the Cherokee and the area's early settlers through forests of red cedar, ash, maple, hickory, sumac, redbud, oak, black walnut, poplar, sweet gum, and pine. Most of the land has been left in its natural state, and hiking allows you to study firsthand the local flora and fauna. For more information on Eagle Awareness weekends and other special packages at the park, visit alapark.com/lakeguntersville or call (256) 571-5440.

Continue to nearby **Fant's Department Store** (256-582-3845) at 355 Gunter Avenue. The rambling structure offers a bargain basement and plenty of treasures. Open Tues through Sat 10 a.m. to 4 p.m. Your sightseeing excursion may take you past the **Guntersville Museum** (256-571-7597) at 1215 Rayburn Avenue. Built under the Works Progress Act (WPA), this handsome structure of rough limestone and mortar dates to 1936 and houses an art gallery, archives, and intriguing collections. Guntersville's past comes alive here with exhibits from Native American artifacts to sepia pictorial views of the Tennessee Valley Authority's dam construction and lake creation. Guntersville is named for John Gunter, great-grandfather of famed humorist and social commentator Will Rogers. Rogers is an honorary son of the city. The museum also hosts traveling exhibits. Hours are Tues through Fri 10 a.m. to 4 p.m.; Sat and Sun 1 to 4 p.m. Admission is free. See guntersvillemuseum.org.

Other local events include a series of fall and spring evening concerts on Thursdays. For more information or to see a current art exhibit, stop by the Mountain Valley Arts Council (MVAC) office at 300 Gunter Avenue, or call (256) 571-7199. The office is open Tues through Sat 10 a.m. to 5 p.m. Gallery hours are Tues through Fri 10 a.m. to 5 p.m., and Sat 10 a.m. to 2 p.m. For an updated schedule, see mvacarts.org

Guntersville's popular two-day *Art on the Lake Show* draws crowds on the third weekend in April. The show features more than 130 artists and craftsmen, plus food vendors, outdoor games and rides, and a bake sale. The show promotes the arts while providing scholarship programs for local high school graduates. Held along beautiful Lake Guntersville, the show takes place rain or shine from 9 a.m. to 5 p.m. Admission is $2 for ages 13 and older. Visit the website for more information, artonthelake-guntersville.com.

On the Saturday before Labor Day, *St. William's Seafood Festival* features more than 5,000 pounds of fresh shrimp, oysters, crab, flounder, and other fish imported from coastal waters. Parish members prepare the seafood, which includes making about 400 gallons of gumbo. The festival is held on the shores of beautiful Lake Guntersville at Civitan Park. For more information, contact St. William's Catholic Church (929 Gunter Avenue; 256-582-4245; stwilliamchurch.com/seafood_festival).

If you prefer the privacy of a vacation rental, check out *Guntersville Getaway* (256-582-3013 or 256-571-5080) on Buck Island near Gunter's Landing and the Yacht Club. Only five minutes from downtown Guntersville and one mile from the public boat launch, this waterfront home at 280 Morrow Drive comes with private pier and many amenities.

The house, which offers three bedrooms and can accommodate nine, is ideal for families or a group of fishing buddies. Enjoy the lake view, natural wooded setting, and wildlife. Say hello to the great blue heron who seems to have a proprietary interest in the place, as do the turtles sunning on a log in the lake out back. Devise your own easygoing schedule and relax in the backyard hammock with a good book. Grill your catch or a steak on the rear patio and dine outside. Owner Lyndall Hamlett has decorated the place with whimsical touches and provides information on local restaurants and attractions. Amenities include free Wi-Fi, good cell phone reception, cable TV, TVs in the

Strange as It Sounds

If a boat outing fits into your travel schedule, try to catch the evening exodus of bats from *Hambrick Cave*. Some 350,000 American gray bats, a protected species, consider this cave home from late April to mid-October (although the females migrate the first of August). You'll probably join a bevy of other boaters, clustered around the water-level cave mouth at the base of a bluff, all waiting for the sunset performance as a cloud of bats swoops overhead on its nocturnal foraging flight. Going downriver toward Guntersville Dam, look for a cave (marked by a small overhead sign) on your right. Flashlights are prohibited. (For more information on this and other area bat caves, call the *Wheeler National Wildlife Refuge* at 256-353-7243 or visit fws.gov/wheeler.)

living room and each bedroom, and a washer and dryer. Remodeled in 2017, the home got a new large master bedroom and two luxury bathrooms, plus a new laundry room, new fireplace stone and mantle. Guests now have their own boat slip. Moderate to deluxe. See guntersvillegetaway.com.

For some good old-fashioned fun and a mess of "poke salat," take State Route 69 to *Arab* during the first weekend in May. When the Arab Liars' Club (the self-appointed title for a group of local men who meet daily for coffee at L Rancho Cafe) came up with the idea for the *Poke Salat Festival*, they probably did not expect it to become an annual affair with everything from street dances and craft shows to beauty contests and drama productions.

In downtown Arab, notice the weather-beaten Farmer's Exchange, a local landmark that now houses a garden center. Also, you may wish to explore the city's dozen or so antiques shops. For more information, contact Downtown Arab at (256) 586-0345 or visit downtownarab.com

At the southern edge of town on Arad Thompson Road, you'll find the inviting Arab City Park with the Shoal Creek Trail, ball fields, a pool, and modern, well-equipped playground. The park is also home to several historical structures including the Hunt School, Rice Church, Elvin Light Museum, and Smith's Country Store. Look for a statue of town founder Tuttle Thompson in Tuttle Thompson Park at the corner of Highway 89 and Main Street. Tuttle named the town in honor of his son, Arad Thompson, but the post office mistakenly changed the spelling to Arab. So it has remained. Afterward head toward Huntsville to launch an exploration of Alabama's northwestern region.

Places to Stay in Northeast Alabama

ALBERTVILLE

Microtel Inn & Suites by Wyndham
220 Alabama Hwy. 75 North
(256) 894-4000 or
(800) 771-7171

Quality Inn
315 Martling Rd.
(256) 891-2600 or
(800) 526-3766

ATTALLA

Days Inn by Wyndham of Attalla
801 Cleveland Ave.
(256) 538-7861 or
(800) DAYSINN

BOAZ

Key West Inn
10535 State Rte. 168
(256) 593-0800 or
(800) 833-0555

FORT PAYNE

DeSoto State Park
7104 Desoto Pkwy.
(256) 845-5380 or
(800) 568-8840
alapark.com/
Desoto-state-park

GADSDEN

Gadsden Inn & Suites
200 Albert Rains Blvd.
(256) 543-7240 or
(800) 637-5678
gadsdeninn.com

Hampton Inn
129 River Rd.
(256) 546-2337 or
(800) HAMPTON

GUNTERSVILLE

Guntersville Getaway
280 Morrow Dr.
(256) 582-3013 or
(855) 499-0001
guntersvillegetaway.com

Hampton Inn of Lake
Guntersville
14451 US 431
(256) 582-4176

Wyndham Garden Lake
Guntersville
2140 Gunter Ave.
(256) 582-2220 or
(877) 999-3223

Lake Guntersville Bed
and Breakfast
2204 Scott St.
(256) 505-0133
lakeguntersvillebedand
breakfast.com

Lake Guntersville State
Park Lodge
1155 Lodge Dr.
(256) 571-5440 or
(800) 548-4553
alapark.com/lakeguntersville

HUNTSVILLE

Bevill Conference Center
and Hotel
550 Sparkman Dr.
Northwest
(256) 721-9428 or
(888) 721-9428
uah.edu/bevill-center

Courtyard by Marriott
4804 University Dr.
(256) 837-1400 or
(800) 321-2211

Dogwood Manor
707 Chase Rd.
Northeast
(256) 859-3946
dogwoodmanorbandb.com

Clarion Inn
4815 University Dr.
(256) 830-9400

Huntsville Marriott
5 Tranquility Base
(256) 830-2222 or
(888) 299-5174

The Westin Huntsville
6800 Governor's West
Northwest
(256) 428-2000 or
(866) 716-8808

LEESBURG

The Secret Bed &
Breakfast Lodge
2356 State Rte. 68 West
(256) 523-3825
secretbedandbreak
fastlodge.com

MENTONE

Crystal Lake Lodge
3291 County Rd. 165
(256) 634-8209
angelfire.com/al4/
crystallakelodge

Raven Haven
651 County Rd. 644
(256) 634-4310
ravenhavenbandb.info

PISGAH

The Lodge at Gorham's
Bluff
101 Gorham Dr. Gorham's
Bluff
(256) 451-2787
gorhamsbluff.com

SCOTTSBORO

Goose Pond Colony
417 Ed Hembree Dr.
(256) 259-2884 or
(800) 268-2884
goosepond.org

Quality Inn
208 Micah Way
US 72
(256) 574-6666

VALLEY HEAD

Winston Place
353 Railroad Ave.
(256) 635-6381

MAINSTREAM ATTRACTIONS WORTH SEEING IN NORTHEAST ALABAMA

Alabama Fan Club & Museum
101 Glenn Blvd. Southwest
Fort Payne
(256) 845-1646 or (800) 557-8223

This museum showcases the band's
musical achievements, which are
many: The group has garnered
numerous awards, gold albums, and

plaques for such releases as "My Home's in Alabama," "Mountain Music," and "Fallin' Again." Fans can purchase souvenirs ranging from T-shirts and jackets to photographs and mugs—and of course albums. The museum features individual sections on band members Randy Owen, Teddy Gentry, Jeff Cook, and Mark Herndon. For a little background and a Web tour, visit thealabamaband.com.

Huntsville Museum of Art
300 Church St. Southwest
Huntsville
(256) 535-4350 or (800) 786-9095

Save time for browsing through the $7.5 million home of the Huntsville Museum of Art. This beautiful building stands in Big Spring International Park, the heart of the city, and offers a wide range of exhibitions, art classes, and educational programs. You'll see an outstanding permanent collection with works by Picasso, Matisse, Toulouse-Lautrec, Goya, and other renowned artists as well as exhibits on loan from major institutions. The Pane e Vino Cafe on the Plaza Level offers pizza, pasta, and sandwiches. Admire student artwork in the Children's Community Gallery, sign up for an art class at the museum academy, and shop for treasures at the Museum Store. Visit hsvmuseum.org.

US Space & Rocket Center1
Tranquility Base
Huntsville
(256) 837-3400 or
(800) 637-7223
rocketcenter.com

At One Tranquility Base on Huntsville's western side, you may feel like a character out of a science fiction movie as you wander through a world of rockets, spaceships, shuttles, nose cones, and lunar landing vehicles. Other interesting exhibits include a moon rock, Apollo 16's command module, the overpowering *Saturn V* moon rocket, history of the space shuttle with artifacts, and an SR-71 Blackbird reconnaissance plane. Don't miss the featured film presentation at the Spacedome Theater, or, for a unique adventure, sign up for Space Camp. You'll find Space Camp dates, rates, registration information, and everything else you need to know for blasting off at spacecamp.com.

Places to Eat in Northeast Alabama

ALBERTVILLE

Asia Garden Restaurant
210 State Rte. 75 North
(256) 891-1616

Bee-Gee's Restaurant
1105 Baltimore Ave.
(256) 878-9294
beegeesrestaurant.com

Catfish Cabin
8524 US 431 North
(256) 878-8170
Mycatfishcabin.com

The Food Basket
715 Sampson Circle
(256) 878-1261

Giovanni's Pizza Italian Restaurant
711 Miller St.
(256) 878-7881

ARAB

Fonseca Factory
1082 N. Brindlee
Mountain Pkwy.
(256) 931-7687

L-Rancho Café
41 N. Main St.
(256) 586-9913

Son's House of Barbecue
2425 N. Brindlee
Mountain Pkwy.
(256) 931-7667

BOAZ

Bubba Ritos
363 US Highway 431
(256) 281-6070
bubbaritos.com

Grumpy's
425 S. McCleskey St.
(256) 593-0599
Grumpys.restaurant

CENTRE

Pat's Perfections
1820 E. Bypass
(256) 927-4060
patsperfections.com

Tony's Steak Barn
804 Alexis Rd.
(256) 927-2844
Tonyssteakbarn.com

GADSDEN

The Choice
531 Broad St.
(256) 546-9055

Cafe 5
501 Broad St.
(256) 547-1066

Top O' the River
1606 Rainbow Dr.
(256) 547-9817
topotheriverrestaurant.com

GRANT

Mi Mi's Cafe
12 Third St.
(256) 728-7483
mimiscafe.com

Porky's 2
4697 Main St.
(256) 728-5539

GUNTERSVILLE

El Camino Real
14274 US 431
(256) 571-9089

Papa Dubi's Cajun Kitchen
3931 Brasher's Chapel Rd.
(256) 894-7878
Papadubis.com

Top O' the River
7004 Val Monte Dr.
(256) 582-4567
topotheriverrestaurant.com

Wintzell's Oyster House
14455 US 431
(256) 582-5600
wintzellsoysterhouse.com

HUNTSVILLE

Cantina Laredo
330 The Bridge St.
6872 Old Madison Pike
(256) 327-8580
cantinalaredo.com

Hildegard's German Cuisine
2357 Whitesburg Dr. Southeast
(256) 512-9776
hildegardsgermancuisine.com

Landry's Seafood House
5101 Governor's House Dr. Southwest
(256) 864-0000
landrysseafood.com

Ol' Heidelberg
6125 University Dr.
(256) 922-0556
olheidelberg.com

Surin of Thailand
975 Airport Rd. Southwest
(256) 213-9866
surinofthailand.com

MADISON

Fulin's Asian Cuisine
8141 Highway 72
(256) 721-7005
fulins.com

Main St. Cafe
101 Main St.
(256) 461-8096
mainstreetcafemadison.com

MENTONE

Green Leaf Grill
6080 State Rte. 117
(256) 634-2110
Greenleafgrillmentone.com

The Wildflower Cafe
6007 State Rte. 117
(256) 634-0066
mentonewildflower.com

PISGAH

The Lodge at Gorham's Bluff
101 Gorham Dr.
(256) 451-8439
gorhamsbluff.com

SARDIS CITY

Garcia's Grill & Cantina
13026 US 431
(256) 840-5694

SCOTTSBORO

McCutchen's Magnolia House
303 East Willow St.
(256) 259-3077

Carlile's Restaurant
23730 John T. Reid Pkwy.
(256) 574-5629
carliles.net

The Docks
Goose Pond Colony
417 Ed Hembree Dr.
(256) 574-3071
goosepond.org

50 Taters
1497 County Park Rd.
(256) 259-3222

Liberty Restaurant
907 E. Willow St.
(256) 574-3455

Payne's
101 E. Laurel St.
(256) 574-2140

STEVENSON

Friday's
507 Second St.
(256) 437-8201

FOR MORE INFORMATION ABOUT NORTHEAST ALABAMA

Alabama Mountain Lakes Tourist Association
402 Sherman St.
PO Box 2537 Mooresville 35649
(800) 648-5381
northalabama.org info@northalabama.org
This organization covers 16 north Alabama counties that are home to some 100 attractions in a 100-mile radius.

DeKalb Tourism
1503 Glenn Blvd. Southwest
PO Box 681165 Fort Payne 35968
(256) 845-3957 or (888) 805-4740
visitlookoutmountain.com
info@tourdekalb.com

Greater Gadsden Area Tourism
90 Walnut St.
PO Box 8269 Gadsden 35901
(256) 549-0351 or (888) 565-0411
greatergadsden.com
info@greatergadsden.com

Mountain Lakes Chamber of Commerce
407 E. Willow St.
PO Box 973
Scottsboro 35768
(256) 259-5500 or (800) 259-5508
mountainlakeschamberofcommerce.com

Huntsville/Madison County Convention & Visitors Bureau
500 Church St.
Huntsville 35801
(256) 551-2230 or (800) 843-0468
huntsville.org info@huntsville.org

Marshall CountyConvention & Visitors Bureau
200 Gunter Ave.
PO Box 711 Guntersville 35976
(256) 582-7015 or (800) 582-6282
marshallcountycvb.com

Northwest Alabama

Tennessee Valley

Mooresville, just east of I-65 at exit 2 on I-565 between Huntsville and Decatur, makes a good place to start a tour of Alabama's northwest region. For information on local and area attractions, call the Alabama Mountain Lakes Tourist Association's office at (800) 648-5381.

To best see Mooresville, a town that dates to 1818 (it's one year older than the state itself), plan to take a walking tour. Not only does everybody know everybody in this community of some twenty families, everybody knows everybody's dog. Don't be surprised if the local canines choose to accompany you on your stroll through town. Listed on the National Register of Historic Places, this charming village occupies an area of one-quarter square mile and can easily be covered in half an hour. Cedar trees and wild hydrangeas make lovely accents as you wend your way through the town. Strolling along streets lined by picket fences and fine old shade trees, you'll see a variety of vintage structures including lovely old federal-style homes.

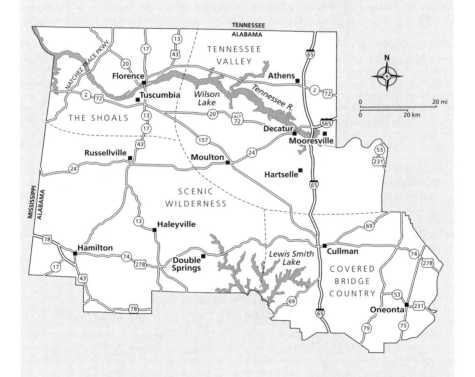

On Lauderdale Street you'll pass a brick church that dates to 1839 and contains its original pews. Although regular worship services no longer take place here, the historic structure is sometimes used for weddings and meetings. Notice the herringbone pattern of the brick walkway in front of the church. Mooresville's former postmistress, Barbara Coker, using many of her lunch hours, excavated through grass and layers of dirt to expose the original brickwork.

Be sure to stop by the tiny post office on the corner of Lauderdale and High Streets. Built around 1840, this small weathered poplar building, with tin roof, pegged joints, and square-head nails, contains the town's forty-eight original post boxes (first installed at the nearby Stagecoach Inn and Tavern).

The Stagecoach Inn, built sometime before 1825, once sold "supper for two bits." Across the street from the inn stands a small cottage, an example of Downing Gothic architecture. Dating to about 1890, the home was built and owned by Uncle Zack Simmons, a black carpenter, and his wife, Aunt Mandy. Former Mooresville mayor Kathleen Lovvorn says that Aunt Mandy, famous for her jellies and pickles, often handed out homemade treats to the village youngsters.

Turning Back the Clock to Mark Twain's Time

If you saw the Disney production *Tom and Huck*, you visited the well-preserved village of Mooresville via video. Jonathan Taylor Thomas (of TV's *Home Improvement* fame) and Brad Renfro (*The Client*) starred in this remake of a Mark Twain classic.

"The moment I saw Mooresville, I knew this was the perfect setting for Tom Sawyer," said the film's production manager, Ross Fanger, after searching for a town that fit the 1876 era of Mark Twain's novel.

For the movie, Mooresville's paved streets became dirt-covered lanes, and a Hollywood facade of nineteenth-century stores sprang up. Film crews shot some scenes along the Tennessee River and inside **Cathedral Caverns**, a state park in Marshall County. The caverns served as a backdrop for the novel's account of Tom and his girlfriend Becky Thatcher's lost-in-a-cave adventure.

If you missed the movie, don't despair—the film is available on DVD, and you can still visit Mooresville.

Mooresville Walking Tours

Village residents often lead walking tours for groups, large and small. Contact Susan Goldby, who can gear the tour focus to the group's common interest—architectural, gardening, or historical. Tours take about one and a half hours and the cost is $5 per person for a minimum of four people. All proceeds benefit the Historical Preservation Fund, used for preservation of Mooreville's town-owned structures and trees. For more information, call (256) 355-2683 or (256) 509-9249.

After departing Mooresville you may want to travel north to **Athens**, Limestone County's seat. Start your local tour by visiting the downtown courthouse square with its surrounding stores and stately old churches. Founded in 1818, Athens barely missed being the state's oldest incorporated town. (Nearby Mooresville won the race by only three days.) To see some of the town's antebellum and Victorian homes—many are identified by historic markers—drive along Beaty, Pryor, Jefferson, and Clinton Streets.

You may want to stop by the **Houston Memorial Library and Museum** (256-233-8770). Located at 101 North Houston Street, this house dates to 1835 and served as the home of George S. Houston (a former Alabama governor and US senator) from 1845 to 1879. Exhibits include family portraits, period furniture, Native American artifacts, Civil War relics, and various items relating to local history. Hours are 10 a.m. to 5 p.m. Mon through Fri, and 9 a.m. to noon Sat.

For a toe-tapping good time, plan to take in the **Tennessee Valley Old Time Fiddlers Convention** held at Athens State University each October. Visitors converge on campus for two days of outdoor competitions featuring harmonica, banjo, fiddle, mandolin, dulcimer, and guitar playing and buck dancing sessions. For more information about the fiddlers, call (256) 233-8141 or visit tvotfc.org.

The Greater Limestone County Chamber of Commerce office at 101 South Beaty Street (256-232-2600; tourathens.com) stocks brochures the visitor will find helpful. Pick up the *Beaty Historic District Walking Tour* guide to explore this area. Listed on the National Register, this historic district was named for Robert Beaty, cofounder of Athens. Although some of the district's homes date back before the Civil War, most were built during the early 1900s.

Beaty Street takes you to Athens State University, Alabama's oldest institution of higher learning. While on this street, be sure to notice the Beaty-Mason

Traveling the Antebellum Trail

Greater Limestone County boasts a rich legacy of antebellum and late-nineteenth- and early-twentieth-century architecture. Near the neighboring industrial and technological centers of Decatur and Huntsville, you'll find an area of contrasting culture—think past, present, and future tenses if you will. The trail begins in Athens and ends in Mooresville. The trail delineates a driving tour with a number of antebellum structures, which translates to the time period between 1812 and 1861. You'll drive past twenty-four homes, three churches, a college, two working cotton plantations, a post office, and stagecoach inn and tavern. Call the Greater Limestone County Chamber of Commerce at (256) 232-2600 or (800) 648-5381, click on the website at tourathens. com, or visit at 101 South Beaty Street in Athens for more information.

House built in 1826, now the college president's home. Located at 302 North Beaty Street, the lovely 1840s Greek revival **Founder's Hall** houses school offices, a library, and a chapel. This building's original portion escaped being burned by the Yankees when a letter allegedly written by President Lincoln appeared in the nick of time. On the second floor, the Altar of the New Testament features fine woodcarvings in tulip poplar. Founder's Hall may be visited Mon through Fri from 8 a.m. to 4:30 p.m. Admission is free. For more information, call (256) 233-8215.

Before leaving Athens, plan to tour the **Donnell House**. Completed in 1851, the T-shaped home contains some period furnishings and is located at 601 South Clinton Street on the Middle School campus. A chinked log cabin kitchen with working fireplace stands nearby. The home is open Fri 1 to 3 p.m., or by appointment. For more information call (239) 249-2211 or visit donnellhouse.net. Modest admission.

Reeves also offers several walking tours including the Maple Hill Cemetery Walk, which visits the graves of five Alabama governors, Revolutionary War and Civil War soldiers, the first Secretary of War for the Confederacy, and the family of actress Tallulah Bankhead. Tours are tailored to fit your needs and cost a modest fee.

alabamatrivia

America's first wave pool was built in 1970 at Point Mallard Park in Decatur.

After exploring Athens, head south to **Decatur** for another dose of history along with wildlife. Founded on the banks of the Tennessee River and originally called Rhodes Ferry, Decatur acquired its current name in 1820. At that time Congress and President James Monroe decided to honor Commodore Stephen Decatur by naming a town after him. A daring naval hero who commanded a three-ship squadron during the War of 1812, Decatur once proposed the following toast: "Our country: In her intercourse with foreign nations may she always be in the right; but our country, right or wrong."

Cook Museum of Natural Science (256-351-4505; cookmuseum.org) is scheduled to reopen in 2019 in downtown Decatur.

Nearby at 1715 Sixth Avenue Southeast, the folks who work at **Big Bob Gibson's** (256-350-6969) say they cook "the best barbecue in town." A Decatur tradition since 1925, the restaurant serves real hickory-smoked pit-barbecued pork, beef, and chicken. Barbecued potatoes (baked and topped with meat) also prove popular menu items. You can grab a bite here or get an order to go.

Hours are "can to can't" (9:30 a.m. to 8:30 p.m.) seven days a week, excluding Easter, Thanksgiving, Christmas, and New Year's Day. Economical prices. The restaurant is so popular, it has another Decatur location at 2520 Danville Road Southwest (256-350-0404; bigbobgibson.com). Oh, yes, and be sure to pick up a bottle of barbecue sauce here—they make several varieties.

Stop by the Decatur-Morgan County Convention and Visitors Bureau at 719 Sixth Avenue Southeast for a pamphlet called *A Walking Tour of Historic Decatur*, which notes many of the city's late-nineteenth-century homes that can be seen in the Old Decatur and New Albany historic districts. Call (256) 350-2028 or (256) 232-5449 or visit decaturcvb.org for more information on local attractions.

Head to the city's northern section to tour the handsome ***Old State Bank*** (256-350-5060), established during Andrew Jackson's presidency. Located at 925 Bank Street Northeast, Alabama's oldest surviving bank building now serves as a museum. Upstairs you'll see the head cashier's spacious living quarters, furnished in the 1830s style.

During the Civil War this classic-style structure served as a hospital for both Union and Confederate soldiers. The bank's thick vault possibly became a shielded surgery chamber during the heat of battle. Outside, the large limestone columns still retain traces of Civil War graffiti along with battle scars from musket fire. The bank was among Decatur's few buildings to survive the Civil War. Bank tours are free, and the building is open Mon through Fri from 9:30 a.m. to noon and 1 to 4:30 p.m., or by appointment. To sample a good mix of shops featuring antiques, clothing, toys, and gifts, take a stroll down Bank Street.

BEST ATTRACTIONS IN NORTHWEST ALABAMA

Alabama Music Hall of Fame, Tuscumbia

Ave Maria Grotto, Cullman

Bankhead National Forest, Double Springs

Blount County Covered Bridges, Oneonta

Dismals Canyon, Phil Campbell

Indian Mound and Museum, Florence

Ivy Green, Tuscumbia

Natural Bridge, Natural Bridge

The Shrine of the Most Blessed Sacrament of Our Lady of the Angels Monastery, Hanceville

Nearby, at 207 Church Street Northeast, you can view some great traveling exhibits and work by regional artists at **Carnegie Visual Arts Center** (256-341-0562). One of millionaire philanthropist Andrew Carnegie's projects, the building dates to 1904 and served as Decatur's library until 1973. Hours run Tues through Fri from 10 a.m. to 5 p.m.; Sat 10 a.m. to 2 p.m. Check out carnegiearts.org for current offerings and exhibits.

When hunger pangs hit, head to **Simp McGhee's** (256-353-6284; simpmcghees.com), at 725 Bank Street Northwest. Named for a colorful early-twentieth-century riverboat captain, this pub-style eatery offers Simp's stuffed Gulf flounder as well as many pasta, poultry, and beef entrees. The upstairs section, Miss Kate's Place, takes its name from a famous former madam, who ran a turn-of-the-twentieth-century bordello nearby. Dinner hours are Mon through Thurs from 5 to 9 p.m.; Fri and Sat from 5 to 9:30 p.m.

Standing in Decatur's New Albany downtown area at 115 Johnston Street Southeast, you'll see the **Old Cotaco Opera House** (334-887-3007). Often called the Old Masonic Building, the big brick structure dates to 1890. Although you won't see a touring vaudeville act here today, you'll find the complex offers other enticing treats. For instance, hungry travelers can visit **Curry's on Johnston Street** (256-350-6715; currysrestaurant.com), located on the building's lower level at 115½ Johnston Street, for lunch or pick-up items. The eatery serves homemade soups, sandwiches, casseroles, fresh bread, and desserts. Moderate rates. Open Mon through Fri 8 a.m. to 5 p.m.

To visit one of *The 100 Best Small Towns in America* (selected by Norman Crampton for his nationwide guide), head south for **Hartselle**, now a mecca for antiques shoppers. (For a list of the other ninety-nine towns, you'll have to buy the book.) Hartselle boasts the largest number of contiguous buildings on the Historic Register in Alabama.

Make your first stop the historic **Depot Building** at 110 S. Railroad Street, which houses the Hartselle Area Chamber of Commerce (256-773-4370; hartsellechamber.com). On one wall you'll see a Works Progress Administration (WPA) mural painted in 1937 that illustrates the major role cotton played in the area's early economy. While here collect a map and guide to local shops. Open by 10 a.m., most shops close on Wed and Sun. Also, some shops close on Mon.

Afterward stroll to **The Freight House** (256-773-4600; freighthousehartselle.com), located at 200 Railroad Street Southwest in a former freight building. You can occasionally hear a passing train. Try the Freighthouse Tilapia or steaks, chicken, or seafood. The restaurant also features a lunch express weekdays from 11 a.m. to 2 p.m. Open Mon through Wed, 11 a.m. to 2 p.m.; Thurs 11 a.m. to 8 p.m.; Fri and Sat, 11 a.m. to 9 p.m.; Sun, 11 a.m. to 2 p.m. Standard to moderate.

Browsing along Main Street, you'll see **Ragtime Antiques** at 112 West Main Street (256-773-2188; ragtimeonmain.com) and other specialty shops, with an array of everything from bric-a-brac and potpourri to primitive antiques and quilts. At **Slate Gallery**, you'll find work by local artists at the shop at 333 West Main Street (256-773-6353).

After leaving Hartselle, follow State Route 36 west, watching for the **Oakville** turn and signs directing you to **Jesse Owens Memorial Park** (256-974-3636) at 7019 County Road 203. The park's focal point is an 8-foot, one-ton bronze statue of Owens, who won four gold medals in the 1936 Olympics. Branko Medenica, a native of Germany who now lives in Birmingham, sculpted the piece, which depicts Owens running and incorporates the familiar Olympic rings. Mounted on a 6-foot granite base, the statue was unveiled in a 1996 ceremony attended by members of the athlete's family when the Olympic torch passed through Oakville en route to Atlanta's games.

alabamatrivia

Alabama symbols include: the yellowhammer, the state bird; the camellia, the state flower; and the Southern pine, the state tree.

The park also offers a visitor center, museum, softball field, basketball court, walking trail, picnic pavilions, and replicas of the 1936 Olympic torch and Owens's modest home. Owens, who was born in Oakville and spent his early life here, once said, "It behooves a man with God-given ability to stand 10 feet tall. You never know how many youngsters may be watching." The park is open during daylight hours, and admission is free. The museum is open Mon through Sat from 10 a.m. to 4 p.m.; Sun 1 to 4 p.m. Free admission to the museum. Check out jesseowensmemorialpark.com.

Before leaving the vicinity, take time to visit the **Oakville Indian Mounds**, a park and museum (256-905-2499; oakvilleindianmounds.com) at 1219 County Road 187. Located eight miles southeast of Moulton just off State Route 157, the complex features a massive 2,000-year-old Woodland Indian Mound, a Copena Indian burial mound, and a museum modeled after a seven-sided Cherokee Council House. The museum contains a 12-foot wooden statue of Sequoyah plus thousands of artifacts—some dating back to 10,000 BC. Generally, hours are Mon through Fri 8 a.m. to 4 p.m.; Sat 10 a.m. to 4 p.m. Admission is free.

Afterward continue your journey toward **Moulton**. Try to hit Moulton at mealtime so you can sample the terrific lemon-pepper grilled catfish fillet at **Western Sirloin Steak House** (256-974-7191), with a huge grain-bin entrance and tin walls. Located at 11383 State Route 157 (behind Foodland), the restaurant also features charbroiled chicken breast and rib-eye steak at economical to moderate rates. Open daily from 11 a.m. to 9 p.m.

Continue west on State Route 20 to **Courtland**, named to the National Register of Historic Places for its 1818 development of the early town plan. Local architectural styles span almost two centuries. For a brochure on Courtland, which details a driving tour of the historical district, stop by Town Hall.

After exploring Courtland, continue to **Doublehead Resort & Lodge** (800-685-9267; doublehead.com) for some relaxation and outdoor recreation. Located at 145 County Road 314 near Town Creek, the complex underscores a Native American theme from its name to its design and furnishings. A split-rail fence defines pastures, and wooden poles frame the metal entrance gate with its "Welcome Friends" greeting in Cherokee characters.

The property takes its name from Doublehead, a Cherokee chief who once lived on this land. The management wants to sustain a Native American

TOP ANNUAL EVENTS IN NORTHWEST ALABAMA

Festival of the Cranes
Decatur, January
(256) 350-6639

Bloomin' Festival at St. Bernard
Cullman, early April
(256) 739-6682 ext. 7133
bloominfestival.com

North Alabama Birding Festival
Wheeler Wildlife Refuge
Highway 67 East
Decatur, May
decaturcvb.org
(256) 350-2028 or (800) 232-5449

Alabama Jubilee Hot-Air Balloon Classic
Point Mallard Park, Decatur
Memorial Day weekend
(256) 350-2028 or (800) 232-5449
alabamajubilee.net

Helen Keller Festival
Tuscumbia, late June
(256) 383-4066 or (888) 329-2124
helenkellerfestival.com

The Spirit of America Festival
Point Mallard Park, Decatur, July 3–4
(256) 350-2028 or (800) 232-5449
spiritofamericafestival.com

W. C. Handy Festival
Florence, late July to early August
(256) 766-7642
wchandymusicfestival.org

September Skirmish
Point Mallard Park, Decatur
Labor Day weekend
(256) 350-2028 or (800) 524-6181

Oktoberfest
Cullman, early October
(256) 727-0949
cullmanoktoberfest.com

Alabama Renaissance Faire
Florence, fourth weekend of October
(256) 740-4141 or (888) 356-8687
alrenfaire.org

Covered Bridge Festival
Oneonta, fourth weekend of October
(205) 274-2153
blountoneontachamber.org

awareness as it continues to develop this distinctive resort. The main lodge features a 5,000-square-foot deck overlooking Wilson Lake. Hammered metal designs of free-floating feathers and an upward-pointing arrowhead frame the double hand-carved front doors. A locally found Cherokee medallion inspired the lodge's unique chandelier.

Nestled among the trees are thirty-eight split-level cedar log cabins, each with three bedrooms, two baths, and a completely equipped kitchen. Other features include a wood-burning fireplace, satellite TV, and washer and dryer. (After all, Doublehead's appreciation for creature comforts is well documented.) Beds are constructed from rustic cedar posts, and Indian wall hangings echo the motif. Each cabin comes with a beckoning hammock, grill, picnic table, and private pier. Recreational activities range from fishing, boating, and hunting to horseback riding. Golfers will want to inquire about special packages with land and water shuttles to the nearby Robert Trent Jones championship golf courses, **Fighting Joe** and **The Schoolmaster**, at the Shoals. Other amenities include two tennis courts, a basketball court, and a 2.5-mile walking/nature trail. The facility offers rentals for Jet Skis, pontoons, canoes, other watercraft, a sporting clays course (shooting range), and a private 1,100-acre hunting preserve. Deluxe rates.

Afterward head west toward Tuscumbia.

The Shoals

You will be transported back in time when you arrive in **Tuscumbia**. At 301 South Dickson Street stands **The Log Cabin Stagecoach Stop at Cold Water**, an authentic structure from the pioneer period. The Stagecoach Stop is open by appointment and on special occasions. Call (256) 383-0783 for more information or check out visittuscumbiaal.com. Continue to Commercial Row, located on the north side of West Fifth Street between Water and Main Streets. This block of seven bordering brick buildings, dating to the 1830s, represents local antebellum commercial architecture. During the 1880s, Capt. Arthur Keller (Helen Keller's father) published his newspaper, the *North Alabamian*, here in the corner building.

While exploring downtown, step inside the restored **Palace Drugstore** at 100 Main Street (256-386-8210) for a bit of nostalgia and maybe a milk shake at the 1950s soda fountain. Also, you'll want to see Spring Park's 51-jet fountain with water surging to heights of more than 150 feet. On weekend evenings, you can take in a special show, choreographed to lights and the music of Alabama's nationally known artists with a focus on those who recorded in Muscle Shoals. The large fountain serves as a memorial to Princess Im-Mi-Ah-Key, wife of

Chickasaw Chief Tuscumbia, for whom the town is named. For more information, call (256) 383-0783 or visit colbertcountytourism.org.

Nearby at 300 West North Commons stands **Ivy Green**, the birthplace of **Helen Keller**. After her graduation from Radcliffe College, Miss Keller worked tirelessly on behalf of those with disabilities by lecturing, writing articles and books (some of which have been translated into more than fifty languages), and appealing to legislative bodies to improve conditions for those with impaired sight and hearing. Because she conquered her own disabilities and gained an international reputation for inspiring other persons with disabilities to live richer lives, she became known as America's "First Lady of Courage."

Of Ivy Green Miss Keller wrote, "The Keller homestead . . . was called 'Ivy Green' because the house and surrounding trees and fences were covered with beautiful English Ivy." On the grounds you'll also see English boxwood, magnolia, mimosa, roses, and honeysuckle. The family home contains many original furnishings, photographs, letters, awards, books, and Miss Keller's braille typewriter.

Summer visitors can watch a miracle reenacted at a performance of William Gibson's drama *The Miracle Worker* staged on Ivy Green's grounds. The play culminates with a vivid portrayal of the poignant incident at the water pump when teacher Anne Sullivan helped the blind and deaf child break through her black void into "a wonderful world with all its sunlight and beauty."

Except for major holidays, Ivy Green is open year-round. The home can be toured Mon through Sat from 8:30 a.m. to 4 p.m. Admission: adults $6, seniors $5, and students (ages 5 to 18) $3. For more information on Ivy Green, the play, or the annual **Helen Keller Festival** (scheduled for a weekend in late June each year), call (256) 383-4066. Visit helenkellerbirthplace.org for more background information.

About 3.5 miles south of Tuscumbia, you'll find another interesting home, **Belle Mont** (256-637-8513) at 1569 Cook Lane. Constructed between 1828 and 1832, the U-shaped brick structure suggests the influence of Thomas Jefferson. Dr. Alexander William Mitchell, who moved here from Virginia, built this home, now considered the state's finest example of Jefferson Palladian architecture. Partially furnished, most of the home's pieces date to the period between 1840 and 1860. Owned by the Alabama Historical Commission, Belle Mont is open Wed through Sat from 10 a.m. to 4 p.m. Admission: adults $6, senior citizens $5, children (ages 6 to 18) $3. Check out this property and other historic sites at preserveala.org.

At some point during your visit, you may want to learn more about this area, called **the Shoals**. Looping through north Alabama, the Tennessee River comes into its own here in the state's northwest corner. At one time navigators found the Muscle Shoals rapids too formidable to negotiate, but the Tennessee Valley Authority (TVA) solved this problem with a series of strategically placed dams. The jagged rocks that created perilous swirling currents and wrecked boats now lie "buried" far below the water's surface.

To get a good idea of the river's impact on the region, you can visit the TVA Reservation at Muscle Shoals to see *Wilson Dam*. With its north end in Lauderdale County and its south end in Lawrence County, the dam stretches almost a mile and serves as a bridge for State Route 101. Named for President Woodrow Wilson, the dam was initiated during World War I to supply power for making munitions. Today, visitors enjoy camping, boating, and fishing at Wilson Reservoir. The site features a network of hiking and walking trails. While on a trek, enjoy the nature area's ideal habitat for lovely ferns. Look for the walking fern, rarely seen in Alabama but a favorite natural inhabitant of the Wilson Dam area. For more information, visit tva.gov/Energy/Our-Power-System/Hydroelectric/Wilson-Reservoir.

Afterward follow Veteran's Drive to downtown *Florence*, which features a number of interesting attractions such as the *Indian Mound and Museum* at 1028 South Court Street near the river. The ancient mound looms to a height of forty-two feet, the largest of several in the Tennessee Valley. Near the mound, called *Wawmanona* by Native Americans, stands a museum containing displays of tools, ornaments, pottery, fluted points, and other artifacts along with exhibits on the Mississippian culture's mysterious mound builders. Museum admission: adults $5, students $2. No charge to walk to the top of the mound. Except for major holidays, the site is open Tues through Sat from 10 a.m. to 4 p.m. For more information call (256) 760-6427; visitflorenceal.com.

Nearby, at 601 Riverview Drive, you'll find the *Frank Lloyd Wright's Rosenbaum Museum* (256-718-5050). Conceived by Wright in 1939 and completed in 1940, the home so reflected Wright's iconoclastic approach to organic domestic architecture that Stanley and Mildred Rosenbaum could not find a local contractor to take on this project. Along with his final plans, Wright sent an apprentice to supervise the construction of this Usonian house, now on the National Register of Historic Places.

Designed for a two-acre site overlooking the Tennessee River, the house uses large areas of glass to take advantage of the view and innovative radiant heating because of the proximity of Tennessee Valley Authority's low-cost electricity. "Mr. Wright wanted to use all natural materials," Mrs. Rosenbaum said, "no paint or plaster—only cypress wood, brick, glass, and concrete." After the couple's four sons arrived, Wright designed an addition—its clean lines flow naturally (and imperceptibly) from the original structure. The home is open for tours Tues through Sat from 10 a.m. to 4 p.m. and Sun from 1 to 4 p.m.

Admission: adults $10, senior citizens and students $5. Visit wrightinalabama
.com for more information.

To see the birthplace of the "Father of the Blues," head for 620 West
College Street, where you'll find the **W. C. Handy Home and Museum**
(256-760-6434), fronted by a fence of split rails. The hand-hewn log cabin,
birthplace of William Christopher Handy, contains furnishings representa-
tive of the period around 1873. The adjoining museum features Handy's
legendary trumpet and the piano on which he composed "St. Louis Blues."
Handy also wrote more than 150 other musical compositions, including
such standards as "Memphis Blues" and "Beale Street Blues." You'll see
handwritten sheet music, photographs, correspondence, awards, and other
items pertaining to Handy's life and legacy. An addition houses Handy's
extensive book collection and serves as a resource center for black history
and culture. The museum is open Tues through Sat from 10 a.m. to 4 p.m.
Admission: adults $2, students $0.50.

For a week of swinging jazz, plan to visit Florence from late July to early
August and take in the **W. C. Handy Music Festival**. Special events include

Strange as It Sounds

South of Russellville and west of Phil Campbell (that's the town's name) lies a unique
attraction known locally as the Dismals. Located at 901 County Road 8, **Dismals
Canyon** once served as a ceremonial ground for Native Americans and a hiding
place for outlaws. In addition to caves, waterfalls, craggy rock formations, rainbows,
and unusual vegetation, the canyon contains phosphorescent creatures called
"dismalites" that glow in the dark. By signing up for a guided night tour, offered Friday
and Saturday (the time depends on the degree of darkness), you can actually see the
rare dismalites. According to a research scientist from Auburn University, these little
glow worms only can be found here in this canyon, New Zealand, or China.

Geologists speculate that a prehistoric earthquake produced the place's chaotic
geography with its many natural grottoes and bridges. This eerie but intriguing site
also features both a natural arboretum and winding staircase.

After hiking through this place primeval, you may decide to take advantage of other
activities—canoeing down Bear Creek, biking a 4-mile mountain trail, or swimming in
Dismals Creek. For overnight visitors the site offers lodges (with fireplaces), a country
store, and camping facilities. To wet your whistle, take a walk back in time to the
Soda Fountain and Grill inside the Country Store. Open every day, the soda fountain
offers old-fashioned milk shakes, malts, sundaes, and sodas. Open only on Saturday,
the grill features Slug Burgers, cornbread salad, and much more. For more information call (205) 993-4559. Pay a virtual visit via dismalscanyon.com.

Memorial Wall for "Woman with Dancing Eyes"

As a youngster, Tom Hendrix would listen to his grandmother talk about her grandmother, a Native American who was forced as a teen to walk from her Alabama home to an Oklahoma Indian reservation. Tagged around the neck like an animal, the young girl had her name taken away and was identified as No. 59.

Thousands of men, women, and children died on that 1,000-mile Trail of Tears during the 1830s. Hendrix's great-great-grandmother survived. But that is only part of her miraculous tale.

As a grown man, Hendrix decided he wanted to do something to honor his ancestor whose real name was Te-lah-nay which in the Yuchi language means "Woman with Dancing Eyes."

Around 1985, Hendrix said he began having a recurring dream about an Indian woman who repeatedly touched her hand to her mouth. Hendrix's wife, Doreen, suggested that it was Te-lah-nay, asking him to tell her story. That year at a Native American gathering in Lebanon, Tennessee, Hendrix met an old Yuchi woman.

When Hendrix told the woman about his great-great-grandmother and expressed his desire to commemorate her, the Yuchi woman responded, "We shall all pass this earth, Tom, but only the stones will remain."

That's when Hendrix knew what he had to do. In 1988, he began constructing a commemorative stone wall on the property of his home outside Florence at 13890 County Road 8 (256-764-3617, ifthelegendsfade.com). Although Hendrix had worked with his hands at the Ford Motor Company as a die caster for decades, he had never built a stone wall. He didn't draw up any blueprints. He didn't have any final plan in mind. He just started collecting rocks discarded along roadsides by farmers and pulling rocks from creek beds. Then he piled the rocks and improvised as he went along.

The wall, Hendrix used to say, wore out three trucks, twenty-two wheelbarrows, 2,700 pairs of gloves, three dogs, and one old man.

Built without mortar or cement, the 3-to-5-foot-high wall is the largest unmortised rock wall in the United States and the largest monument to an American woman.

For his ancestor, Hendrix said that living on the Indian reservation meant sure death. "When she got to Oklahoma, she said she searched for a river that sang to her. We call this the Tennessee River but all tribes called it the Singing River. They believed a young woman lived in this river, sang to them and protected them."

When the displaced teen could find no singing river in Oklahoma, she determined to return home. "If she stayed in that dark place, she knew she would die."

So, his great-great-grandmother ran away from the reservation and started the long trek home. It took her five years. From 1839 to 1844, the young woman struggled through the wilderness. "If she got caught, she would have been hung."

His great-great-grandmother made it home. She married a man named Jonathan Levi Hipp, had three children, and died at a young age. "Grandmother said she walked herself to death," Hendrix said.

The two walls symbolize his great-great-grandmother's trip to Oklahoma and her journey back.

A section of the wall is dedicated to all those on the Trail of Tears. It is four feet tall and starts out at about twenty-five feet wide. But, as you walk, the wall gets thinner and thinner until it is about four feet across at the end. "They're dying, all the way to Oklahoma," Hendrix said.

Nestled by the wall is a prayer circle where Hendrix would pray most every morning. It features four tiers that represent birth, life, death, and rebirth. Through word of mouth, people from all over began coming to see the wall that Hendrix was building. They walked through the circles, they sat in silence, some knelt in prayer.

Over the years, people began bringing and sending rocks to add to the wall. Hendrix received stones from all fifty states and rocks and fossils from 127 nations, territories, and islands.

On February 24, 2017, ten days past his 83rd birthday, Tom Hendrix left this earth to join Te-lan-nay in the Great Circle. Tom's Wall remains open to visitors daily from 8 a.m. to 4 p.m.

parades, jam sessions, the "DaDooRunRun" for joggers, a picnic-jazz evening on the Tennessee River's banks, the colorful "Street Strut" led by the Grand Oobeedoo, and a concert with celebrated musicians.

The Handy Festival evolved from a chance meeting in the Muscle Shoals Airport when two men struck up what turned out to be more than a casual conversation. Local veterinarian David Mussleman happened to ask Willie Ruff, a Yale music professor, about the horn he carried. This led to a discussion about native son W. C. Handy and his tremendous musical contribution—and subsequently to the annual festival held in Handy's honor. For more information call the festival office at (256) 766-7642 or visit wchandymusicfestival.org.

While exploring Florence, you'll pass Wilson Park on the corner of Tuscaloosa Street and Wood Avenue. This setting serves as a backdrop for a number of local festivities, such as the *Alabama Renaissance Faire* (256-740-4141 or 888-356-8687; alrenfaire.org). In fact, if you visit the park during this October gala, you can enjoy diversions ranging from derring-do with sword and shield to music, dance, and drama as residents bring to life some of the color, action, and excitement of the Renaissance period.

Beside the park you'll see the *Kennedy-Douglass Center for the Arts* at 217 East Tuscaloosa Street (256-760-6379; kdartcenter.org). This 1918

Georgian-style mansion and adjacent structures serve as a performing arts center. Stop by to view the current art exhibit and visit the gift shop.

At 316 North Court Street, you'll find ***Trowbridge's*** (256-764-1503), which offers sandwiches, soups, chili, ice cream, and Oh My Gosh—a brownie piled high with vanilla ice cream and topped with hot caramel, whipped cream, and a cherry. The dessert gets its name from what most people say when they see it.

A mirrored soda fountain lists ice cream flavors and drink choices. Third generation owner Don Trowbridge credits the eatery's longevity to keeping the menu simple. Don's grandfather built Trowbridge's Creamery in 1918, and local farmers brought their milk and cream in to be processed. The family occupied the second floor over the ice cream shop, and the dairy stood behind. The founder's original recipe for Orange-Pineapple Ice Cream, now shipped from New Orleans, remains a favorite with today's patrons.

A large painting on the rear wall depicts Trowbridge's interior from previous years—with almost no changes. Posters publicizing past local festivals pay tribute to Helen Keller and W. C. Handy, "Father of the Blues." Framed photos depict early Florence scenes and the construction of Wilson Dam, which originated as a World War I project to supply power for making munitions. Open Mon through Sat from 9 a.m. to 5:30 p.m. Economical rates.

A short distance away at 203 Hermitage Drive stands ***Pope's Tavern*** (256-760-6439), now a history-filled museum. Originally built as a stagecoach stopover and tavern, the attractive structure of white-painted bricks dates back to 1811. Travelers on the Natchez Trace stopped here, and so did Andrew Jackson

Tee Time at the Shoals

The Robert Trent Jones Golf Trail continues to lure golfers from near and far with an unbeatable combination of great golf and value. In the Shoals, you can tee off at two 18-hole championship RTJ courses and dip into a little history, too. Named for Civil War Gen. Joseph Wheeler, the Fighting Joe has earned high marks for new courses from golfing publications and attracts near overflow crowds. The Schoolmaster pays tribute to President Woodrow Wilson, "the schoolmaster" of politics, who was instrumental in getting the Wilson Dam built here. To play either or both of these courses situated between the Wheeler and Wilson Dams on the Tennessee River, call (256) 446-5111. Visit rtjgolf.com or pchresorts.com for more information on the Trail's offerings.

For the record, Florence makes a great starting point if you want to research the new RTJ Spa Trail. Golf widows (and everyone else, too) will appreciate the opportunity to de-stress at this world-class spa. Just look for the soaring tower and head for **Marriott Shoals Hotel & Spa** at 10 Hightower Place (256-246-3600; marriott.com). You'll emerge feeling like you made an eagle.

The Sound of Swampers

About four miles over the river from Florence is a concrete block building that once rang with some of the best music in the world. *Muscle Shoals Sound Studio* (256-978-5151, muscleshoalssoundstudio.org) at 3614 Jackson Highway in Sheffield was opened in 1969 by a local rhythm section known as the Swampers—David Hood, Jimmy Johnson, Barry Beckett, and Roger Hawkins. Unique because it was the only recording studio owned and operated at the time by session musicians, the studio became a popular recording place for artists such as The Staples Singers, Rolling Stones, Aretha Franklin, Joe Cocker, Willie Nelson, Cat Stevens, Bob Dylan, Bob Seger, Rod Stewart, Leon Russell, Lynrd Skynrd, Paul Simon, and many more. The building was featured on the album cover of Cher's debut solo album in 1969 titled "3614 Jackson Highway."

By 1978, the Swampers had outgrown the small studio and moved. Other businesses used the facility but by late 1990s, the building was abandoned. In 2013, the studio was purchased by the Music Shoals Music Foundation and opened as a museum and recording studio restored to its 1969 look. The studio is open from Sept through Apr, Mon through Sat from 10 a.m. to 5 p.m. May through Aug hours are 10 a.m. to 5 p.m. daily. Hours may vary if recording sessions are taking place. Call before visiting. Tours are $15 for adults, $13 for seniors and military, $10 for students, and free for children (ages 10 and under).

when he passed through in 1814 on his way to fight the British at the Battle of New Orleans. During the Civil War the inn served as a hospital where wounded Confederate and Union soldiers lay side by side to receive medical treatment from local doctors and the townswomen.

Inside the tavern you'll see period furnishings, kitchen utensils, tools, firearms, Civil War uniforms, photos, letters, and pioneer artifacts. Be sure to notice the worn silk Stars and Bars. This flag, hand-stitched by local ladies, traveled to Virginia with the Lauderdale Volunteers (one of northwestern Alabama's first Confederate military units) when they left to fight in the first Battle of Manassas. Before you leave, notice the Florence Light Running Wagon, made in a local factory that at one time was the world's second-largest wagon-building operation. Admission: adults $2, students $0.50. Open Tues through Sat, 10 a.m. to 4 p.m., except for major holidays.

Scenic Wilderness

Leaving the Shoals, you might enjoy taking the ***Natchez Trace Parkway***. A portion of the historic Trace cuts across this corner of Alabama through Lauderdale and Colbert Counties. Once a pioneer footpath, this route took travelers from Natchez, Mississippi, to Nashville, Tennessee. To intercept the Trace, which offers plenty of scenic stops, picnic spots, and nature trails, head northwest on State Route 20. For more information, visit nps.gov/natr.

Heading south to **Winfield** takes you to another fascinating attraction, **Natural Bridge** (205-486-5330). Located on US 278 about a mile west of the

Meet Jerry Brown, Ninth-Generation Potter

While exploring this region of scenic wilderness, consider a visit to **Jerry Brown Pottery** (205-921-9483 or 800-341-4919; jerrybrownpottery.com), located at 166 Boyett Dr. in Hamilton. Here, Jerry Brown carries on a family tradition of pottery making that spans nine generations. In 1992 Jerry and his wife, Sandra, made a trip to Washington, DC, where he received a National Heritage Fellowship Award, presented by President and Mrs. Bush. Jerry's work is exhibited in galleries across the country as well as the Smithsonian, where he has been invited several times to demonstrate pottery making. The traditional Southern folk potter has captured numerous awards at shows and festivals, and his work is sought by collectors. "Folk pottery increases in value," said Jerry, who signs and dates his pieces. In a "Quest for America's Best," QVC shopping network featured his work on national television. For this show Jerry filled an order for 1,500 pitchers, which sold out in two minutes.

One of the nation's few practicing traditional potters, Jerry remembers "playing around on the potter's wheel before I was old enough to start school." He performs his magic by combining water with local clay, which "looks almost blue. The South is known for its good clay," he added. Using a backhoe to dig the clay from a 150-year-old pit, Jerry then turns the process over to his four-legged assistant who does the mixing by walking circles around a mule-powered clay grinder. Jerry designed and built the brick oval kiln, in which he fires his work at temperatures that exceed 3,000 degrees Fahrenheit.

The pottery's showroom features blue-speckled pitchers, bowls, churns, candleholders, crocks, mugs, pie plates, bluebird houses, and more. Face jugs, Jerry's specialty, were historically used to hold harmful substances. Sometimes called ugly jugs, the vessels feature faces that don't win beauty contests but do earn awards and are coveted by collectors. The jugs sell for prices ranging from $30 to $200 and vary in size up to the largest, a five-gallon container. Jerry's newest additions include bacon cookers, egg separators (with faces), and mule mugs. (And yes, the mule's tail serves as the handle.)

To view the pottery-making process as it was done in the olden days or to buy unique gifts (for yourself and others), head to Hamilton, near the Mississippi border. The Pottery's hours run Mon through Sat 9 a.m. to 5 p.m.; Sun by appointment only. For a fun event, visit the Jerry Brown Arts Festival held in March at the Tombigbee Electric Cooperative, 3196 Hwy 55 in Hamilton. The indoor juried arts festival draws artists from around the Southeast for the two-day free festival.

intersection of State Routes 5 and 13, this double-span, 60-foot-high sandstone bridge, thousands of years in the making, looms majestically in its pristine setting. Surrounding this impressive formation, presumably the longest natural bridge east of the Rockies, you'll see massive moss-covered boulders and lush vegetation. Local flora includes ferns, bigleaf magnolias, mountain laurel, and oakleaf hydrangeas. Inviting nature paths and picnic areas make this a pleasant place for an outing. Admission: adults $3.50, children (ages 6 to 12) $2.50, children (age 5 and under) free. Except for Thanksgiving and Christmas days, the facility is open daily year-round from 8 a.m. till sunset. You are not allowed to walk across Natural Bridge. You can only view it from below.

Continuing east through Winston County, you'll find the town of **Double Springs**, located in the **William B. Bankhead National Forest**. This huge forest (named for the distinguished political family of actress Tallulah Bankhead) spreads over most of Winston County and north into Lawrence County.

In front of the Winston County Courthouse at Double Springs stands *Dual Destiny*, the statue of a Civil War soldier flanked by billowing Confederate and Union flags. Contrary to common assumption, many Alabamians remained staunch Unionists during the Civil War, and "the Free State of Winston" represented such a contingent. After Alabama's secession (which passed by a narrow vote), these hill-country people, led by local teacher Christopher Sheats, took the position that if a state could secede from the Union, then a county could secede from a state.

While visiting the Free State of Winston, take time to explore some of the surrounding **Sipsey Wilderness**. With 25,988 acres, Sipsey provides plenty of off-the-beaten-path territory, including twenty miles of hiking trails.

Afterward take US 278 east and head toward Cullman.

On the Coon Dog Trail

Way off the beaten path in northwest Alabama, the **Key Underwood Coon Dog Memorial Graveyard** projects a sense of serenity—at least for 364 days of the year. But that changes each Labor Day when this site, located beyond Tuscumbia and near tiny Cherokee, attracts a throng of visitors for a rollicking celebration.

Festivities include an afternoon of live bluegrass music, buck dancing, and a liars' contest. "And they can really tell some whoppers," said one visitor. If it's an election year, political hopefuls often show up for this occasion.

Now a park, the site features markers and tombstones for more than 185 coon dogs—with each grave decorated on Labor Day. The graveyard's origin dates to the death of Troop, a famous coonhound owned by Key Underwood. On September 4, 1937, Underwood and some friends buried his faithful coon dog in this wooded area, where they often congregated to compare dogs, spin yarns, and launch their hunts. On an average day, the surroundings look pretty much like they did way back when Troop picked up the scent of a coon here.

"When I buried Troop, I had no intention of establishing a coon dog cemetery," Underwood said. "I merely wanted to do something special for a special coon dog." Other hunters started doing the same when their favorite coon dogs died. Take time to walk around and read the names and tributes. Hunter's Famous Amos, a hound named Ralston Purina's Dog of the Year in 1984, is buried here as well as several World Champion coon dogs. Others honored include Preacher, Old Blue, Queen, Patches, Smoky, Barney, Bean Blossom Bomma, Bluetick, Old Roy, Strait Talk'n Tex, and Night Ranger.

Some headstones contain only names and dates. On others, the owners memorialize their dogs with such tributes as "A joy to hunt with" and "He wasn't the best, but he was the best I ever had." Black Ranger, who died in 1976, "was good as the best and better than the rest." Monuments range from those made of wood and sheet metal to field stones and marble.

Only bona fide coon dogs can qualify for burial in this unique cemetery, and three requirements must be met: First, the owner needs to claim his pet is an authentic coon dog and present proper credentials. Then a witness, who has observed the animal tree a coon in the past, must declare the deceased is indeed a coon dog. Finally, a member of the local coon hunters' organization must be allowed to view the coonhound and verify it as such.

"It is good to see a place like this exists. I bet there are a hundred stories to go along with each gravestone," reads an entry in the Coon Dog Cemetery's online guestbook. (Visit the Coon Dog Memorial Graveyard at coondogcemetery.com for photos and comments or call 256-412-5970.)

Another reader observes, "The younger generation of today will never know just how great the sport is because of the expansion of the cities into rural America and a sport that is slowly dying."

Apparently, many moviegoers from across the country learned of the cemetery's existence while watching *Sweet Home Alabama*. Using their literary license, however, the producers placed the Coon Dog Graveyard in south Alabama.

Labor Day visitors can dig into some finger-licking Southern barbeque—free for those who belong to the Tennessee Valley Coon Hunters Association, and membership applications are available on the spot. Otherwise, attendees can purchase barbecue plates. Soft drinks and bottled water along with T-shirts and caps featuring the Coon Dog Graveyard logo are for sale for this occasion, but don't forget your lawn chair. Admission is free. Coon hunters will want to put this event on their list, and maybe you will, too—especially if you're running for office.

For more information, call (256) 412-5970 or check out coondogcemetery.com. The site is open year-round during daylight hours.

Covered Bridge Country

To see Alabama's largest covered truss bridge, continue east from Winston County on US 278. Watch for the left turn to **Clarkson Covered Bridge** (sometimes called the Legg Bridge), located a short distance north of the highway on Cullman County Road 11. The bridge, situated in a picturesque park setting, stretches 270 feet across Crooked Creek. Supported by four large stone piers, this "town-truss" structure features latticed timbers, clapboard siding, and a roof of cedar shingles. The bridge, restored in 1975, dates to 1904.

Once the site of a Civil War battle, the surrounding area offers picnic grounds and woodland hiking trails. The park is open year-round during daylight hours, and there's no admission charge.

Continuing east on US 278 takes you to **Cullman**, a city that dates to 1873 when Col. John G. Cullmann bought a large tract of land and established a colony for German immigrants here. A reproduction of the founder's Bavarian-style home (which burned in 1912) now serves as the **Cullman County Museum** (256-739-1258 or 800-533-1258), located at 211 Second Avenue Northeast. The museum's eight rooms, each with a theme, preserve some of the city's German heritage and the area's history. You'll see a 7-foot wooden sculpture of a Native American warrior, china, jewelry, vintage clothing, fainting couches, early tools, and other local items. Admission: adults $5, senior citizens $4, children (under age 12) $3. Hours run from 9 a.m. to 4 p.m. Mon through Fri. Sun hours are 1:30 to 4:30 p.m. Visit cullmancountymuseum.com for more information.

For a good meal, stop by **The All Steak** (256-734-4322), located just a few blocks away on 323 Third Avenue Southwest. Contrary to its name, the restaurant serves a wide variety of entrees, including seafood and poultry. In addition to its beef specialties, the eatery is famous for homemade breads and desserts, especially the orange rolls, as well as its vegetable lunches. Prices are moderate. Hours are 10:30 a.m. to 10 p.m. Tues through Thurs; 7:30 a.m. to 10 p.m. Fri and Sat; 7:30 a.m. to 3 p.m. on Sun.

Continue to **The Duchess Bakery** and pick up some doughnuts. This family-owned business at 222 First Avenue Southeast opened in 1939. The bakery is open Tues through Sat 7 a.m. to 4 p.m.

At **Southern Accents** (256-734-0684 or 877-737-0554), you'll find an array of architectural antiques—everything from carved mantels, leaded-glass windows, statuary, and stately columns to chandeliers, hitching posts, molding, staircases, and claw-foot bathtubs. Housed in historic quarters at 308 Second Avenue Southeast, the inventory draws clients from across the US. Owner Garlan Gudger Jr. searches the globe for treasures from the past. His father,

Dr. Garlan Gudger, started the business in 1969 when he began rescuing architectural objects from local buildings slated to be demolished. Gudger offers an antique floor salvaging and cutting service plus door and window framing, which makes today's carpenters happy.

A sign near the entrance reads: your husband called . . . he said to buy anything you want. Hours run Tues through Fri 9 a.m. to 5 p.m.; Sat 9 a.m. to 3 p.m. Take a look at sa1969.com and order anything you want.

"We will serve no swine before its time," promise Ron Dunn and Gary Wiggins, first cousins who operate *Johnny's Bar-B-Q* (256-734-8539; johnnysbarbq.com), a family business at 1401 Fourth Street Southwest that opened in the early 1950s. Here, you can opt for a barbecue sandwich or a plate with all the fixings: coleslaw, beans, and potato salad. Other popular items include smoked chicken with white barbecue sauce, catfish, or barbecue-topped baked potatoes. "Closed on Sunday for church and closed on Monday for rest," the restaurant's hours run Tues through Sat from 10 a.m. to 9 p.m. Economical rates.

Afterward continue to 1600 Saint Bernard Drive Southeast, off US 278, on the town's east side. At *Ave Maria Grotto* (256-734-4110), on the grounds of a Benedictine monastery, visitors can take a Lilliputian world tour in a unique garden filled with more than 150 miniature reproductions of famous landmarks. Brother Joseph Zoettl, a Bavarian who arrived at St. Bernard Abbey in 1892, constructed these reduced versions of various buildings. At age 80 the gifted monk completed his final work, the Lourdes Basilica. His architectural miniatures also include the Hanging Gardens of Babylon, ancient Jerusalem, Rome's Pantheon, and St. Peter's Basilica.

Using ingenuity and an unlikely assortment of materials, from playing marbles and fishing floats to cold-cream jars and even a discarded bird cage (for the dome of St. Peter's), along with the more standard cement, limestone, and marble, Brother Joe fashioned a small world that continues to delight travelers. Check it out at avemariagrotto.com. Except for Christmas and New Year's Days, the grotto can be visited daily Oct through Mar from 9 a.m. to 5 p.m.; Apr through Sept, 9 a.m. to 6 p.m. Admission: adults $8, seniors $6, children (ages 6 to 12) $5.

In south Cullman County near Hanceville, you can make a personal pilgrimage to *The Shrine of the Most Blessed Sacrament of Our Lady of the Angels Monastery*. To reach the shrine, take State Route 91 through Hanceville, watching for signs that lead to County Road 747 and then to 3222

alabamatrivia

County Road 548. A long, white-fenced approach winds through a portion of the site's 380 acres of rolling farmland. More than three years in construction, the shrine opened in December 1999, and has become a major mecca for visitors. Home to the Poor Clare Nuns of Perpetual Adoration, the building of this facility was dear to the heart of Mother Angelica, founder of the Eternal Word Television Network (EWTN).

The shrine's Romanesque–Gothic style of architecture echoes Franciscan churches and monasteries of thirteenth-century Assisi. To reach the shrine, you'll cross an expansive colonaded piazza. As you approach, notice the T-shaped cross. The original top portion was struck by lightning, leaving the form of a Tau cross, the symbol that St. Francis used in signing his letters.

From inlaid Italian-marble floors and stately columns to vaulted ceiling, the awe-inspiring interior leaves no detail to chance. Made of carved cedar, the main altar is covered in gold leaf. The stained-glass windows were created in Munich, Germany, and the stonework embellishments were crafted by artisans in Spain. Other features include mosaics fashioned by Italian artisans using a four-century-old method of hand-chiseling and fitting.

Castle San Miguel stands below the piazza and houses a great hall, conference facilities, and a gift shop; hours are Mon through Sat from 8 a.m. to 4:45 p.m. The shrine is open to the public on Sun from 6 a.m. to 6 p.m. and until 9:30 p.m. on Mon through Sat. The nuns' Conventual Mass takes place at 7 a.m. daily. To learn more about the circumstances that led to the erection of this magnificent structure in the hills of Alabama, you can attend one of the brothers' commentaries, generally scheduled at 9 a.m. daily, depending on the crowd. For more information call (256) 352-6267 or visit olamshrine.com, where you will find a map and specific directions.

For a relaxing base on crystal blue waters, head to Crane Hill and **Smith Lake Bed & Breakfast** (256-747-6057). Located at 994 County Road 4230 and situated on the Rock Creek branch of the finger-shaped Lewis Smith Lake (the nation's third cleanest), the property promises all the amenities laced with warm hospitality and gorgeous natural surroundings, plus water recreation.

Owners Alexandra (better known as Alex) and Jim Cox offer two suites, the Loft and the Dock, and a vintage Airstream trailer. Both suites have balconies overlooking the lake—wonderful spots for sipping your morning coffee. Jim's job as a civil engineer took the couple to countries all over the world, including Germany, Israel, Saudi Arabia, and Japan. During the decade they lived in Japan, Alex taught cooking classes and conversational English to Japanese ladies and started thinking about a B&B of her own when she returned to the States. Now, that's a reality, and guests can enjoy this inviting getaway filled with antiques and fine Asian art.

Breakfast here starts with a fresh fruit medley and might feature quiche or stuffed French toast. Alex offers information on area restaurants, but some guests enjoy grilling their own dinner while watching a sunset. Perfect for couples or families, the suites can accommodate four comfortably, and the owners welcome kids. When weather permits, Jim takes guests out on his pontoon boat and also provides a double kayak and bikes for their use. The couple will send you to interesting spots nearby, perhaps to an artist's studio in Crane Hill or a year-round trout fishery in Jasper or to nearby Bankhead National Forest with its miles of hiking and biking trails. Visit smithlakebandb .com and check out the views. Moderate rates.

Continue east on US 278 until it intersects US 231, then turn south to see the ***Blount County Covered Bridges***. Known as the Covered Bridge Capital of Alabama, this area features three covered bridges, all still in daily use and marked by road signs on nearby highways. If you're on a tight schedule, choose the Horton Mill Covered Bridge, probably the most picturesque of the bunch. Located about five miles north of Oneonta on State Route 75, the latticed structure looms some seventy feet above the Warrior River's Calvert Prong—higher above water than any other covered bridge in the US. Adjacent to the highway there's a parking area with nearby picnic facilities and nature trails, making this a relaxing place to take a driving break.

Continuing your exploration, you'll find the county's shortest covered bridge southeast of Rosa. The 95-foot-long, tin-topped Easley Covered Bridge stands about a half-mile off Blount County Road 33 and spans Dub Branch.

Northwest of Cleveland, a mile off State Route 79, Swann Bridge appears rather suddenly as you're rounding a curve. The three-span bridge extends 324 feet over the Locust Fork of the Black Warrior River. You can park in a turn-off lane on the bridge's opposite side to explore the nearby terrain, where Queen Anne's lace, ferns, mountain laurel, wild hydrangeas, and muscadine vines grow. You might hear a mockingbird's serenade in the background.

Each October on the fourth weekend, the ***Oneonta*** area stages an annual ***Covered Bridge Festival*** featuring bridge tours, arts and crafts exhibits, and other festivities. For additional information on the festival, award-winning Palisades Park, or other area attractions, call the Blount County/Oneonta Chamber of Commerce at (205) 274-2153 or visit blountoneontachamber.org.

At ***Capps Cove*** (205-625-6045 or 800-583-4750), you'll find a country get-away with a mountain on one side and a river on the other. Located at 4126 Blount County Road 27, the complex offers two cabins and much, much more. Owners Sybil and Cason Capps, native Alabamians who lived in several states over fifteen years before moving back to Alabama from St. Louis when Cason retired from a broadcasting career.

"We think we're unique," Sybil says, "a country village with a barn, wedding chapel, and two old-style country cabins." Guests can enjoy a continental breakfast basket. Moderate rates. Visit the property at cappscove.com.

Continue to the state's central section. Nearby Ashville, easily reached by taking US 231 south, makes an interesting stop.

Places to Stay in Northwest Alabama

ATHENS

Econo Lodge
1500 US 72 East
(256) 232-1520

CRANE HILL

Smith Lake Bed & Breakfast
994 County Rd. 4230
(256) 747-6057
smithlakebandb.com

CULLMAN

Hampton Inn
6100 State Rte. 157
(256) 739-4444 or
(800) 426-7866

DECATUR

Comfort Inn
3239 Point Mallard Pkwy.
(480) 568-4632

Courtyard by Marriott

1209 Courtyard Circle
(256) 355-4446 or
(800) 321-2211

DoubleTree by Hilton Hotel Decatur Riverfront
1101 Sixth Ave. Northeast
(256) 355-3150 or
(800) 553-3150

Hampton Inn
2041 Beltline Rd. Southwest
(256) 355-5888 or
(800) 426-7866

FLORENCE

Marriott Shoals Hotel & Spa
10 Hightower Place
(256) 246-3600 or
(800) 593-6450

ONEONTA

Capps Cove Bed & Breakfast
4126 County Rd. 27
(205) 625-6045 or
(800) 583-4750
cappscove.com

ROGERSVILLE

Joe Wheeler State Park Lodge
4401 McLean Dr.
(256) 247-5461 or
(800) 544-5639 or
(800) 252-7275
Alapark.com/Joe-Wheeler-State-Park-Lodge

TOWN CREEK

Doublehead Resort & Lodge
145 County Rd. 314
(800) 685-9267
doublehead.com

TUSCUMBIA

The ColdWater Inn
712 US 72
(256) 383-6844
coldwaterinn.com

Key West Inn
1800 US 72 West
(256) 383-0700 or
(800) 833-0555

WINFIELD

Hampton Inn Winfield
7005 State Hwy 129 North
(205) 487-1270

FOR MORE INFORMATION ABOUT NORTHWEST ALABAMA

Alabama Mountain Lakes Tourist Association
402 Sherman St. Southeast
Decatur 35602
(256) 350-3500 or (800) 648-5381
northalabama.org

This organization covers 16 north Alabama counties that are home to some 100 attractions in a 100-mile radius.

Colbert County Tourism Bureau
719 Hwy. 72 West
PO Box 740425
Tuscumbia 35674
(256) 383-0783
colbertcountytourism.org

Cullman Area Chamber of Commerce
301 Second Ave. Southwest
Cullman 35055
(256) 734-0454 or (800) 313-5114
cullmanchamber.org
info@cullmanchamber.org

Decatur/Morgan County Convention & Visitors Bureau
719 Sixth Ave. SE
PO Box 2349
Decatur 35601
(256) 350-2028 or (800) 232-5449
decaturcvb.org info@decaturcvb.org

Florence/Lauderdale Tourism
200 Jim Spain Dr.
Florence 35630
(256) 740-4141 or (888) 356-8687
visitflorenceal.com

Places to Eat in Northwest Alabama

CULLMAN

The All Steak
323 Third Ave. Southwest
(256) 734-4322

Johnny's Bar-B-Q
1404 Fourth St. Southwest
(256) 734-8539
johnnysbarbq.com

Rumors Deli
601 Fourth St. Southwest
Suite 100
(256) 737-0911
rumorsdeli.com

DECATUR

Big Bob Gibson Bar-B-Q
1715 Sixth Ave. Southeast
(256) 350-6969
bigbobgibson.com

Brick Deli & Tavern
112 Moulton St. East
(256) 355-8318
brickdeli.com

Curry's on Johnston Street
115 Johnston St. Southeast
(256) 350-6715
currysrestaurant.com

Simp McGhee's
725 Bank St. Northeast
(256) 353-6284
simpmcghees.com

Simply Delicious
2215 Danville Rd.,
Southwest
(256) 355-7564

The Railyard
209 Second Ave. Southeast
(256) 580-5707
therailyarddecatur.com

DOUBLE SPRINGS

Lakeshore Inn Restaurant
364 E. Lakeshore Dr.
(205) 489-2462
lakeshoreinnandmarina.com

Sapore Grill
26641 Hwy. 195
(205) 489-1172
saporegrill.com

FLORENCE

Ricatoni's Italian Grill
107 North Court St.
(256) 718-1002
ricatonis.com

Trowbridge's
316 North Court St.
(256) 764-1503

The 360 Grill
10 Hightower Place
(256) 246-3660

HALEYVILLE

Cazadores
1918 21st St.
(205) 486-2108

Dixie Den
907 20th St.
(205) 486-8577

HARTSELLE

The Freight House
200 Railroad St. Southwest
(256) 773-4600
freighthousehartselle.com

Las Vias Mexican Grill
711 Nance Ford Rd.
Southwest
(256) 751-1402
lasviasmexicangrill.com

MOULTON

**Western Sirloin
Steak House**
11383 State Rte. 157
(256) 974-7191

MUSCLE SHOALS

Donna and Friends
1325 Avalon Ave.
(256) 314-2494

Sweet Peppers Deli
619 Avalon Ave.
(256) 383-8800
sweetpeppersdeli.com

ONEONTA

Swamptails Restaurant
130 First Ave. East
(205) 274-2525
swamptailsrestaurant.com

SHEFFIELD

George's Steak Pit
1206 Jackson Hwy.
(256) 381-1531
georgessteakpit.com

TUSCUMBIA

**Brown's Heavenly Fish
and Soul Food**
1306 E. Sixth St.
(256) 381-4001

Claunch Cafe
400 South Main St.
(in Spring Park)
(256) 386-0222

MAINSTREAM ATTRACTIONS WORTH SEEING IN NORTHWEST ALABAMA

Alabama Music Hall of Fame
617 US 72 West Tuscumbia
(256) 381-4417 or (800) 239-2643
Alahof.org

You can immerse yourself in the state's musical heritage at this facility, which features exhibits, audiovisual galleries, and memorabilia related to musicians either from Alabama or associated with the state. Artists represented include Hank Williams, Elvis Presley, Emmylou Harris, the Temptations, and many others.

Point Mallard Park
2901 Point Mallard Cir. Decatur
(256) 341-4900
pointmallardpark.com

Named for nearby Wheeler National Wildlife Refuge's wintering ducks, this park for all seasons offers aquatic fun in the summer and year-round golfing on a championship course. You may even see Capt. Mike Mallard, a human-size mascot in nautical attire, wandering about. Not only does the 750-acre complex contain a wave pool, an Olympic-size diving pool, water slides, sand beach, and "Squirt Factory," you'll also find a 173-acre campground, hiking and biking trails, and picnicking facilities here.

Central Alabama

Ridges, Springs & Valleys

Alabama's midsection presents a pleasing pastoral landscape, a panorama of ridges, springs, and valleys. Heading south, the Birmingham area serves as a convenient base from which to branch out into the state's central region. From here, too, you can easily sweep down into Alabama's southeastern section to explore the historic *Chattahoochee Trace* (877-766-2443) as well as the state capital area.

Start your area exploration with a trip to downtown *Ashville*, home of one of St. Clair County's two courthouses (the other is in Pell City). This neoclassical revival structure, an enlargement of an earlier courthouse, dates from the early 1840s.

A charming southern town, Ashville offers many historic structures. Start off at the circa-1852 *Inzer House* at 229 Fifth Street, a striking structure now reincarnated as a Civil War museum, the John W. Inzer Museum (205-594-2116). A number of black cast-iron Confederate crosses dot the grounds of nearby *Ashville Cemetery*.

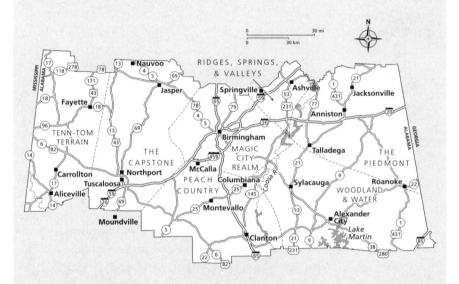

RIDGES, SPRINGS, & VALLEYS

Nauvoo

Jasper

Springville

Ashville

Jacksonville

Fayette

Anniston

MISSISSIPPI

ALABAMA

TENN-TOM TERRAIN

Birmingham

MAGIC CITY REALM

Talladega

THE PIEDMONT

GEORGIA

THE CAPSTONE

McCalla

Columbiana

Northport

Roanoke

PEACH COUNTRY

Sylacauga

WOODLAND & WATER

Carrollton

Tuscaloosa

Aliceville

Montevallo

Alexander City

Lake Martin

Moundville

Clanton

Coosa R.

0   30 mi
0   30 km

N

BEST ATTRACTIONS IN CENTRAL ALABAMA

Aliceville Museum, Aliceville

The American Village, Montevallo

Anniston Museum of Natural History, Anniston

Birmingham Civil Rights Institute, Birmingham

DeSoto Caverns Park, Childersburg

International Motorsports Hall of Fame, Talladega

McWane Science Center, Birmingham

Moundville Archaeological Park, Moundville

Paul W. Bryant Museum, Tuscaloosa

Tannehill Historical State Park, McCalla

The Westervelt Warner Museum of American Art, Tuscaloosa

To learn more about local history, drive out to see the *John Looney House*, one of Alabama's oldest two-story log dogtrot structures. (The term "dogtrot" refers to a central hallway connecting two rooms also known as "pens." Although covered, this passage was left open and often proved a popular napping place for the family canines, hence its name.) Located a little over four miles southeast of Ashville at 4187 Greensport Road, this rare example of pioneer architecture dating to about 1820 may be visited on weekends. Current hours are Sat and Sun from 1 to 5 p.m. Modest admission. For more information, call (205) 594-7849.

While in Ashville, stop by the *Ashville House Quilt Shop* (35 Third St.; 205-594-7046; ashvillehousequiltshop.com), with its wonderful display of quilts, fabrics, notions and other items. The shop also offers quilting lessons. For a tasty snack, visit *The Two Sisters Homestyle Cafe* (36438 Hwy 231; 205-594-5777). The cafe is known for its fried chicken, roast beef, and chicken salad, which often sells out.

From Ashville take State Route 23 south until you reach US 11 leading to *Springville*, a town that takes its name from several area springs. First called Big Springs and settled about 1817, the town became Springville with the post office's establishment in 1834; the entire downtown district is on the National Historic Register.

Take time to explore some of this state historic district's nostalgic shops. Nearby *Homestead Hollow* at 1161 Murphrees Valley Road (205-467-3681, homesteadhollow.com), a 55-acre pioneer homestead with a blacksmith shop, log cabin, barn, and gristmill, serves as a quaint backdrop for art-and-craft festivals throughout the year. During such events, visitors may sample sorghum and apple cider made on the premises.

The Piedmont

Located in the Appalachian foothills, Calhoun County occupies a portion of the state's Piedmont region. Start your tour in **Anniston**, an attractive, arts-oriented city that named William Shakespeare its citizen of the year in 1984—before the Alabama Shakespeare Festival left its birthplace here and moved to Montgomery.

"It's your world. Explore it!" urges the staff at the **Anniston Museum of Natural History** (256-237-6766; exploreamag.org), located a couple of miles from downtown at 800 Museum Drive. Some adventures promised by the museum's slogan include treks through jungles, deserts, and savannahs at this handsome facility surrounded by 187 acres on Anniston's northern outskirts. Entering the museum's Lagarde African Hall, you'll see a rogue elephant

Strange as It Sounds

Deadly beauty and intrigue await at the **Berman Museum** (256-237-6261) in Anniston's LaGarde Park. Here you'll find an arsenal of rare weapons collected from all over the world by a former secret agent. Suits of armor that now stand still once clanked as knights did battle. Beheading axes and swords from ancient China and Japan hang in silence—not divulging their roles in past dastardly deeds.

A stunning royal Persian scimitar set with 1,295 rose-cut diamonds, 60 carats of rubies, and an exquisite 40-carat emerald in a three-pound gold handle mesmerizes sightseers here just as it once did Russian audiences during the reign of Catherine the Great. Other rare items include a Greek helmet dating to 300 BC. Jefferson Davis's traveling pistols, Adolf Hitler's silver tea service, and Napoleon Bonaparte's ivory comb and brush set. Also displayed is a saber used in the dramatic "Charge of the Light Brigade." The collection contains eighty-eight guns from the American West, Fraser's famous End of the Trail sculpture, and bronzes by Frederic Remington, Charles Russell, and Karl Kauba.

Army colonel Farley Lee Berman worked in counterintelligence, and he and his wife, Germaine (a Parisian with a comparable position in French Intelligence), met during World War II. Afterward they traveled the world on a decades-long quest for historical weapons and art.

Personnel from several metropolitan museums approached Berman about acquiring his collection, but he chose to donate it to the city of Anniston, saying he knew "the people of Alabama would enjoy it." Located at 840 Museum Drive next to the Museum of Natural History, the Berman Museum's hours June to Aug are Mon through Sat, 10 a.m. to 5 p.m. and Sun 1 to 5 p.m. Sept to May hours are Tues through Sat from 10 a.m. to 5 p.m.; Sun from 1 to 5 p.m. Self-guided tours $4 per person. Guided tours $7 per person.

keeping vigil beside a towering baobab tree (the world's largest replica of an "upside-down" tree). Preserved specimens of more than a hundred creatures inhabit this African complex, most collected by Annistonian John B. Lagarde, a big-game hunter who donated his award-winning assemblage to the museum.

From antelope to zebras, all animals appear in the most realistic habitats possible. And through it all visitors see the versatility with which nature's creatures adapt to their world. Every effort has been made to achieve the effect of authenticity; for example, light in the bamboo forest filters through a type of Venetian blind to create a network of slanted rays.

Spacious corridors wind from the African depths to the Ornithology Hall with its impressive array of more than 600 specimens of North American birds, many now either extinct or on the endangered species list. Naturalist William Werner assembled this priceless bird collection more than a century ago, and several diorama groupings include nests (some with eggs) built by the birds themselves. The museum boasts one of the world's finest models of a pteranadon, a prehistoric flying reptile with a 30-foot wingspan. In Dynamic Earth Hall, which features a life-size model of an albertosaurus, you can explore an Alabama cave complete with waterfall, stalactites, and stalagmites. The museum's hall, "Alabama: Sand to Cedars," features a walk through the state from seashore to mountains. NatureSpace encourages children to explore beyond backyard boundaries with a unique exhibit of natural resources.

Accredited by the American Association of Museums and a Smithsonian affiliate, the Anniston facility has received national recognition for its innovative participatory exhibits. The museum also offers rotating art exhibits, a fine gift shop, picnicking facilities, and several nature trails, including the popular Bird of Prey Trail. The museum is open Tues through Sat from 10 a.m. to 5 p.m. (plus Mon during summer) and Sun from 1 to 5 p.m. Admission: adults $6, senior citizens $5.50, children (ages 4 to 17) $5, children (age 3 and under) free.

Don't miss the historic Episcopal ***Church of St. Michael and All Angels*** (256-237-4011; stmichaelsanniston.org) at 1000 West 18th Street. With an exterior of Alabama stone, this 1888 Norman-Gothic structure features a magnificent marble altar backed by an alabaster *reredos* (ornamental screen). Bavarian woodworkers carved the church's entire ceiling by hand, and angels on corbels all face the altar at slightly different angles. Admission: adults $6, senior citizens $5.50, children (ages 4 to 17) $5, and children (age 3 and under) free. You can visit year-round Tues through Sat between 10 a.m. and 5 p.m.; Sun 1 to 5 p.m.

Take time to drive through the Tyler Hill Historic District and along tree-lined Quintard Avenue, where you'll see grand Victorian homes. At one such mansion, **Hotel Finial** (256-236-0503; hotelfinial.com), you can drop in for a fine meal or an overnight stay. Look for a turreted, three-story structure, painted taupe and trimmed in white with an awning covering a walkway in front, on a hill at 1600 Quintard Avenue. Formerly the Victoria Inn, the renovated and restructured home was reopened in 2016 as the Hotel Finial. The boutique hotel is owned by Senator Del Marsh and his wife Ginger Marsh. Hotel Finial has fifty-six deluxe rooms along with an additional five specialty suites.

alabamatrivia

Alabama's name comes from a Native American tribe, the Alibamu.

While in the area, head to **Munford** via State Route 21 for a visit to **Talladega National Forest, Cheaha State Park**, and other nearby spots for nature lovers. After basking in the country's serenity, head to nearby **Talladega** and immerse yourself in history. If you take the Jackson Trace Road, you'll follow a wagon route cut by Gen. Andrew Jackson and his Tennessee Volunteers as they marched southward through the Creek Indian nation. For a self-guided driving map of the town's historical sites, head to the Greater Talladega and Lincoln Area Chamber of Commerce office (256-362-9075; talladegalincolnchamber.com), just off the courthouse square in the old L&N Depot at 210 East Street South. Start with the Silk Stocking District (outlined on your map), a sizable concentration of homes listed on the National Register of Historic Places. Stop by **Heritage Hall Museum** (256-761-1364, heritagehallmuseum.org), a restored 1908 Carnegie Library at 200 South Street East, for a look at its current exhibits. The museum is open Tues through Fri from 10 a.m. to 4 p.m. Afterward drive by **Talladega College** at 627 Battle Street West (256-761-6100; talladega.edu), established in 1867, to see Hale Woodruff's striking *Amistad* murals at Savery Library. Other points of interest include the campus chapel and Swayne Hall, the college's first building.

For a delightful history lesson and a fun-filled family adventure, don't miss nearby **DeSoto Caverns Park** (256-378-7252; desotocavernspark.com), five miles east of Childersburg at 5181 DeSoto Caverns Parkway. A one-hour tour presents highlights of the cave's role in history and features a spellbinding laser light and sound show in the magnificent onyx chamber, taller than a 12-story building and bigger than a football field.

After the tour children can climb DeSoto's cave wall, wander through a lost trail maze, pan for gemstones, do battle with water balloons, enjoy a picnic on the grounds, and camping in the campgrounds. A café offers soups, salads, sandwiches, pizza, and other snacks. The facility features more than twenty-six attractions, and you can make arrangements to stay overnight in the cave. Hours Mon through Sat 9 a.m. to 5:30 p.m.; Sun 1 to 4:30 p.m. (or to 5:30 p.m.

TOP ANNUAL EVENTS IN CENTRAL ALABAMA

Sakura Festival
Tuscaloosa, April
(800) 538-8696
International.us.edu

Dogwood Festival
Aliceville, second weekend of April
(205) 373-2820
Thecityofaliceville.com

Operation New Birmingham
Magic City Art Connection
Linn Park, Birmingham, April
(205) 595-6306
magiccityart.com

Dickens Downtown
Northport, first Tuesday in December
(205) 339-7000
cityofnorthport.org

Heritage Week
Tuscaloosa, third week in April
(800) 538-8696

Kentuck Festival of the Arts
Kentuck Park, Northport, mid-October
(205) 758-1257
kentuck.org

Moundville Native American Festival
Moundville Archaeological Park, October
(205) 371-2234
moundville.ua.edu

Geico 500 Talladega Superspeedway
Talladega, October
(256) 761-4976
talladegasuperspeedway.com

Christmas Village Festival
Birmingham-Jefferson Convention
Complex Exhibition Hall, Birmingham
First weekend in November
(205) 836-7178 or (800) 458-8085
christmasvillagefestival.com

Apr through Oct). Admission: cave tours are $24.99 for adults, and $19.99 for children (ages 4 to 11). Other attractions are $4.99 each or $29.99 for a cave tour and two attractions, and $34.99 for a cave tour and five attractions.

Magic City Realm

Before exploring busy, bustling Birmingham, you can enjoy another back-to-nature experience at *Oak Mountain State Park* (205-620-2524; alapark.com/oakmountain), fifteen miles south of Birmingham off I-65 at 200 Terrace Drive in Pelham. This state park offers canoeing, fishing, swimming, golfing, picnicking, horseback riding, and a demonstration farm. Children especially enjoy seeing the geese, peacocks, rabbits, pigs, calves, donkeys, horses, and other animals. The park, most of it in a natural state, occupies almost 10,000 acres. A drive to the top of Double Oak Mountain affords some sweeping views of the park's steep slopes and rugged terrain.

Other features include some forty miles of hiking trails and four lakes. Don't miss the Treetop Nature Trail, where the Alabama Wildlife Rescue Service houses injured birds of prey. Climbing a boardwalk through woodsy surroundings takes you past large enclosures containing hawks, great horned owls, and other raptors. Call for park information or reservations at Oak Mountain's lakeside cabins or campground. Admission: adults $5, senior citizens and children (ages 4 to 11) $2. The park is open 7 a.m. until 7 p.m.

After basking in serenity you can pick up the pace with a jaunt to **Birmingham**. Named for the British industrial city, Birmingham acquired its nickname, Magic City, when soon after its 1871 incorporation it burgeoned into Alabama's major metropolis. No longer a fire-breathing, smoke-spewing dragon, the city projects a much-changed image—from gray smog to crisp skyline and green-bordered boulevards. As a leading medical and technological center, the city boasts an economic base broadened far beyond its mineral resources. The financial impact of the University of Alabama at Birmingham (UAB) Medical Center beefs up the local economy enormously.

As the state's biggest city, Birmingham boasts many choice restaurants. For a memorable dinner with a focus on freshness and simplicity, add **Highlands Bar & Grill** (205-939-1400) at 2011 11th Avenue South to your itinerary. Classically trained chef Frank Stitt's regional Southern creations have been dubbed "New American" cuisine, and his accolades fill walls and books. *Gourmet* magazine awarded Highlands Bar & Grill its number five slot for the "50 Best American Restaurants" in 2001. The James Beard Foundation named Stitt "Best Chef of the Southeast" the same year and nominated him as "Outstanding Chef in America in 2008. *Bon Appétit* listed him as one of the culinary "Legends of the Decade."

Start with an appetizer of baked grits, and select an entree ranging from beef, duck, and seafood to rabbit and veal. Renowned for its crab cakes, the restaurant also serves such specialties as pan roast quail with corn pudding and grilled leg of lamb with basil aioli and ratatouille. Try the Fudge Farms pork, fresh bacon, and braised shoulder with potatoes and Snow Bend's spring onions. Or savor the pork cheek and lobster with parsnip puree, pickled onions, and natural jus. The popular dessert list includes strawberry shortcake with sweet biscuits from Cullman, Alabama strawberries and mascarpone cream, and a petite strawberry milk shake. Moderate to expensive. Dinner hours are 5:30 to 10 p.m. Tuesday through Saturday. Visit highlandsbarandgrill.com for more background.

If you love to cook, be sure to pick up a copy of *Frank Stitt's Southern Table*, featuring recipes from the Highlands Bar and Grille. If you don't, this handsome book will make you want to learn. In either case, you'll enjoy the stories. Also, look for the companion book, *Frank Stitt's Bottega Favorita: A Southern Chef's Love Affair with Italian Food.*

alabamatrivia

Birmingham ranks as the state's largest city.

All about Art

While in the Birmingham area, stop by *Artists Incorporated* (205-979-8990; artistsincorporated.com) at 3365 Morgan Drive in Vestavia Hills. Representing the work of about fifty artists, this cooperative gallery offers a feast for the eyes. Here, you'll find oils by Les Yarbrough and Troy Crisswell, fiber art by Murray Johnston, bronzes by Frank Fleming, and more. Housed in a former dairy barn built in 1928, the gallery boasts the distinction of being Vestavia's oldest commercial building.

"This gallery offers a great variety of art forms in a wide range of prices," says Bill Charles, a fan and former Birmingham resident. "I'm the proud and happy owner of several works including two affordable Frank Fleming pieces, and I'm glad for the chance to have seen any number of [for me] unaffordable pieces, too. The crew here loves art and delights in sharing that love with their customers, be they buyers or browsers."

Hours are Tues through Thurs from 10 a.m. to 5 p.m.; Fri 10 a.m. to 8 p.m.; Sat 10 a.m. to 4 p.m. A reception, featuring artists, food, wine, and sometimes music, takes place from 4:30 to 7:30 p.m. on the first Friday of every month—and you're invited.

While sightseeing in the Magic City, be sure to visit towering *Vulcan* (205-933-1409), the world's largest cast-iron statue, at 1701 Valley View Drive. To reach Vulcan Park atop Red Mountain, take 20th Street South and watch for the sign. An observation deck affords a panoramic view of Birmingham and surrounding Jones Valley. Cast from Birmingham iron, *Vulcan* represents the mythological god of metalworking, fire, and forge. Designed for the 1904 St. Louis Exposition by Italian sculptor Giuseppe Moretti, *Vulcan* lifts his torch in tribute to the city's iron industry. At the base of the 55-foot statue, a museum presents *Vulcan's* history along with an overview of steel production. The museum is open daily 10 a.m. to 6 p.m. The Observation Tower is open daily 10 a.m. to 10 p.m. Admission from 10 a.m. to 6 p.m. is $6 for adults, $5 seniors, $4 children (ages 5 to 12). Evening admission from 6 to 10 p.m. is $5 per person (ages 13 and up), $4 for children (ages 5 to 12). For a virtual tour, visit visitvulcan.com.

Consider stopping by *Birmingham Botanical Gardens* (205-414-3950; bbgardens.org) at 2612 Lane Park Road, on the lower southern slope of Red Mountain. Stroll through the Japanese garden complete with a fourteenth-century teahouse reproduction. Also on the grounds, *Southern Living* magazine maintains demonstration gardens with plantings that might be duplicated at home. The museum's gift shop offers a fine selection of items, from note cards and prints to unusual plants and garden statuary—great for giving or keeping. Free admission. The gardens are open year-round, from dawn to dusk

Letter from Birmingham Jail

Locked in solitary confinement in Birmingham jail, the inmate was slipped a newspaper. Hungrily reading it, the prisoner saw a printed advertisement of a letter aimed directly at him.

Angry and indignant, the jailed man wanted to answer his critics' letter. So he began scrawling in the margins of the newspaper. That was the start of a letter that would eventually be translated into more than forty languages and become the cornerstone for the civil rights movement and nonviolent protests around the world.

On April 16, 1963, **Dr. Martin Luther King Jr**. wrote his famed "Letter from Birmingham Jail."

"There are two types of laws, just and unjust," King wrote from his narrow jail cell on Easter weekend. "One has a moral responsibility to disobey unjust laws."

This civil disobedience was exactly what landed 34-year-old King in jail in the first place.

Spurred by the success of the Montgomery bus boycott, Birmingham residents were determined to gain equal rights and King decided to join them. The focus of the Birmingham struggle, King and other leaders decided, would be the boycott of the business community during the second biggest shopping season of the year—Easter—which fell on April 14, 1963. Sit-ins with freedom songs kicked off the Birmingham campaign. And it started rather peacefully with few arrests.

How did King end up in jail? By the end of the first three days of Birmingham lunch counter sit-ins, there had been thirty-five arrests. On April 6, 1963, protestors marched on City Hall and the marches and business boycotts increased. On April 10, city government obtained a court injunction for protestors to cease their activities until a court decided their legal right to demonstrate. Two days later, the protestors did something unheard of—they disobeyed the court order, precisely what Henry David Thoreau had written about in his "Civil Disobedience," published in 1849.

On Good Friday, April 12, King and fellow civil rights activist Ralph Abernathy took the next step, knowing full well that they would be arrested. Deciding to march anyway, King, Abernathy, and others were arrested. King was thrown in solitary confinement, unable to communicate with anyone, even his lawyer. King spent nine days in the Birmingham jail.

On April 12, eight local white clergymen wrote an open letter printed in the *Birmingham News* denouncing King and demanding an end to the demonstrations. The ministers argued that the battle against racial segregation should be fought solely in the courts, not in the streets. Using what scraps of paper he could get, King crafted a lengthy response that his attorneys were later able to smuggle out of the jail in installments.

"Never have I written so long a letter," King wrote. "I can assure you that it would have been much shorter if I had been writing from a comfortable desk, but what else can one do when he is alone in a narrow jail cell, other than write long letters, think long thoughts, and pray long prayers?"

The letter became an instruction manual for people everywhere to stand up to injustice through nonviolent direct action. The philosophy that King had articulated in his letter from Birmingham Jail triumphed when President Lyndon Johnson signed the Civil Rights Act in 1964, smashing Jim Crow laws.

Less than five years after the Birmingham campaign, Martin Luther King Jr. was killed. Coming to Memphis in support of striking sanitation workers, King was standing on the balcony of the Lorraine Motel on April 4, 1968, when he was shot dead.

At the **Birmingham Civil Rights Institute**, visitors can see bars from the jail cell where King wrote his famous letter. The Institute also offers free admission every year on Martin Luther King Jr. Day, the third Monday in January. President Ronald Reagan signed the holiday into law in 1983.

each day. The gift shop is open Mon through Sat 9:30 a.m. to 5:30 p.m.; Sun 1 to 4 p.m.

The Gardens Cafe by Kathy G at the gardens offers a lovely lunch Tues through Fri from 11 a.m. to 2 p.m. Inspired by local greens and produce, the menu changes seasonally. A favorite is the salmon nicoise with mixed greens, lemon vinaigrette, boiled eggs, haricots verts, red pepper, red onion, olives, grilled potatoes, and feta cheese for $13.

Hampton Inn & Suites Birmington-Downtown-Tutwiler (205-322-2100 or 866-850-3053) at 2021 Park Place North makes a comfortable and convenient base for seeing Birmingham's attractions. The staff at this charming historic hotel will make you glad you came to the Magic City. With its rose-marble foyer, original coffered ceilings, moldings, plasterwork, and brass hardware, the hotel recaptures the elegance of another era. Your room or suite, which might come with a balcony or a marble fireplace, features high ceilings, restored woodwork, marble bathrooms, and custom-designed antique reproductions. Built in 1913 as a prestigious apartment/hotel, the redbrick, Italianate Tutwiler underwent a renovation. The Tutwiler's meticulous restoration resulted in charter membership in Historic Hotels of America, a select group recognized for preserving historic architectural quality and ambience. The original Tutwiler, the hotel's namesake, made news in 1974 when it became one of the country's first structures to be leveled by "implosion" (also the inspiration for the hotel's specialty drink by the same name).

The first Tutwiler hosted such dignitaries and celebrities as Eleanor Roosevelt, President Warren G. Harding, Charles Lindbergh, Will Rogers, Nelson Eddy, Tallulah Bankhead, Rocky Marciano, and Marilyn Monroe. Carrying on tradition, the current Tutwiler counts former President George Bush, Dan Quayle, Henry Kissinger, Colin Powell, Casper Weinberger, Mick

Solving Crimes with the Southern Sisters

Before **Anne George** wrote her critically acclaimed novel, *This One and Magic Life,* she penned award-winning poetry and became a Pulitzer Prize finalist. She also wrote an award-winning mystery series about two "Southern Sisters." Perhaps her most lasting legacy is the legion of mystery fans who eagerly followed the zany antics of Patricia Anne and Mary Alice, an unlikely pair of sleuths who live in Birmingham. As the Southern Sisters go about their crime solving, the reader gets a light-hearted look at the local landscape and a lot of laughs. Buy a book in this series, pour yourself a tall glass of iced tea, and enjoy an easy summer afternoon.

Jagger, Billy Joel, and Henry Mancini among its honored guests. As another honored guest of the Tutwiler, you can enjoy such amenities as complimentary shoe shines and newspapers, airport transportation, and valet parking. A complimentary continental breakfast is served daily from 6 to 10 a.m. Rates are moderate to deluxe.

For a glimpse of the city's Iron Age, take First Avenue North over the viaduct to 1236 32nd Street North toward the towering smokestacks of **Sloss Furnaces** (205-254-2025; slossfurnaces.com). Designated a National Historic Landmark, the ironworks that served Birmingham from 1881 to 1971 now serve as a massive walk-through museum portraying the city's industrial past. Near the park gate, a visitor center features exhibits on the various aspects of combining coal, limestone, and ore at high temperatures to produce iron. In its prime, Sloss turned out 400 tons of finished pig iron a day. Hours are Tues through Sat from 10 a.m. to 4 p.m. and Sun from noon to 4 p.m. Admission is free. Free hour-long guided tours are offered on Sat and Sun at 1 p.m. The museum also offers self-guided tours. Guests are asked to wear closed-toe shoes for safety.

For some down-home country cooking, head for **The Irondale Cafe** (205-956-5258)—the inspiration for the Whistle Stop Cafe in the movie *Fried Green Tomatoes*. Located at 1906 First Avenue North in the historic area of Irondale, the cafeteria offers a variety of meats and fresh vegetables including that Southern favorite, fried green tomatoes, that actress/writer Fannie Flagg put in the spotlight. Open Sun through Fri 11 a.m. to 2:30 p.m. Check the website at irondalecafe.com.

Heading toward the Birmingham International Airport, you'll find the **Southern Museum of Flight** (205-833-8226; southernmuseumofflight.org). Look for the big McDonnell-Douglas F-4N Phantom II on the front lawn of the museum at 4343 73rd Street North, two blocks east of the airport. Aviation buffs can spend hours here delving into the mystery and history of flying. This out-standing facility features a reproduction of a 1910 Curtis "Pusher," the second powered plane to follow on the heels of the Wright brothers' success; a 1925 crop duster that launched Delta Airlines; a dozen Cold War aircraft from the F-84 and F-86 through the A-12 Blackbird, including a MiG-15 and MiG-21; and hundreds of models that trace aviation's history. You'll see decades of mem-orabilia relating to Amelia Earhart, Gen. Claire Chenault's Flying Tigers, and the infamous Red Baron.

"We've doubled our collection during the last four years," said a staff member, and expansion continues. Visitors can view short movies, shown continuously, on such subjects as the Tuskegee Airmen and women in avi-ation as well as humorous newsreels on early attempts to fly. Take time to look through the Alabama Aviation Hall of Fame and the Air Force's 50th Anniversary Collection of Aircraft Art on the second floor. The museum, which also offers an aviation reference library, is open Tues through Sat from 9:30 a.m. to 4:30 p.m. Admission: adults $7, senior citizens and students $6, children (age 3 and under) free, and free for active military members and families.

Afterward return downtown to the ***Birmingham-Jefferson Civic Center*** for a spectator outing at the ***Alabama Sports Hall of Fame*** (205-323-6665).

Irondale Cafe Corn Bread

When you can't stop by the famed Irondale Cafe in Irondale, cook up a batch of the cafe's popular cornbread at home.

1 1/2 teaspoons baking powder

2 1/2 teaspoons vegetable oil

2 1/2 teaspoons melted butter

2 beaten eggs

1 1/2 cups fat-free cultured buttermilk

1 1/2 cups whole milk

1 1/2 cups self-rising white cornmeal

1 1/2 cups self-rising White Lily flour

Combine all ingredients and mix well. Let batter rest under refrigeration for 1–2 hours. Pour batter into a well-buttered 9x13 pan. Bake at 350°F in convection oven for 17–20 minutes or until knife inserted into center comes out clean. Brush top liber-ally with melted butter. Can also bake in a pre-heated, cast iron skillet for a dark and crunchy bottom crust.

Located at 2150 Richard Arrington Jr. Boulevard, this unique two-floor facility focuses on some of the state's greatest sports figures. Walls of bronze plaques pay tribute to athletes from Olympic diving champion Jenni Chandler to Joe Louis, who boxed his way to the world heavyweight title. You'll also see displays on such sports luminaries as John Hannah, Joe Namath, Bo Jackson, Pat Sullivan, Bart Starr, Ozzie Newsome, Hank Aaron, Willie Mays, Jesse Owens, Hubert Green, Bobby Allison, Pat Dye, and Bear Bryant. Wall cases and displays feature trophies, uniforms, photographs, and other memorabilia from the sports world.

Even though exhibits cover Hall of Fame inductees who made names for themselves in archery, auto and harness racing, golf, baseball, boxing, track, and waterskiing, the name of the game in Alabama is Football (with a capital F). A black-and-white photo exhibit, depicting un-helmeted players in skimpy uniforms, captures some historic moments during the first Alabama–Auburn clash on February 22, 1893, in Birmingham. Football fever rages in many other parts of the country, but the intensity seems several degrees higher in the South and reaches a boiling point in Alabama during the annual collegiate battle between the Crimson Tide and the War Eagles. You can visit the Hall of Fame Mon through Fri from 9 a.m. to 5 p.m. Check out ashof.org for more information. Admission: adults $5, senior citizens $4, students $3.

Nearby at 2000 Reverend Abraham Woods Jr. Boulevard stands the **Birmingham Museum of Art** (205-254-2565), noted for its excellent Wedgwood collection, the finest outside England. The museum houses a diverse collection of more than 25,000 paintings, pieces of sculpture, prints, drawings, and examples of the decorative arts dating from ancient to modern times. You'll see works by Monet, Sargent, Corot, Cassatt, Bierstadt, Motherwell, Stella, Chihuly, and others. Other museum treasures include the Kress collection of Renaissance paintings and the largest collection of Asian art in the South.

Check with the staff regarding current offerings. Don't miss the multilevel Charles W. Ireland Sculpture Garden, which provides a splendid backdrop for outdoor exhibits. Oscar's at the Museum restaurant serves lunch Tues through Sat from 11 a.m. to 2 p.m. and features a musical brunch on select Sundays. Stop by the Museum Store for an extensive selection of books, posters, jewelry, crafts, and unique gift items. Except for major holidays, the museum is open Tues through Sat from 10 a.m. to 5 p.m. and Sun noon to 5 p.m. Check on current exhibits and other happenings at artsbma.org. Free general admission. Admission may be charged for special exhibitions.

Don't miss the **Birmingham Civil Rights Institute** (205-328-9696), located at 520 16th Street North. The focal point of the Civil Rights District,

Christmas in Nauvoo

When Gene McDaniel planned a Christmas celebration in **Nauvoo**, population 249, he expected maybe 250 to 500 people. Between 2,000 to 3,000 people showed up for that first holiday festival in 1989, and that's how it's been ever since. **Christmas in Nauvoo** takes place the first Saturday in December with an open house at the **Old Harbin Hotel** (205-697-5652), myriad lights, attendant festivities, and a parade led by Miss Alabama, who makes the hotel her overnight base.

Other special events in Nauvoo include an Antique Car and Truck Show in June. Visit nauvooalabama.com to check out special events in town.

Once a booming coal-mining town, Nauvoo takes its name from a Hebrew word meaning "pleasant." A railroad worker, who said the place reminded him of his hometown in Illinois, christened it Nauvoo. After two mines and a lumber mill closed in the 1950s, Nauvoo started to shrivel and dry up.

The town's largest structure, the two-story brick Old Harbin Hotel, stands on the corner of McDaniel Avenue and Third Street. Built in 1923 at a cost of $24,574, the hotel boasted sixteen furnished rooms and seventy-six electric lights. The structure, which retains its original pine walls, downstairs pressed-tin ceilings, and four center rooms with skylights, was added to the Alabama Landmark Register in 1990.

Owners Gene and Earlene McDaniel, who live on the premises, have collected a variety of furnishings, antiques, and memorabilia to decorate each of the nine guest rooms individually.

"We don't advertise for customers," said Gene, a retired union coal miner and hardware store owner. "Don't expect a person on duty at the desk. Most weekends in summer, we're booked with family reunions because the whole clan can gather here." Gene, who owns several other buildings in Nauvoo, said he's had from 20,000 to 25,000 visitors at the hotel since 1989. Breakfast is included, and rates are standard.

which also embraces historic 16th Street Baptist Church and Kelly Ingram Park, the facility features innovative exhibits, which re-create in graphic fashion a sad chronology of segregation's inequities. Visitors start their journey through darkness with a film, followed by a startling entrance to the "Barriers" Gallery, where exhibits trace the struggle that led to the passage of civil rights laws. The Richard Arrington Jr. Resource Gallery offers an interactive multimedia experience and creates a "living library" honoring persons who participated in the civil rights struggle. Video segments from the institute's Oral History Project interviews are available for learning and research. Admission: adults $15; senior citizens $5; college students $6; children (grades 4 to 12) outside Jefferson County $5; children (age 17 and under) living in Jefferson County free. Hours are Tues through Sat 10 a.m. to 5 p.m., and Sun 1 to 5 p.m. Visit bcri.org for more information.

While exploring the Magic City, take in nearby Homewood, where you'll find a delightful neighborhood market and cafe specializing in Mediterranean fare. *Nabeel's Cafe* (205-879-9292) at 1706 Oxmoor Road offers a menu with a global theme and a market filled with imported herbs, coffees, teas, olive oil, beans, nuts, and more. Vats of olives, bins of spices, and wedges of Greek, Italian, Bulgarian, Russian, and Lebanese cheeses tempt the shopper here.

The Krontiras family, John and Ottavia with their son Anthony, own and operate this establishment, housed in the white-painted brick building with an exterior wall mural and green canopies. The cafe evokes the intimacy of a European dining experience with a leisurely sharing of food and drink. Wine barrels and a wooden rack for wine storage along the dining-room wall suggest the old country. Anthony, Nabeel's chef, focuses on family recipes and prepares food with home-cooked flavor. Nabeel's numerous awards include "Birmingham's Favorite Restaurant" in a former readers' poll conducted by *Birmingham Magazine.* "We try to treat customers as if they were guests at our home," said John.

Sip some of the cafe's celebrated and refreshing mint tea and scoop up some taramasalata dip, made of red caviar and salted carp roe, with a pita wedge while you decide what to order. From homemade soups and piquant Greek salads to sandwich specialties like *fior di latte* (made with fresh mozzarella cheese, roasted peppers, and fresh basil), Nabeel's crew prepares everything fresh daily. Favorites include eggplant parmesan and a spinach pie (*spanakopita*). Made of fresh spinach and layered with phyllo, Greek feta cheese, and herbs, *spanakopita* is served with a salad and pita bread. Other popular menu items include grouper Greek style and filet mignon. End your meal on a sweet note with baklava, cannoli, butter cookies, or honey crescents. Restaurant hours are Mon through Wed 11 a.m. to 8 p.m.; Thurs through Sat 11 a.m. to 9:30 p.m. Market hours are Mon through Sat 8:30 a.m. to 6 p.m. Click on nabeels.com for more information and some mouth-watering recipes.

Before leaving the Birmingham area, stop by *The Bright Star* (205-424-9444) in nearby *Bessemer.* Housed in a tall brick building at 304 North 19th Street, this restaurant beckons diners with an extensive menu prepared with Greek flair. Brothers Jimmy and Nicky Koikos continue a family culinary tradition that started in 1907.

The attractive interior features roomy brass and glass-topped booths and murals dating from 1915, painted by a European artist traveling through the area. The Bright Star offers daily luncheon specials, such as fresh trout amandine or Greek-style beef tenderloin tips with such side dish choices as fresh fried eggplant, corn on the cob, and candied yams.

For dinner start with a cup of the restaurant's scrumptious gumbo. (All fish dishes here feature fresh seafood straight from the coast.) For the main course, you might choose broiled snapper (Greek style) or the beef tenderloin. Other enticing entrees include lobster and crabmeat au gratin, a broiled seafood platter, and a tasty blackened snapper, prepared New Orleans style, with a creamy wine sauce. Top off your meal with a slice of fresh homemade pineapple-cheese or lemon icebox pie. Economical to moderate prices. Lunch hours are 11 a.m. to 3 p.m. daily. Dinner is served Sun through Thurs 4:30 to 9 p.m.; Fri and Sat 4:30 to 10 p.m. View the property at thebrightstar.com.

The Capstone

Traveling southwest from Birmingham about fifty miles takes you to **Tuscaloosa**. This college town, rich in tradition, served as Alabama's capital from 1826 to 1846.

Before exploring the area's many attractions, you might like to fortify yourself with a slab of ribs at **Dreamland Bar-B-Que** (205-758-8135; dreamlandbbq.com), two miles from the intersection of US 82 and I-59, off Jug Factory Road in Jerusalem Heights at 5535 15th Avenue East. Here you don't have to agonize over what to order—the choice is ribs along with slices of white bread to sop up the sauce. You'll also get a bib that says ain't nothin' like 'em—nowhere, a stack of napkins, and a wet paper towel to assist you in this gustatory project that must be performed with no inhibitions. If you want more variety in your meal, get a bag of potato chips. Beer or soft drinks, followed by toothpicks, complete the feast.

True, Dreamland stays crowded and the noise level runs high, but regulars say these things add to the place's appeal. Dreamland's hours are Mon through Thurs 10 a.m. to 9 p.m. On Fri and Sat the restaurant is open from 10 a.m. to 9 p.m. and Sun from 11 a.m. to 9 p.m. Rates are economical to moderate.

Continue to nearby **Cypress Inn** (205-345-6963; cypressinnrestaurant. com) at 501 Rice Mine Road North. Located on the Black Warrior's banks, this restaurant offers fresh seafood, prime steaks, and traditional Southern fare as well as a relaxing river view. House specialties include Hoppin' John (a combination of black-eyed peas, rice, scallions, and bacon), smoked chicken with white barbecue sauce, crispy fried catfish, and fresh broiled red snapper. Also popular are the homemade yeast rolls, fresh raisin-bran muffins, and peanut butter pie. The Cypress Inn serves lunch Mon through Sat from 11 a.m. to 2 p.m.; Sun from 11 a.m. to 3 p.m. Dinner hours run Mon through Thurs from 4:30 to 9 p.m.; Fri 4:30 to 10 p.m.; Sat 5 p.m. to 10 p.m., and Sun 5 to 8 p.m. Economical to moderate prices.

Art lovers will want to search out a rare museum at 1400 Jack Warner Parkway Northeast. The *Tuscaloosa Museum of Art: Home of the Westervelt Collection* (205-562-5280; tuscaloosamoa.org) showcases Jack W. Warner's remarkable assemblage resulting from four decades of collecting. In addition to paintings and sculpture, the collection includes American decorative arts and antiques such as furniture by Duncan Phyfe, silverware by Paul Revere, exquisite porcelain, early American firearms, and more. Most of the furniture dates to the period between 1820 and 1840, and every piece is museum quality.

alabamatrivia

Founded in 1819 near the site of an early Indian village, Tuscaloosa occupies the highest navigable point on the Black Warrior River.

Here, you'll view portraits of Washington, Jefferson, and Lafayette all painted from life as you wend your way through galleries and color-coordinated suites in the Blue, Yellow, Green, and Salmon rooms. Visitors to the Gulf States Paper offices will remember seeing some of the works previously exhibited there. The extensive collection, which has been called an "unparalleled assembly of 18th, 19th and 20th century American art," was moved to the facility in 2011.

Artists represented include Andrew Wyeth, Frederic Remington, George Catlin, Mary Cassatt, and Georgia O'Keeffe. Also, you'll see works by John Singer Sargent, Winslow Homer, Albert Bierstadt, James McNeil Whistler, Childe Hassam, James Peale, Thomas Cole, Asher B. Durand, and many others. The world-class collection can be viewed by the public Tues through Sat 10 a.m. to 6 p.m., and Sun 1 to 6 p.m. Admission is free.

Afterward head for the *University of Alabama campus*, the site of a beautiful historic district as well as the home of the Crimson Tide. Since student William Gray Little organized the college's first football club in 1892, Alabama has celebrated "A Century of Champions." A good place to learn about the school's more than 100-year football history is the *Paul W. Bryant Museum* (205-348-4668; bryantmuseum.com). To reach the museum from US 82, take the University Boulevard exit and follow the signs. If you arrive via I-59, exit onto I-359, take the 35th Street exit to 10th Avenue, go north to Bryant Drive, and then turn east. You'll find the museum on campus at 300 Paul W. Bryant Drive.

For some background on the legendary figure called "The Bear," the man who became college football's most acclaimed coach, start your museum visit by viewing *The Bryant Legacy*, a film narrated by sports commentator Keith Jackson. While browsing among the displays, you'll see a replicated setting of Bear Bryant's office and a dazzling version of his famous hat. Sculptor Miraslav

Havel translated the familiar crimson-and-white houndstooth pattern into a multifaceted Waterford crystal showpiece. A courier transported the real hat from Tuscaloosa to Ireland for its magic rendering—and back again.

Although dedicated to the memory of Bryant, who headed Alabama's football teams from 1958 to 1982, the museum also pays tribute to other coaches and players prominent in the school's history. You'll see photos, memorabilia, and audiovisual displays pertaining to such superstars as Joe Namath, Kenny Stabler, Cornelius Bennett, and Bart Starr. To supplement vintage film clips, montages, and recordings, the museum offers taped highlights of recent games.

In addition to the large exhibit hall, the museum houses a comprehensive library of media guides, game programs, photographs, books, films, scrapbooks, and other materials covering Southeastern Conference and college sports. Admission: adults $2, senior citizens and children $1. Except for major holidays, hours run from 9 a.m. to 4 p.m. daily.

While exploring the campus, stop by the *Gorgas House* (205-348-5906) at 810 Capstone Drive. One of four university buildings to survive the Civil War, this 1829 two-story brick federal-style cottage with a curving cast-iron staircase originally served as a college dining hall. Inside you'll see period furnishings, an outstanding collection of Spanish colonial silver, and memorabilia of William Crawford Gorgas, who was noted for his work in the prevention and cure of yellow fever. Free admission. The Gorgas House is open Mon through Fri from 9 a.m. to noon and 1 to 4:30 p.m. with tours by appointment. Admission is $2. Tap into gorgashouse.ua.edu for more details.

Housed at nearby Smith Hall at 427 Sixth Avenue Northeast, the *Alabama Museum of Natural History* (205-348-7550) features extensive fossil and mineral collections. Entering this 1909 classical revival building, you'll see a spacious hall and a sweeping marble staircase with iron railings. Exhibits include pottery, tools, weapons, and various artifacts from South Pacific and Central and South American cultures.

On display in the gallery upstairs, you'll find the Hodges meteorite—an outer-space missile weighing 8.5 pounds that struck a Sylacauga woman in 1954. Featured fossils include mammoth, mastodon, mosasaur, and marine turtle, along with a 65-foot whale fossil. You'll also see a Studebaker buggy from the 1880s and a free-standing exhibit illustrating the research methods used by Professor Eugene Allen Smith, for whom the building is named, in gathering his geological and biological collections. Except for major holidays, you can visit the museum Monday through Saturday from 10 a.m. to 4:30 p.m. Admission: adults $2, children and seniors $1. Check almnh.ua.edu for more background.

Downtown at 2300 University Boulevard in a building that dates to the 1890s, you'll find **DePalma's Italian Cafe** (205-759-1879; depalmasdowntown. com). This Italian cafe is noted for its pizzas, calzones, and dishes such as pine nut–crusted salmon, veal Marsala, or pasta DePalma—angel-hair pasta baked in a cream sauce with garlic, cheeses, and Italian herbs and topped with mushrooms, mozzarella, and a choice of ham, Italian sausage, artichokes, and more. Tiramisu ranks at the top of the dessert list, and the crew offers a great wine selection, too. In fact, the owners make regular scouting trips to Italy for their selections. Here, messages don't come in a bottle—but *on* a bottle—because the staff invites you to sign and date your wine label and pen an appropriate message. Then your special bottle joins a long line of others on the booth-level shelf. DePalma's is open Tues through Thurs from 11 a.m. to 10 p.m.; Fri and Sat until 11 p.m.; and Sun from 11 a.m. to 9 p.m. Prices are economical to moderate. Reservations not accepted.

After your campus tour take time to explore Tuscaloosa (a Choctaw name that means "black warrior"). While downtown, stop by the **Battle-Friedman House** (205-758-6138; historictuscaloosa.org), a handsome Greek revival mansion located at 1010 Greensboro Avenue. Built in 1835, this structure now serves as a house museum and city cultural center. Free tours are offered Tues through Sat at 2:30 p.m.

Continue to 1512 Greensboro Avenue, where you'll find **The Waysider Restaurant** (205-345-8239) in a small early-twentieth-century house. Because this is the place for breakfast in Tuscaloosa, you may have to stand in line, so bring along a newspaper to read while you wait for a table. No wimpy affair, breakfast at The Waysider means homemade biscuits (with a deserved reputation), eggs, grits (get the cheese version), and a meat of your choice: from sugar-cured ham to grilled pork chops or steak. An order of real country-cured ham with two eggs and red-eye gravy runs in the economical range. You can also opt for pancakes.

The Waysider is open Tues through Fri 5:30 a.m. to 2 p.m.; Sat 5:30 a.m. to noon. Sun breakfast hours run from 6:30 a.m. to 1 p.m.

Next, head to nearby **Northport**, just a short drive across the Black Warrior River. Once called Kentuck, Northport has developed into an important craft center with a complex of studios and galleries. The third weekend of October the **Kentuck Festival of the Arts** features more than 300 selected artists and craftspeople from all over the country. Kerry Kennedy, Steve Davis, Ann Betak, Robby Roberts, Daniel Livingston, and a number of other artists maintain individual studios at the **Kentuck Museum Association** (205-758-1257), located at 503 Main Avenue. The gift shop, which offers photography, pottery, glass, jewelry, musical instruments, textiles, baskets, and other items, is open Tues through Fri from 10 a.m. to 6 p.m. and Sat from 10 a.m. to 4:30 p.m. Call for information on the center's artists, exhibits, or Kentuck Museum's gallery or visit kentuck.org.

If you have a green thumb, be sure to stop by the **Potager** (205-752-4761; theadamsantiques.com), next door at 428 Main Avenue. The shop offers everything from books and tools to gardening accessories. Zebra finches provide the chirping background music. Afterward step through the connecting door to **Adams' Antiques** (205-758-8651; theadamsantiques.com) for more browsing. Both shops are open Tues through Sat from 10 a.m. to 5 p.m.

After your Northport excursion, head for **Moundville**, named "the Big Apple of the fourteenth century" by *National Geographic*. To reach **Moundville Archaeological Park** (205-371-2234), located about fifteen miles south of Tuscaloosa, take State Route 69 South to 634 Mound Park. Said by archaeologists to be the best-preserved prehistoric settlement east of the pueblos, Moundville is an internationally known archaeological site with more than twenty flat-topped earthen mounds, plus other less prominent ones, spread over a 317-acre setting on the Black Warrior River. For a sweeping overview of the grounds, you can climb to the top of a 60-foot ceremonial mound. The **Jones Archaeological Museum** spotlights a re-created marriage ceremony from 500 years ago featuring life-size figures. You'll also see hundreds of Mississippian artifacts, ceremonial vessels, and tools made by the advanced group of prehistoric people who occupied this area between AD 1000 and 1450. Don't miss the Rattlesnake disc, the most famous artifact ever found at Moundville. Although scholars disagree on the meaning of the entwined rattlesnakes on the disc, the hand with the eyelike motif in the palm is common in Mississippian art. The Edward T. Douglass Nature Trail winds through a half-mile of scenic woodlands. The level boardwalk offers a fascinating trek that takes visitors from ground level to treetop height. The ring road at the park is also a great place to ride a bike.

For a welcome break, the **Black Warrior Coffee Company** (205-371-2572; moundville.ua.edu) is a good cafe to enjoy a variety of Native American specialty coffees and teas along with cakes, pies, pastries, and homemade cream sodas. Park grounds are open daily from dawn to dusk. Except for major holidays, the museum is open 9 a.m. to 5 p.m. The museum closes at 4 p.m. Nov through Feb. Camping, hiking, and picnicking facilities are available. Admission: adults $8, senior citizens $7, students $6, children (under age 5) free; Native Americans free with tribal membership card. The annual four-day **Moundville Native American Festival**, featuring southeastern Native American crafts and cultural activities, takes place during the first week in October.

Afterward return north to US 82, and travel west toward Pickensville and the Tennessee-Tombigbee (Tenn-Tom) Waterway, which offers exceptional fishing, hunting, and recreational facilities.

Tenn-Tom Terrain

Don't miss the **Tom Bevill Visitor Center** (205-373-8705) at Pickensville, half-mile south of the junctions of State Routes 14 and 86 at 1382 Lock and Dam Road. The white-columned Greek revival–style mansion you see here looks as if it dates from the mid-1800s but actually was completed in 1986. Definitely not your average rest stop, this facility primarily represents a composite of three historical homes in the vicinity, and you'll see portraits of these grand mansions in the central hall. Ascend the sweeping stairway to the second floor, where various exhibits interpret the Tennessee-Tombigbee Waterway's history. A 22-foot relief map illustrates the waterway's course through several locks and dams, and a model display demonstrates the lockage process. Even better, you can climb to the roof level and perhaps watch a vessel pass through the Tom Bevill Lock and Dam. Whether or not said event happens during your visit, the splendid view from the cupola justifies the climb.

After your house tour, stop by the US Snagboat *Montgomery* near the visitor center. A National Historic Landmark, this steam-powered sternwheeler once kept Southern rivers navigable by removing tons of debris, such as fallen trees and sunken logs that impeded river traffic. Except for some federal holidays, and weekends during November through March, the center is open daily year-round. Open Wed through Sat 9 a.m. to 5 p.m. year-round.

Strange as It Sounds

Carrollton offers a unique site—a face imprinted on a windowpane at the **Pickens County Courthouse**. To learn the strange story behind the image of a prisoner's face preserved here since 1878 (the visage remains despite repeated scrubbings and harsher attempts at removal), step inside the courthouse and pick up a leaflet that provides some background information. You can also read an intriguing account of the mysterious face in Kathryn Tucker Windham's book *13 Alabama Ghosts and Jeffrey* (published by the University of Alabama Press in Tuscaloosa).

Don't miss the **Aliceville Museum** (205-373-2363), downtown at 104 Broad Street Northeast. During World War II some 6,000 German prisoners—most from Field Marshall Erwin Rommel's Afrika Korps—were interned at Camp Aliceville, site of the present-day **Sue Stabler Park** about two miles due west of town on State Route 17. In 1993 the city hosted its 50-year Prisoner of War Reunion. During this three-day event, officials, residents, and visitors—including fifteen German ex-POWs and their families—gathered to dedicate the only World War II German POW museum in the US. The last Prisoner of War Reunion was in 2007. A 15-minute video, featuring first-person interviews with the camp guards and prisoners, provides background on the museum's focus. Historians will want to view a 45-minute video produced by the History Channel. Exhibits include drawings, paintings, sculpture, musical instruments, furniture, newspapers, photos, and other artifacts from Camp Aliceville. Also, visitors can see an American military collection from World War II in the adjacent building and a 1948 Coca-Cola bottling works. Museum hours Mon through Fri 10 a.m. to noon, and Sat 1 to 4 p.m. Admission: adults $10, senior citizens $7, and students $5.

From Aliceville you can either dip southeast via State Route 14 to Eutaw (a charming town covered in the Southwest section of this book) or return east to tour Tannehill, about midway between Birmingham and Tuscaloosa.

Peach Country

To reach **Tannehill Ironworks Historical State Park** (205-477-5711; tannehill.org) near McCalla, take exit 100 off I-59 and follow the signs to 12632 Confederate Parkway. This 1,500-acre wooded park spills into Tuscaloosa, Jefferson, and Bibb Counties. On the grounds you'll see the remains of the Tannehill Iron Furnaces and more than forty pioneer homes and farm outbuildings. A cotton gin, blacksmith shop, and gristmill (that grinds cornmeal one weekend a month from March to November) add to the authenticity of this mid-1800s re-creation. Exhibits at the **Iron and Steel Museum of Alabama** spotlight the history of technology prior to 1850. The facility offers hiking trails and camping. The park is open from sunrise to sunset year-round. Museum hours run from 10 a.m. to 4 p.m. daily. Park admission: adults $5, senior citizens $4, children (ages 6 to 11) $3, children (age 5 and under) free. Museum admission: $2 with regular gate admission.

Afterward you might like to shift south to **Montevallo**, located in the middle of Alabama. Here the **University of Montevallo**, situated on a beautiful campus complete with brick streets, tree-lined drives, and historical buildings such as the 1823 King House and Reynolds Hall, makes a pleasant stopover. An arbor walk features a variety of trees labeled by their common and scientific names. Better yet, pick up a *Red Brick Walking Tour* guide, available in versions highlighting several interests—from architectural and horticultural to ghosts. These guides and other information on local sites are available at the Montevallo Chamber of Commerce office (205-665-1519; montevallocc.com) at 845 Valley St. and the Montevallo Welcome Center based at the historic Will Lyman House at 720 Oak Street, adjacent to the campus. The public can also attend campus concerts, plays, films, lectures, art exhibits, and sporting events; most activities are free. Call the university's public relations office at (205) 665-6230 to check on current happenings during the time of your visit or check out montevallo.edu.

For overnighters, the on-campus ***Ramsay Conference Center*** (205-665-6280) offers double rooms on a space-available basis, seven days a week during the school term, at bargain rates. The rooms feature TVs and private bathrooms. A short stroll away you'll find the college dining hall with cafeteria-style meals. Pay-at-the-door prices for breakfast, lunch, and dinner are economical.

Another overnight option is a stay at the ***Fox and Pheasant Inn*** (205-665-3080; foxandpheasantinn.com) at 540 Shelby Street. Innkeeper Janice Seaman rescued the historic home and turned it into the luxurious inn it is today. The 1915 English manor-style home offers four suites—East, West, North, and South—with private baths, cable TV, luxury bedding, towel warmers, and much more. Days start with a gourmet breakfast, maybe eggs Benedict or blueberry pancakes with applewood smoked bacon. Guests can also order a lunch to enjoy on the premises or to pack in a hamper for a picnic in the countryside. Dinner menus also are available with such popular items as steak Diane and honey-roasted pork tenderloin stuffed with apricots, walnuts, and shiitake mushrooms. For dessert, it is difficult to pick a favorite between the delicious chocolate pecan bourbon pie and flourless chocolate cake.

Before leaving town, visit ***Orr Park***, where you can stroll along Shoal Creek, a natural habitat for Tim Tingle's life-size wood carvings of birds, animals, and wizard faces.

Continuing south to ***Clanton*** in the heart of peach country, you'll find several places to purchase this locally grown fruit. ***Peach Park*** (205-755-2065, peachparkclanton.com), for instance, features fresh peaches (in season) along with homemade peach ice cream, milk shakes, yogurt, and other delicious desserts as well as pecans and boiled peanuts. The Peach Park barbecue menu offers pulled pork, brisket, chicken, ribs, and more.

A Revolutionary Experience

Prepare yourself for a revolutionary experience and step into the action at **The American Village** (205-665-3535 or 877-811-1776), located four miles off I-65 at exit 234 in Montevallo at 3727 State Road 119. Actually, you don't have to do much preparation if your visit coincides with that of school groups because their teachers have already primed them to participate and appreciate the exciting turn of events that brought about a struggling young nation's independence.

Authentically costumed interpreters bring to life the fervor of that time when our forebears made choices that formed the fabric of our lives today. You'll get caught up in such events as the Stamp Act Rally and interact with colonial residents expressing their growing resentment against the mother country. You'll hear Patrick Henry's fiery oratory and attend the 1787 Philadelphia Convention to form a new national government. You'll voice your opinions, vote, and maybe even sit behind the desk in the Oval Office.

The backdrop for this revolutionary experiment is a complex of various colonial buildings including the centerpiece Washington Hall, inspired by Mount Vernon, and a Williamsburg-style courthouse. But this 113-acre development is not about buildings—handsome though they are—it's about ideas. And the dreamer who envisioned this place, Tom Walker, wants citizens of today and tomorrow to realize they also have choices—just as our early leaders did. The village's mission of strengthening and renewing the foundations of American citizenship can be witnessed in action weekdays from 10 a.m. to 4 p.m. with public tours at 10 a.m., noon, and 2 p.m. The village is closed Saturday and Sunday. You can make a virtual visit via americanvillage.org. Admission: adults $10, senior citizens and children (ages 5 to 17) $9, children (age 4 and under) free.

Village visitors can see a Southern Living Showcase House replica of the Philadelphia residence occupied by George and Martha Washington and then John and Abigail Adams, adding another facet to the on-site history lesson.

To learn about the area's history, visit the new ***Aldrich Coal Mine Museum*** (205-665-2886) housed in the former Montevallo Coal Mining Company at 137 Highway 203. Owners Henry and Rose Emfinger are proud to tell visitors about the only monument in Alabama dedicated to all coal miners. The museum is located in the old company store and features a simulated coal mine. Open Thurs through Sat from 10 a.m. to 4 p.m., Sun 1 to 4 p.m., and other times by appointment. Admission: adults $5, children $3.

While in the area, plan a visit to ***Confederate Memorial Park*** (205-755-1990), just off US 31 near I-65 at 437 County Road 63 in Marbury. The site of a former home for Confederate veterans and their widows, the park features a museum with historical displays, Civil War relics, flags, Confederate uniforms, and weaponry. On the grounds you'll also find two cemeteries, a chapel, the old Mountain Creek Post Office, picnic pavilions, and hiking trails. Except for major holidays, the museum is open from 9 a.m. to 5 p.m. The park may be visited year-round from 6 a.m. to dusk. Admission: adults $4, college students and senior citizens $3, children (ages 6 to 18) $1; and children (under age 6) free.

Head back north to **Calera** to see several antiques shops and the **Heart of Dixie Railroad Museum** (205-668-3435). From I-65 take exit 228 and travel less than a mile west on State Route 25, following signs to the museum at 1919 Ninth Street. Exhibits include World War II photos, framed timetables, waiting room benches, old railroad lanterns, signal equipment, special tools used to repair steam locomotives, a caboose stove, and an arrival/departure board from the demolished Birmingham Terminal. A glass case contains dishes made by Marshall Field and Company in 1925 for the Rock Island Lines. You'll see a centralized train control board (CTC) with which one person, a railroad counterpart of the airline's air traffic controller, managed a large section of tracks and the trains that traveled it. Locomotives, guard cars (the museum owns four of only six in existence), passenger and freight cars, and the state's largest railroad crane stand outside the green depot museum. The museum is open mid-March to mid-December. Open Tues through Fri 9 a.m. to 2 p.m., and Sat 9 a.m. to 4 p.m. The museum sponsors train rides and special events. Call for more information on the museum and train ride schedule with excursion rates. Trains generally run from mid-March until the weekend before Christmas. Museum admission is free, but donations are accepted. Visit hodrr. org for more information.

Continue a few miles northeast via State Route 25 to **Columbiana**, where you'll discover hundreds of prized possessions from the country's first First Family. People can't believe that all these things belonged to George Washington, and they are amazed to find such a collection in central Alabama at the **Karl C. Harrison Museum of George Washington** (205-669-8767). Housed in a modern building that adjoins the Mildred B. Harrison Library's right side, the facility provides spacious quarters for the extensive collection and permits previously stored pieces to be exhibited. Located at 50 Lester Street, the museum stands behind the handsome Shelby County Courthouse.

The foyer's focal point, a commanding bust of George Washington, was created by French sculptor Jean Antoine Houdan from a life mask. Nearby, a glass case topped by a handsome pair of pink Sevres vases contains family correspondence, documents, jewelry, and a writing instrument from Washington's survey case. Martha Washington's prayer book ranks among the museum's rarest possessions. Two dining room tables feature beautiful settings with exquisite porcelain pieces and coin-silver utensils used at Mount Vernon. A prized 207-piece set of Minton porcelain is displayed on a table and buffet and also fills the shelves of a walnut cabinet signed by William Elfie.

Other treasures include family portraits, various personal items, an original 1787 Samuel Vaughn sketch of Mount Vernon's grounds, and some seventy letters and documents dating to the Revolutionary War period. You can read correspondence from James Madison, Lord Cornwallis, John Adams, Aaron Burr, and other historic figures. The collection's oldest item is the 1710 handwritten will of Col. Daniel Parke, the grandfather of Martha Washington's first husband. You'll also see an original tintype made by Civil War photographer Mathew B. Brady that depicts Robert E. Lee in uniform for the last time.

Amassed by Eliza Parke Custis Law, Martha Washington's granddaughter, the collection passed through six generations of Washington heirs down to Shelby County's Charlotte Smith Weaver. After giving her grandchildren selected items, Mrs. Weaver offered the remainder of the family collection for public preservation. Columbiana banker Karl Harrison acquired two-thirds of it for this museum, and the rest went to Mount Vernon. The Columbiana museum procured additional family pieces from the estate of George Washington's half-brother, Augustin, in 1989. The museum is open Mon through Fri 10 a.m. to 3 p.m., except for major holidays. Admission is free. Visit online at washingtonmuseum.com.

Woodland & Water

Continue east to **Sylacauga**, sometimes called Marble City. While many cities contain marble monuments and buildings, here the entire town rests on a marble bed about thirty-two miles long and more than a mile wide. Sylacauga marble was used in the US Supreme Court Building in Washington, DC, Detroit's General Motors Building, and in many other distinctive edifices. "The Sylacauga area has some of the whitest marble in the world," says a local quarrying company official.

Stop by the ***Isabel Anderson Comer Museum and Arts Center*** (256-245-4016; comermuseum.weebly.com) at 711 Broadway Avenue North. At the museum, housed in a former library building dating from the 1930s, you'll see a big chunk of calcite quartz, unusual because it came from the middle of a local marble quarry. The museum owns several pieces by Giuseppe Moretti, the Italian sculptor who designed Birmingham's statue of *Vulcan*. Moretti came to Sylacauga in the early 1900s to open a marble quarry.

The museum's displays cover everything from beaded evening bags and Victorian hat pins to a reproduction of the Hodges meteorite that hurtled down on Sylacauga from outer space and struck a local woman in 1954. Here, you'll find a gallery of Native American artifacts, antique toys, handmade fabrics from the 1830s, and an extensive collection of photos and scrapbooks on local history. Pioneer exhibits are housed in the basement. One section features albums, awards, photos, costumes, and other memorabilia of native son Jim Nabors, who starred as TV's Gomer Pyle on *The Andy Griffith Show*.

The museum is open Tues through Fri 10 a.m. to 5 p.m., or by appointment. Although there's no admission charge, donations are accepted.

For fine dining with a Southern accent, visit ***Buttermilk Hill Restaurant & Bar*** (256-207-1001) at 300 East Third Street. Housed in a Victorian home built in 1904, the restaurant's name comes from its historic location. The interior features original floors, fireplaces, ornate woodwork, antique chandeliers—and maybe some ghosts, hints Kara McClendon Bacchi, who owns the property.

Depending on the weather, you may opt for lunch or dinner on the marble patio or front wraparound porch. For lunch, try the sautéed buttermilk chicken breast over romaine, tomatoes, locally made goat cheese, toasted walnuts, and sweet onions with Balsamic molasses vinaigrette. A dinner choice might be the pork tenderloin roulade with lavender, sage, Parmesan, and sundried tomatoes drizzled with truffle oil and served with buttermilk mashed potatoes (a signature dish here) and assorted vegetables. Or select from the two or three daily specials. As for dessert, you'll want to try a seasonal treat like the chef's sublime take on strawberry shortcake with sliced berries, whipped cream, sweet corn bread, and a splash of sorghum syrup. Lunch hours run Tues through Fri 11 a.m. to 2 p.m.; dinner hours are Thurs through Sat 5 to 9 p.m. Moderate to expensive. Visit buttermilkhillrestaurant.com.

Meteorite Brings Rude Awakening to Alabama Woman

Taking a nap on her couch, a Sylacauga woman got an unexpected awakening. Crashing through the roof of her home, an 8.5-pound meteorite ricocheted off a console radio and smashed into the woman's hand and hip. It is the only confirmed occurrence of an extraterrestrial hitting a human.

The event on November 30, 1954, caused a flurry of media coverage and an Air Force investigation. Today the hunk of space stone—known as the Hodges meteorite—is on display at the **Alabama Museum of Natural History at the University of Alabama** (427 Sixth Ave. NE, Tuscaloosa; 205-348-7550; amnh.ua.edu).

When 31-year-old Ann Hodges was jolted awake by the noise and the pain, she first thought a gas space heater had exploded and hurled something at her. Then she saw the grapefruit-size rock on the floor. And a gaping hole in the roof.

People in Alabama and nearby states reported seeing a fireball streaking through the sky at about the same time. Neighbors said they saw the falling star, followed by an explosion and billowing smoke. Most onlookers thought it must have been an airplane crash. Geologists said the loud noise was likely a sonic boom created by the meteorite as it traveled many times the speed of sound.

Examined by a local doctor, Hodges was found to have no permanent damage. Her hip and hand were swollen and painful, with a grapefruit-size bruise on her hip, but the hoopla surrounding the event soon engulfed her. Besieged by the media, Hodges was featured in *Life* magazine, as well as many other newspapers and magazines around the nation. She also appeared on Gary Moore's popular TV show, *I've Got a Secret*. Hodges eventually donated the meteorite to the Alabama Museum of Natural History.

Hodges died of kidney failure in 1972 at age 49.

The meteorite itself is still on display underneath a glass case at the Alabama Museum of Natural History. The 7-inch-by-5-inch-by-5-inch rock is covered with a thick black coating from its blazing entry. It has several chips and a patch of tar from the Hodges' roof.

Don't leave town without treating yourself to some ice cream at **Blue Bell Creameries** (256-249-6100 or 888-573-5286; bluebell.com) at 423 North Norton Avenue. What's your pleasure? Choices range from lemon, triple chocolate, chocolate chip, caramel pecan fudge, and banana split to pecan praline and cream, cherry vanilla, and black walnut—and the list goes on. In addition to watching ice cream being made, you can relax (after you finish agonizing over which flavor to order) in the old-fashioned ice-cream parlor or browse in the Country Store. Tours, which last about forty-five minutes, take place Mon through Fri. Call ahead for information on how to schedule or join a tour. The Country Store is open Mon through Fri from 9 a.m. to 4:30 p.m.

After leaving Sylacauga, follow US 280 southeast to *Alexander City* or Alex City, as the locals call it. While in the Alex City area, you might like to explore nearby *Horseshoe Bend National Military Park* (256-234-7111; nps.gov/hobe), the site of the final battle of the Creek War, which made a national hero of Andrew Jackson. Located about twelve miles north of Dadeville on State Route 49 at 11288 Horseshoe Bend Road, the 2,040-acre park features a visitor center with exhibits on the battle, Creek Indian culture, and frontier life. The visitor center is open daily 9 a.m. to 5 p.m. Free admission.

Other local options include boating, swimming, and fishing at *Lake Martin*, which offers a 750-mile shoreline against a backdrop of wooded hills. This body of water spills over the southern half of Tallapoosa County and even splashes into neighboring Elmore and Coosa Counties. Depending on the season and local weather conditions, anglers haul in largemouth and striped bass, bream, bluegill, crappie, and catfish from this lake. For more outdoor recreation continue south to Elmore County.

Places to Stay in Central Alabama

ALEXANDER CITY

Super 8 by Wyndham
4335 US 280
(256) 392-7440

Days Inn by Wyndham
3146 US 280
(256) 234-6311

Mistletoe Bough Bed & Breakfast
497 Hillabee St.
(256) 329-3717
mistletoebough.com

Quality Inn
2945 US 280
(256) 234-5900

ANNISTON

Hotel Finial
1600 Quintard Ave.
(256) 236-0503
HotelFinial.com

Parker House Bed & Breakfast
330 E. Sixth St.
(256) 405-9262
parkerbnb.com

Springwood Inn Bed & Breakfast
1301 Booger Hollow Road
(843) 384-2618
springwoodinn.com

BIRMINGHAM

Birmingham Marriott
3590 Grandview Pkwy.
(205) 968-3775 or
(800) 627-7468

Cobb Lane Bed and Breakfast
1309 19th St. South
(205) 918-9090
cobblanebandb.com

Hotel Indigo Birmingham
1023 20th Street South
(205) 933-9555
ihg.com

Redmont Hotel
2101 Fifth Ave. North
(205) 957-6828
redmontbirmingham.com

Hyatt Regency Birmingham
1000 Riverchase Galleria
(205) 705-1234

Renaissance Ross Bridge Golf Resort & Spa
4000 Grand Ave.
(205) 916-7677 or
(800) 593-6419

Sheraton Birmingham Hotel
2101 Richard Arrington Jr. Blvd. North
(205) 324-5000 or
(888) 627-7095

Hampton Inn & Suites Birmingham-Downtown-Tutwiler
2021 Park Place North
(205) 322-2100 or
(866) 850-3053

DELTA

Cheaha State Park
2141 Bunker Loop
(256) 488-5115 or
(800) 610-5801
alapark.com/cheaharesort

MONTEVALLO

Fox & Pheasant Inn Bed & Breakfast
540 Shelby Street
(205) 665-3080
foxandpheasantinn.com

Ramsay Conference Center
University of Montevallo
24 Vine St.
(205) 665-6280

OXFORD

Holiday Inn Express Hotel & Suites
160 Colonial Dr.
(256) 835-8768 or
(888) 465-4329

PELHAM

Oak Mountain State Park
200 Terrace Dr.
(205) 620-2524 or
(800) ALA–PARK
alapark.com/oakmountain

SYLACAUGA

Quality Inn
89 Gene Stewart Blvd.
(256) 245-4141 or
(800) 526-3766

TUSCALOOSA

Bama Bed and Breakfast
46 Sherwood Dr.
(205) 750-0990
bamabedandbreakfast.com

Hotel Capstone
320 Paul Bryant Dr.
(205) 752-3200 or
(800) 477-2262
hotelcapstone.com

Centerstone Inn
4700 Doris Pate Dr.
(205) 556-3232 or
(800) 311-3811
centerstonehotels.com

Courtyard by Marriott
4115 Courtney Dr.
(205) 750-8384 or
(800) 321-2211

FOR MORE INFORMATION ABOUT CENTRAL ALABAMA

Alexander City Chamber of Commerce
175 Aliant Parkway
Alexander City 35010
(256) 234-3461
alexcitychamber.com

Calhoun County Chamber of Commerce
1330 Quintard Ave.
PO Box 1087 Anniston 36201
(256) 237-3536
calhounchamber.com
info@calhounchamber.com

Greater Birmingham Convention & Visitors Bureau
2200 Ninth Ave. North
Birmingham 35203-1100
(205) 458-8000 or (800) 458-8085
birminghamal.org info@birmingham.org

Montevallo Chamber of Commerce
845 Valley St.
Montevallo 35115
(205) 665-1519
montevallocc.com
montevallochamber@gmail.com

Tuscaloosa Tourism & Sports Commission
1900 Jack Warner Pkwy.
Tuscaloosa 35401
(205) 391-9200 or (800) 538-8696
visittuscaloosa.com

Places to Eat in Central Alabama

ALEXANDER CITY

Jake's
16 Broad St.
(256) 234-4300
jakesonbroad.com

Kowaliga Restaurant
295 Kowaliga Marina Rd.
(256) 215-7035
Kowaligarestaurant.com

ALICEVILLE

Gate's Restaurant
403 Third Ave. Northwest
(205) 373-8100

ANNISTON

Betty's Bar-B-Q
401 South Quintard Ave.
(256) 237-1411

Classic on Noble
1024 Noble St.
(256) 237-5388
classiconnoble.com

Effina's
919 Noble St.
(256) 770-4830
effinas.com

Top O' the River
3330 McClellan Blvd.
(256) 238-0097
topotheriverrestaurant.com

BESSEMER

The Bright Star
304 North 19th St.
(205) 424-9444
thebrightstar.com

Homestyle Kitchen
1901 Second Ave. North
(205) 565-7278

BIRMINGHAM

Bottega
2240 Highland Ave. South
(205) 939-1000
bottegarestaurant.com

Serendipity
1500 First Ave. North
(205) 847-1610
serendipitybham.com

Cafe Dupont
113 20th St. North
(205) 322-1282
cafedupont.net

Chez Fonfon
2007 11th Ave. South
(205) 939-3221
fonfonbham.com

Gianmarco's Restaurant
721 Broadway St.
(205) 871-9622
gianmarcosbhm.com

Highlands Bar & Grill
2011 11th Ave. South
(205) 939-1400
highlandsbarandgrill.com

Hot & Hot Fish Club
2180 11th Court South
(205) 933-5474
hotandhotfishclub.com

Ocean
1218 20th St. South
(205) 933-0999
oceanbirmingham.com

Parish Seafood & Oyster House
1911 Gadsden Hwy.
(205) 655-4117
parishoysterhouse.com

CALERA

Zapopan Mexican Restaurant
4416 US 31
(205) 668-4008

HOMEWOOD

Johnny's Restaurant
2902 18th St. South
(205) 802-2711
johnnyshomewood.com

Nabeel's Cafe
1706 Oxmoor Rd.
(205) 879-9292
nabeels.com

HOOVER

Brock's
Renaissance Ross Bridge
Resort
4000 Grand Ave.
(205) 949-3051

Shonos Restaurant
1843 Montgomery Hwy. 107
(205) 988-3319

IRONDALE

Green Acres Café Irondale
1819 Crestwood Blvd.
(205) 956-4648
greenacres-cafe.com

The Irondale Cafe
1906 First Ave. North
(205) 956-5258
irondalecafe.com

MAYLENE

Fox Valley Restaurant
6745 County Rd. 17
(205) 664-8341

MONTEVALLO

Main Street Tavern
710 N. Boundary St.
(205) 665-0336
mainsttavern.com

Zapopan Mexican Restaurant
4551 State Rte. 25
(205) 665-7404

MOUNDVILLE

Pam's Diner
39266 Alabama 69
(205) 371-4300

MOUNTAIN BROOK

Chez Lulu
1909 Cahaba Rd.
(205) 870-7011
chezlulu.us

NORTHPORT

Brown Bag
9425 Jones Rd.
(205) 333-0970

China Bob
5550 McFarland Blvd.
(205) 339-9993
chinabobnorthport.com

OXFORD

China Luck
503 Quintard Dr.
(256) 831-5221

Garfrerick's Café
655 Creekside Dr.
(256) 831-0044
garfreickscafe.com

SYLACAUGA

**Buttermilk Hill
Restaurant & Bar**
300 East Third St.
(256) 207-1001
buttermilkhillrestaurant.com

Faye's Bar-B-Que
2600 Old Birmingham Hwy.
(256) 245-0490

**LaCosta Mexican
Restaurant**
215 North Broadway Ave.
(256) 249-3360

TRUSSVILLE

**Chocolate Biscuit
Tearoom**
335 Main St.
(205) 655-0119
chocolatebiscuit.cafe

TUSCALOOSA

Cypress Inn
501 Rice Mine Rd. North
(205) 345-6963
cypressinnrestaurant.com

DePalma's Italian Cafe
2300 University Blvd.
(205) 759-1879
depalmasdowntown.com

Dreamland Bar-B-Que
5535 15th Ave. East
(205) 758-8135
dreamlandbbq.com

Evangeline's
1653 McFarland Blvd. North
(205) 752-0830
evangelinesrestaurant.com

Urban Cookhouse
1490 Northbank Pkwy. #110
(205) 561-6999
urbancookhouse.com

The Waysider Restaurant
1512 Greensboro Ave.
(205) 345-8239

MAINSTREAM ATTRACTIONS WORTH SEEING IN CENTRAL ALABAMA

Arlington Antebellum Home & Gardens
331 Cotton Ave. Southwest Birmingham
(205) 780-5656
arlingtonantebellumhomeandgardens
.com

This circa 1850 Greek revival mansion contains a fine collection of period antiques. Located on six acres of landscaped gardens, the two-story frame house and gardens offer lovely special lunches, dinners, and events throughout the year.

Birmingham Zoo
2630 Cahaba Rd.
Birmingham
(205) 879-0408 or (205) 879-0409
birminghamzoo.com

Both big and little kids enjoy outings to this facility, the home of some 900 animals from all over the globe. A 3,000-square-foot Butterfly Encounter is home to hundreds of butterflies, more than twenty species all native to Alabama. The Rhino Encounter lets visitors get up close and personal with two 4,000-pound rhinos. The zoo also has a carousel, train ride, and a restaurant named Nourish 205 which features healthy food options using fresh locally grown ingredients for soups, sandwiches, salads, and more.

International Motorsports Hall of Fame & Talladega Superspeedway
3198 Speedway Blvd. Talladega
(256) 362-5002
talladegasuperspeedway.com
motorsportshalloffame.com

This unique facility, which occupies a complex of circular-shaped buildings, captures the speed of movement and thrill of competitive racing. You'll see the Budweiser Rocket Car, a missile on wheels that broke the sound barrier, and record-breaking vehicles once guided by Richard Petty, Bill Elliott, Bobby Allison, and other racing greats. Additional exhibits include vintage autos, drag racers, motorcycles, trophies, photos, and a simulator that puts you in the driver's seat. You can also tour the adjacent Talladega Superspeedway, the world's fastest speedway.

McWane Science Center
200 19th St. North Birmingham
(205) 714-8300
mcwane.org

Definitely not off the beaten path, this science-adventure museum occupies the historic Loveman's department store building in the heart of downtown. Youngsters will especially enjoy the IMAX theater's presentations and simulated space-flight experiences offered by the Challenger Center for Space Science Education, a nonprofit organization founded by the families of the seven Challenger crew members who died in the tragic 1986 space shuttle explosion. The Ocean Pool, World of Water, and various interactive science exhibits all add to the excitement.

Alabama Splash Adventure
4599 Alabama Adventure Pkwy.
Bessemer
(205) 481-4750
alabamasplash.com

This fun-filled family park offers water adventure galore in Bessemer, just southwest of Birmingham. Choose from watery fun on Acapulco Drop, Castaway Island, Kahuna Waves, and a zipline. Or pick the world's first 360-degree interactive water-based obstacle course. The Wipeout Adventure Course features a series of ropes, bridges, and towers along with hand- and foot-activated water elements.

Southeast Alabama

The Plains

On your way to "The Plains" (home of Auburn University) in the historic Chattahoochee Trace's upper section, you might want to strike out east to **Tuskegee**. Stop by the **Tuskegee Human & Civil Rights Multicultural Center** (334-724-0800), which also serves as a welcome center. Located in a former bank building at 104 South Elm Street, the facility houses exhibits on the history of Macon County, including one on the Tuskegee Syphilis Study and local civil rights activities. Here, you can pick up tourist information. The staff will answer your questions and suggest nearby off-the-beaten-path spots to visit. Hours are Tues through Sat from 10 a.m. to 3 p.m. Admission is free.

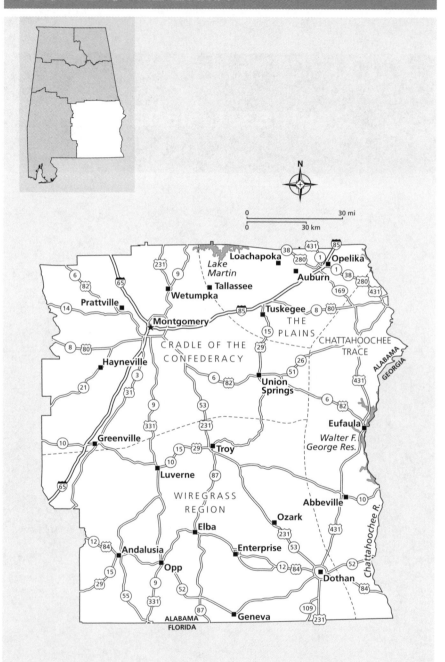

Next make your way to 1212 West Montgomery Road and *Tuskegee Institute National Historic Site* (334-727-3200, nps.gov/tuin/index), where even peanut-butter buffs will be amazed to learn about the peanut's potential. *The Carver Museum* pays tribute to the creative genius of the agronomist, artist, and inventor who helped change the course of Southern agriculture. *George Washington Carver's* agricultural experiments with peanuts, pecans, sweet potatoes, and cotton resulted in a more educated approach to farming—not to mention hundreds of new products, many featured among the museum's exhibits. You'll also see some of Carver's artwork and a model of the first lab he used to launch research that resulted in the transformation of sweet potatoes into after-dinner mints, a coffee substitute, lemon drops, starch, synthetic ginger, tapioca, library paste, medicine, writing ink, and a multitude of other items. As for the multipurpose peanut, the legendary scientist's list of possible uses ranges from beverages, foods, cosmetics, dyes, and medicines to diesel fuel, laundry soap, and insecticide. Before you leave the museum, be sure to visit the gift section and purchase a copy of the booklet (first published in June 1925) entitled *How to Grow the Peanut and 105 Ways of Preparing It for Human Consumption*, containing recipes from peanut bisque to peanut pudding. Museum open Mon through Sat from 9 a.m. to 4:30 p.m., except for Thanksgiving, Christmas, and New Year's Day. Museum admission is free.

Later take a campus stroll to see some of the handmade brick buildings, which students constructed during the institute's early years. You'll also want to tour *The Oaks* at 905 W. Montgomery Road, home of *Booker T. Washington*, who served as first president of Tuskegee Institute, which was founded in 1881. The home is furnished as it was during the time the Washington family lived there. Admission is free. Tours are available. Call (334) 727-3200 for information.

Head north to the "land where turtles live"—a former Creek Indian settlement called *Loachapoka* that once also thrived as a stagecoach junction. Seven miles west of Auburn on State Route 14, you'll find the *Loachapoka Historic District*, which features several structures dating from the decade 1840 to 1850. *The Lee County Historical Society Museum* (334-887-3007, leecountyhistoricalsociety.org), housed in the old Trade Center building at 6500 Stage Road, contains items ranging from a unique hand-carved cedar rocking chair and an 1840s accounting desk to an oak map case, an antique medical bag, and a punch bowl and dipper made from gourds.

alabamatrivia

George Washington Carver invented peanut butter during his experiments at Tuskegee Institute.

The Intrepid Tuskegee Airmen

During the early 1940s, Moton Field served as the training grounds for the Tuskegee Airmen, who overcame formidable odds to serve their country with bravery and distinction in a segregated America. As escorts to World War II bombing missions in North Africa and Southern Europe, these African-American aviators compiled an enviable combat record and ranked among the military's best pilots. The 332nd Fighter Group never lost a bomber to enemy fighters while escorting the 15th Air Force on bombing missions. Revered by American bomber crews (who called them the "Red-tail Angels" because of their aircrafts' distinctive markings), these flying heroes also commanded the respect of the German Luftwaffe.

At the US Air Force Academy, the Tuskegee Airmen statue acknowledges their extraordinary contribution: "They rose from adversity through competence, courage, commitment, and capacity to serve America on silver wings, and to set a standard few will transcend."

Lending her support to Tuskegee Institute's civilian pilot training program, First Lady Eleanor Roosevelt visited here in March 1941. She requested to be taken on a flight by Charles Alfred "Chief" Anderson, who inspired the founding of Tuskegee's School of Aviation, and newspapers across the country carried a photo of this unprecedented event.

The Tuskegee group's achievements represent a turning point in the role of African-Americans in the US military and factored into President Harry S. Truman's signing Executive Order 9981 in 1948, setting the stage for the military's desegregation and later the Civil Rights Movement.

In 1998, Congress designated the *Tuskegee Airmen National Historic Site* as a unit of the National Park System. Along with the remaining hangar, visitors can see the airfield taxiway, control tower, reservoir, gasoline pits, and fuel storage facilities from the World War II era. The modest airport terminal also features exhibits of photos that chronicle the history of Black aviation and the Tuskegee Airmen.

The National Park Service Visitor Center is located on the outskirts of Tuskegee at 1616 Chappie James Avenue. The site is open Sat 9 a.m. to 4:30 p.m., except for major holidays. Free admission.

To reach the "Home of Black Aviation," take exit 38 off I-85. For more information call (334) 724-0922 or visit nps.gov/tuai.

Upstairs, rooms with individual themes feature vintage costumes such as an 1877 wedding dress, an exhibit on Ella Smith's Roanoke doll creations, antique quilts, and a melodeon. Other displays include military uniforms and equipment, kitchen utensils and gadgets, and an almost complete section of Auburn annuals that date to the 1890s.

On the grounds you'll see a steam-powered cotton gin, gristmill, working blacksmith shop, bandstand, doctor's buggy, and dogtrot cabin (moved here from rural Tallapoosa County and reconstructed). If you visit in October, don't miss **Pioneer Day** in Loachapoka. Folks at this event, harking back to yester-year, demonstrate the entire process of converting sugar cane into syrup—from cane crushing by mule-drawn press to syrup sampling on homemade sweet potato biscuits (sometimes called "cat head biscuits" because of their large size). For information on making an appointment to see the museum, call the Auburn-Opelika Tourism Bureau at (866) 880-8747 or (334) 887-8747, stop by at 714 Glenn Avenue, or visit aotourism.com.

Afterward continue east to "sweet Auburn, loveliest village of the plain." This line from Oliver Goldsmith's poem "The Deserted Village" inspired the university town's name. Founded by the Alabama Methodist Conference in 1856, the school later became a land-grant institution. (Incidentally, if you enter **Auburn** by way of I-85, a trail of big orange tiger paws takes you all the way to the university campus.)

Start your tour of the **Auburn University Historic District** at Toomer's Corner, a busy intersection that gets layered so deeply with toilet tissue after each Tiger victory that sometimes vehicles cannot pass through for an hour or two while a celebration takes place. (Auburn is the only city in the world to have a line item in the city budget for the removal of toilet paper.) Toomer's Corner is named in honor of former state senator Sheldon "Shell" Toomer, a halfback on Alabama's first football team in 1892. Local lore says that the tradition of papering Toomer's Corner can be traced back to the days when Toomer's Drugs had the only handy telegraph for fast (in those days) news delivery. When Auburn played away games, fans would wait to hear results from the drugstore telegraph. If the team won, the ticker tape would be thrown on power lines in celebration.

Before embarking on your campus trek, you might like to step into **Toomer's Drugstore** (334-887-3488; toomersdrugs.com), a local landmark at 100 North College Street, to see the antique marble soda fountain and to order a lemonade. Shell Toomer established the store in 1896. Hours are Mon through Fri 10 a.m. to 6 p.m., Sat 10 a.m. to 5 p.m., and Sun noon to 5 p.m. This section of campus features several buildings that date from the 1850s to the early 1900s. You'll see the Gothic revival University Chapel, Langdon Hall, and Samford Hall. The latter, a four-story brick structure of Italianate design, dates to 1888 and stands on the site of Old Main, a building that burned the year before.

To explore a tucked-away corner on campus, search out the **Donald E. Davis Arboretum**, with pavilion, lake, and some 200 labeled botanical specimens ranging from red Japanese maples and chinquapin oaks to Southern magnolias and chinaberry trees. The 13.5-acre arboretum is open daily from sunrise to sunset. Restrooms are located on the east side of the pavilion.

Don't miss the *Lovelace Athletic Museum and Hall of Honor* (334-844-4750), located at the corner of Samford and Donahue in the Athletic Complex. Honoring Auburn's athletes, the museum recognizes such athletes as Heisman Trophy winner and football/baseball hero Bo Jackson, NBA star Charles Barkley, star baseball player Frank Thomas, Heisman Trophy winner/coach Pat Sullivan, and legendary coaches Pat Dye and Shug Jordan. Check out auburntigers.com to see some Auburn legends and keep up with the renovation project.

To visit a jewel of a museum, head to 901 South College Street. Here you'll find *The Jule Collins Smith Museum of Art* (334-844-1484) overlooking a three-acre lake. Constructed of travertine stone from Italy, the handsome facility features eight exhibition galleries, a museum shop, an auditorium, and a cafe. On entering, you'll see a stunning glass chandelier created for the vaulted rotunda by internationally known glass artist Dale Chihuly.

Other treasures include one of the world's largest collections of Victorian Belleek porcelain, outstanding Tibetan bronzes, and more than 100 of Audubon's most acclaimed prints. But the big story here centers on a collection of thirty-six paintings and drawings that had remained homeless for more than half a century.

Originally assembled by the US State Department in 1946, the collection features works by John Marin, Georgia O'Keeffe, Ben Shahn, Arthur Dove, Ralston Crawford, Yasuo Kuniyoski, and others. Because of its abstract nature and the political leanings of a few of the artists, the traveling exhibit met with so much criticism on the home front that it was recalled, stored, and labeled government "surplus property," thus allowing tax-supported institutions like

BEST ATTRACTIONS IN SOUTHEAST ALABAMA

Alabama Shakespeare Festival, Montgomery

First White House of the Confederacy, Montgomery

The Jule Collins Smith Museum of Art, Auburn

Landmark Park, Dothan

Lovelace Athletic Museum and Hall of Honor, Auburn

Old Alabama Town, Montgomery

Pioneer Museum of Alabama, Troy

Rosa Parks Library and Museum, Montgomery

State Capitol, Montgomery

Town of Eufaula

Tuskegee Institute National Historic Site, Tuskegee

US Army Aviation Museum, Fort Rucker

Auburn to receive a ninety-five percent discount when the collection was subsequently offered at auction. An Auburn professor with foresight, Frank Applebee, spearheaded "the art bargain of the century" when he persuaded art department instructors to pool their yearly salary increase and enter the announced auction. As a result, Auburn University's Advancing American Art Collection was acquired in 1948 for an unthinkable $1,072. Experts call this body of works, now valued somewhere between $7 and $10 million, one of the most important collections of American art from the post–World War II era.

After viewing the exhibits, take time to enjoy the museum's botanical gardens with walking paths. The Museum Cafe is a great place to relax and recharge. The menu changes weekly and specials are posted on the website. A favorite is the delicious crab bisque and the fried goat cheese salad with grapes and pecans. The cafe is open for lunch Tues through Fri from 11 a.m. to 2 p.m. and for dinner on Thurs from 5 to 8 p.m.

Museum hours are Tues through Sat 8:30 a.m. to 4:30 p.m., and Sun 1 to 4 p.m. On Thursday nights, hours are extended to 8 p.m. Free admission. For more information, visit jcsm.auburn.edu.

While in Auburn consider headquartering at *Crenshaw Guest House* (334-821-1131 or 800-950-1131), two blocks north of Toomer's Corner. Shaded by giant oak and pecan trees, this blue Victorian gingerbread–style house stands at 371 North College Street in Auburn's Old Main and Church Street Historic District. The two-story 1890 home is furnished with lovely antiques. Owners Steve and Sarah Jenkins offer five units for overnight guests. The Crenshaw also offers two guest cottages on the property—the Coach Dye Cottage with two bedrooms and two baths, and the Thach Cottage with a loft and bedroom. Guests receive a bountiful hot breakfast. See crenshawguesthouse.com. Standard to moderate rates.

While in the area, golfers will want to tee off at *Auburn Links at Mill Creek* (334-887-5151, aulinksgolfcourse.com), a $5 million facility that occupies 274 acres located about three miles south of town near the intersection of US 29 and I-85 at exit 51 at 826 Shell Toomer Parkway. (The 18th hole's sand traps form a giant tiger paw print.)

Auburn's sister city, *Opelika*, makes a good place to continue your area exploration. In Opelika's "olden days," passengers traveling through by train sometimes saw shootouts across the railroad tracks. Fortunately, today's visitors don't have to dodge stray bullets, so you can relax as you explore the Railroad Avenue Historic District.

As a result of Opelika's participation in Alabama's Main Street program (a project of the National Trust for Historic Preservation), many once-forgotten structures have been rescued and reincarnated as charming shops such as

Easterday Antiques at 805 South Railroad Avenue. Helen Easterday, who's been called "the quintessential town person," and her husband, Kenneth, have embraced the local downtown revitalization program to the point of converting the enormous upper level of their shop into a wonderful home. Mrs. Easterday's passion for art may be observed in the exquisite antique furnishings, oriental rugs, paintings, and accessories displayed in her shop. The shop is open 9:30 a.m. to 4 p.m. weekdays. Appointments are suggested. For more information or an appointment, call (334) 749-6407 or visit easterdayantiques.com.

After your Railroad Avenue stroll, head to *The Museum of East Alabama* (334-749-2751; eastalabama.org), located nearby at 121 South Ninth Street. Here you'll see a dugout canoe of white cypress that dates back as far as 3,500 BC, as well as glass milk bottles, baby bonnets, Shirley Temple and Roanoke dolls, toys, collections of vintage typewriters, pianos, farm implements, war memorabilia, and surgical instruments. Notice the interesting foot X-ray machine

TOP ANNUAL EVENTS IN SOUTHEAST ALABAMA

Bridge Crossing Jubilee
Selma, first full weekend in March
(334) 526-2626
selmajubilee.com

Rattlesnake Rodeo
Opp, March
(334) 493-2122
opprattlesnakerodeo.com

Azalea-Dogwood Trail and Festival
Dothan, late March or early April
(334) 794-6622

Auburn Floral Trail
Auburn, late March or early April
(334) 887-8747
Aotourism.com

Spring Pilgrimage
Eufaula, first weekend in April
(888) 383-2852
eufaulapilgrimage.com

A-Day Football Game
Auburn, April
(334) 844-4040 or (800) AUB-1957
Rolltide.com

Auburn CityFest
Auburn, April
(334) 501-2936
auburncityfest.com

On the Tracks Food & Wine Festival
Opelika, October
(334) 745-0466
onthetracks.org

Pioneer Day
Loachapoka, October
(334) 887-3007
Leecountyhistoricalsociety.org

Alabama Coastal BirdFest
Fairhope, October weeksbay.org

National Peanut Festival
Dothan, November
(334) 793-4323 or (888) 449-0212
nationalpeanutfestival.com

(typical of those once used in shoe stores) and the bicycle-propelled ice-cream cart. The museum's collection also includes an early-twentieth-century kitchen and a full-size fire truck. Open Tues through Fri 10 a.m. to 4 p.m.; Sat 2 to 4 p.m. Admission is free.

Looking to the right as you exit the museum, you'll see the lofty clock tower of the **Lee County Courthouse**, a half block away. Listed on the National Register of Historic Places, the handsome, white-columned, two-story brick structure dates to 1896 and features marble floors and decorative arched windows.

Take time to drive around a bit to see Opelika's lovely homes, which exemplify a wide range of architectural styles. While in the area, golfers will enjoy playing the **Grand National**, one of Alabama's fine courses on the Robert Trent Jones Golf Trail at 3000 Robert Trent Jones Trail. For more information on this award-winning course, built on 1,300 acres encompassing a 650-acre lake, call (334) 749-9042 or (800) 949-4444 or visit rtjgolf.com/grandnational.

Chattahoochee Trace

After touring War Eagle country, continue south toward Eufaula, sometimes called the "Natchez of Alabama." You may want to make your base at lovely **Lakepoint Resort** (334-687-8011 or 800-544-5253; alapark.com/lakepoint-state-park), about seven miles north of town just off US 431 at 104 Old Highway 165. Located on the shores of Lake Eufaula (also known as Lake George), this complex offers accommodations ranging from campsites, cabins, and cottages to resort rooms and suites along with a restaurant, coffee shop, lounge, and gift shop. Recreation options include swimming, golfing, tennis, hiking, picnicking, biking, waterskiing, and boating—not to mention fishing in a 45,200-acre lake known as the Big Bass Capital of the World. Room rates are standard.

Continue to Eufaula, a city filled with multiple versions of the perfect Southern mansion. Located on a bluff above the Chattahoochee River, Eufaula boasts the state's second-largest historic district and offers a feast for architecture aficionados. During the **Eufaula Pilgrimage**, an annual event that takes place the first full weekend in April, visitors can enjoy home tours, antiques shows, concerts, and other festivities. For more information, contact the Eufaula Heritage Association at (334) 687-3793 or (888) 383-2852 or go to eufaulapilgrimage.com.

Stop by the **Hart House** (334-687-9755) at 211 North Eufaula Avenue, an 1850 Greek revival structure that serves as headquarters for the Historic Chattahoochee Commission. Here you can pick up visitors information about the Trace, a river corridor running through portions of Alabama and Georgia.

Throughout this bi-state region, travelers will discover a wealth of historic sites, natural attractions, and recreation facilities. Except for holidays, the Hart House may be visited Mon through Fri from 8 a.m. to 5 p.m.

Continue to **Shorter Mansion** (334-687-3793 or 888-383-2852) at 340 North Eufaula Avenue. This elegant structure dates to 1884 and features seventeen Corinthian-capped columns and an elaborate frieze of molded acanthus leaves and scrolls beneath its lofty balustraded roof. Be sure to notice the front door's beveled leaded glass and the entrance hall's parquet floor and molded plaster cornices. This Neoclassical revival mansion, furnished in fine Victorian period pieces, houses the Eufaula Historical Museum and serves as headquarters for the Eufaula Heritage Association.

One upstairs room contains portraits of six state governors who were either born in or later lived in Barbour County. Another upstairs room pays tribute to retired Adm. Thomas H. Moorer, a Eufaula native who served two terms as chairman of the Joint Chiefs of Staff. Displays include Admiral Moorer's portrait, uniform, awards, and mementos from his naval career.

You'll also see Waterford crystal and cut-glass chandeliers, antiques, Confederate relics, period wedding dresses, Alabama memorabilia, and decorative arts. You may browse through the mansion at your leisure or take a guided tour. Admission: adults $5, children (ages 5 to 12) $3. The home is open Mon through Sat from 10 a.m. to 4 p.m., except for major holidays.

Before leaving Eufaula be sure to visit **Fendall Hall** (334-687-8469; fendallhall.weebly.com), at 917 West Barbour Street. Built between 1856 and 1860, the home features stenciled walls and ceilings painted by a nineteenth-century Italian artist, and the original decor with high Victorian colors remains relatively unchanged. Also noteworthy are the entrance hall's striking black-and-white marble floor and the home's early plumbing system, supplied by attic cisterns. Rumor has it that a ghost named Sammy makes his presence known here from time to time. Currently the house is open for tours Mon through Sat from 10 a.m. to 4 p.m. Admission: adults $7.

After touring this town of lovely mansions, head to **Clayton**, a small town with some unique attractions, such as the **Octagon House** at 103 North Midway Street. Listed on the National Register of Historic Places, this unusual structure, also known as the Petty-Roberts-Beatty House, is the state's sole surviving antebellum octagonal house. The ground floor served as the original kitchen (and also as the setting for a mystery, *The Rusty Key*, written by one of the home's owners). Four chimneys extending above the cupola enclose the staircase of this eight-sided structure. The first floor features four main rooms, two small rooms, and two halls that open to the surrounding porch. Call (334) 775-9176 to arrange a tour. Tours $5 per person.

At nearby Clayton Baptist Church Cemetery (also on North Midway Street), you'll find the **Whiskey Bottle Tombstone**, once featured on *Ripley's Believe It or Not!* television show. The bottle-shaped headstone and footstone, which mark the final resting place of William T. Mullen (1834–1863), still contain their original removable stone stoppers. Such a memorial obviously tells a story, and the story behind the stone goes something like this: Mr. Mullen, a local accountant, acquired a reputation as a heavy drinker. His wife, Mary, a devout teetotaler, threatened that if he drank himself to death, she would let the world know by erecting an appropriate memorial. The Whiskey Bottle Tombstone testifies that she kept her promise.

Wiregrass Region

Continuing south along the Chattahoochee Trace takes you to **Dothan**, in the state's southeastern corner. Here, in a region called the Wiregrass, early settlers battled the odds to cultivate this large stretch of land once completely covered by clumps of stiff, dry grass growing under longleaf pines. To learn more about the Wiregrass region's roots, stop by **Landmark Park** (334-793-4323; landmarkparkdothan.com), in Dothan on US 431, about three miles north of Ross Clark Circle at 430 Landmark Drive. At this living-history farmstead, you may be greeted by sheep, goats, pigs, chickens, cows, and a mule. You'll see a blacksmith shop, pioneer log cabin, smokehouse, cane-mill syrup shed, and other authentic outbuildings of a 1890s farm. The cozy clapboard farmhouse looks as if its occupants just stepped out to milk the cows and may return any minute. An apron hangs on a cupboard door, and a shaving mug and brush wait beside the washstand.

The park offers a full schedule of special events with demonstrations of seasonal farming activities, pioneer skills, and various crafts. In addition to the farmstead, you'll see a country store, church, one-room schoolhouse, drugstore, gazebo, interpretive center, planetarium, nature trails, boardwalks, beaver ponds, and picnic areas. Youngsters will especially enjoy the playground with its barnyard theme. Admission: adults $4, children (ages 3 to 12) $3. Hours are Mon through Sat 9 a.m. to 5 p.m.; Sun noon to 6 p.m.

Continue to downtown Dothan, the area's major trade center. Proclaimed "Peanut Capital of the World," this region produces one-fourth of the nation's peanuts. Each fall Dothan stages the **National Peanut Festival** (334-793-4323; nationalpeanutfestival.com) with a full calendar of events, from demonstrations of square dance rounds by the Goober Gamboleers to a contest for prize-winning peanut recipes. Look for the large peanut sculptures, individually decorated and placed throughout town.

Across the street from the Civic Center, you'll see the **Wiregrass Museum of Art** (334-794-3871; wiregrassmuseum.org) at 126 Museum Avenue. This three-level facility features a full schedule of rotating exhibits attractively displayed in various galleries. The museum contains a classroom/studio and a children's hands-on gallery. Youngsters will find the activity area entertaining as well as educational. Open Wed through Fri 10 a.m. to 5 p.m.; Sat 10 a.m. to 3 p.m. Admission is free, but donations are accepted.

First known as Poplar Head, Dothan took its present biblical name in 1885. Around that time, concerned citizens decided to tone down the town's rowdy image and hired a marshal and deputies to enforce new laws designed to terminate the saloons' regular Saturday-night brawls.

While driving around town, you'll see local history depicted in colorful murals on various city buildings. The **Mule Marker** in Poplar Head Park pays tribute to the animal that played a major role in the Wiregrass region's early development. Nearby at 115 North Saint Andrews Street, you'll notice the impressive **Dothan Opera House**, a neoclassical revival structure that dates from 1915. Another downtown historic site, **E. R. Porter Hardware Museum** (334-794-6622; visitdothan.com), at 136 East Main Street with its rolling ladders, still exudes the nostalgic flavor of its late-1800s origin. After operating for almost 125 years, the historic hardware store officially became a museum in May 2018. Museum hours are Tues through Fri from 10 a.m. to 6 p.m.

Afterward head to nearby Ozark, home of the **Claybank Church** on East Andrews Avenue just off State Route 249. This 1852 log church with hand-split board shingles and original pews is open daily during daylight hours.

Carry on your exploration of the Wiregrass region with a visit to **Enterprise** and don't miss the **Boll Weevil Monument**. Actually, you can't miss this memorial because it stands in the middle of Main Street. And if you aren't sure you'd recognize a boll weevil (a bug about a quarter-inch long with a snout half the length of its body), just watch for a statue of a woman clad in classic drapery who stands on an ornamented pedestal and holds a magnified version of the pest high above her head. A streetside plaque explains that in 1919 the citizens of Enterprise and Coffee County erected the statue in profound appreciation of the boll weevil and what it has done as the herald of prosperity. After the boll weevil demolished two-thirds of Coffee County's cotton in 1915, local farmers started to diversify, planting other crops such as sugarcane, corn, hay, potatoes, and peanuts. Particularly suited to the Wiregrass, peanuts played a primary role in saving the local economy after the boll weevil's destruction and soon became the region's principal cash crop.

About half a block from the Boll Weevil Monument at 116 South Main Street stands the **Rawls Restaurant**, which offers farm-to-table cuisine with a contemporary Southern touch. The restaurant is open Tues through Sat from 5 to 9 p.m. Keep a lookout for the ghost of founder Japheth Rawls, who is said to walk the halls keeping an eye on his beloved hotel. Visit the website at therawlsrestaurant.com. Prices are standard to moderate.

Behind the hotel on Railroad Street, you'll find the **Pea River Historical Society Depot Museum** at 106 Railroad Street. In railroad's golden days, passengers simply stepped off a train here, and a short stroll took them to the Rawls. Today's visitor can browse through the depot's rooms and large freight area filled with historical artifacts. "Many of the arrow and spear points in the Indian Room were discovered by local farmers, while plowing their land," said a volunteer.

History buffs can dip into more local lore at **Pea River Genealogical Library** (334-393-2901; peariver.org) at 108 South Main Street. A stroll along Main Street takes you past eateries like **Annie's Café** and antiques shops.

Before or after exploring downtown, stop by the **Enterprise Welcome Center** and Little Red Schoolhouse (complete with pot-bellied stove and slate boards) near the US 84 bypass.

At the **Boll Weevil Soap Company**, you'll find Southern Belle, Camellia Flower, High Cotton, Gardener's Love, Southern Romance, and other herbal products. The company was founded by Rosemary Howell, a nurse by profession. Chad and Kendra Wester bought the company in June of 2017. Visit bollweevilsoapcompany.com, call (334) 393-7627, or stop by 109 North Main Street and make someone happy with a fine selection of soaps. The shop is open Mon through Sat from 10 a.m. to 6 p.m.

Opp, in neighboring Covington County, hosts a unique annual event: the **Rattlesnake Rodeo**. This spring festival, scheduled the first full weekend in March, features the world's only rattlesnake race along with arts and crafts (including several made from rattlesnake skins), a buck dancing contest, and programs on rattlesnake education and safety. For specific information call (334) 493-4572 or visit opprattlesnakerodeo.com. You can also visit cityofopp.com.

To reach **Troy** follow State Route 87 north from Enterprise. On the southern outskirts of this town, the home of Troy State University, you'll find the **Mossy Grove School House Restaurant** (334-566-4921) just off US 231 at 1841 Alabama Highway 87. Set among moss-draped trees, this rustic structure started out as a one-room schoolhouse in 1856. Later enlarged and renovated, the building still contains its original stage, now part of the back dining room.

Diners can order fried dill pickles to nibble on while waiting for their entrees and admire memorabilia ranging from Confederate money, swords, and a cannonball to antique tools, barrels, and even bear teeth. Also displayed here are an old-fashioned telephone, cheese cutter, barber chair, and many other items.

Popular entrees include broiled shrimp scampi, charbroiled chicken tenders, and charbroiled rib eye. All dinners include hush puppies, coleslaw or salad, wedge fries or baked potato, and white beans with a special pepper relish. Open Tues through Sat 5 to 9 p.m. Moderate prices.

Continuing north through Troy takes you to the **Pioneer Museum of Alabama** (334-566-3597), located at 248 US 231. Situated on thirty wooded acres, this fascinating folk museum contains some 18,000 items from the past two centuries. You'll find extensive collections, all well organized and attractively displayed, plus fifteen outbuildings. Household items range from lemon squeezers, sausage stuffers, and butter molds to cookware, fluting irons, spittoons, and an Edison phonograph with a morning glory–shaped speaker. Although the lovely period furnishings of the three Bass Rooms reflect an upper-class lifestyle, the museum's collections focus on items that played a part in the daily existence of the community's middle- and lower-class members.

Other exhibits include newspaper typesetting and printing machines, an enormous collection of farm equipment, blacksmith and carpenter shop displays, and several horse-drawn vehicles, including an antique hearse. One exhibit, "When Cotton Was King," features a mule with "a lean and hungry look." Upon seeing the sculptor's interesting armature, museum officials had the artist stop working at once to preserve the unique look of the unfinished piece. Other objects on display include a portable boll weevil catcher, a peanut sheller, and a moonshine still.

Don't miss the early-twentieth-century street setting featuring storefronts of barber and millinery shops, a bank, and offices for a dentist, doctor, and lawyer—all appropriately equipped. Save plenty of time for exploring the grounds, too. On your way to see the furnished dogtrot log cabin and nearby tenant house, you'll pass a loblolly pine known as the Moon Tree—the seed from which it grew journeyed to the moon and back with the Apollo astronauts. Before leaving the museum, stop by the country store stocked with essentials such as snuff, castor oil, patent medicines, and bone buttons. You'll also find a restored 1928 schoolhouse, a working gristmill, a corncrib made of hand-hewn logs, a covered bridge, a nature trail, and a picnic area on the grounds. Other interesting exhibits include Native American artifacts and a coal-burning train engine. Thursday visitors can watch quilters at work, and weaving demonstrations take place Friday and Saturday. Except for major holidays, hours are Thurs through Sat 9 a.m. to 5 p.m. Admission: adults $10, senior citizens $9, students (ages 6 to college) $8, children (age 5 and under) free. Preview the property at pioneer-museum.org.

Cradle of the Confederacy

For a hearty meal at **Red's Little School House** (334-584-7955), located at blink-and-you've-missed-it **Grady**, travel north from Troy on US 231, then turn onto State Route 94 in the direction of Dublin and Ramer. At the intersection of Route 94 and Gardner Road, look for a tall water tower, labeled Pine Level, with a small red structure beside it. Or leave the directions up to your GPS at 20 Gardner Road. At this restaurant, housed in a former school and owned by Debbie Deese, you'll find a buffet selection of all-you-can-eat, fresh, home-cooked vegetables such as sweet potato soufflé, fried okra, and collards. (Red, Debbie's father and the former owner, grows acres and acres of vegetables each season and reaps a huge harvest.) The menu also features fried corn-bread, chicken and dumplings, barbecue, and fried chicken. If you manage to save room for dessert, the choices are listed on the blackboard.

Even though the nation's presidents look sternly from their frames over the chalkboard and old maps suggest geography-test anxiety, this is a place to relax. Schoolmarm Debbie banters with the customers, who obviously enjoy both the food and the friendly surroundings. Debbie, who calls herself "a half-decent guitar player," sometimes sings for the crowd. "Everyone brags on the food, and laughs at the entertainment," she writes in the preface of her cookbook.

Debbie converted two school buses into traveling kitchens and takes her catering show on the road for large gatherings. She has cooked for five governors and one president. "I think food is the answer to everything," she says. School is open Wed through Sat from 11 a.m. to 9 p.m.; Sun 11 a.m. to 3 p.m. Prices are economical to moderate.

Afterward continue north on one of several roads that lead to **Montgomery**, about thirty minutes away. Montgomery offers a wealth of attractions appealing to all interests. In the past the city has been home to such luminaries as Tallulah Bankhead, Hank Williams, and Nat King Cole. Montgomery served as a launching ground for the Wright brothers, who gave early flying lessons here; a playground for Zelda and F. Scott Fitzgerald; and a battleground in the Civil Rights Movement. This city also pioneered the nation's first electric trolley system, the Lightning Route, which made its successful trial run in 1886.

There are just two things to remember when you dine at the top-notch restaurant named **Central Restaurant**, located in downtown Montgomery at 129 Coosa Street. First: Anything you order on the menu will be delicious. Second: If you get a chance to chat with owner Jerry Kyser, you'll quickly discover that he loves his hometown and is a very smart businessman. Born in Montgomery, Jerry didn't grow up with a silver spoon in his mouth but he did get something even more valuable—a strong work ethic and an uncanny ability to look ahead and make long-term plans.

Opened in 2012 in a historic 1890s building, Central's décor features 16-foot ceilings, exposed brick walls, big timber beams, flickering gas wall sconces, and unusual chandeliers. An open kitchen with wood-burning ovens and grilles showcases chefs as they prepare each order.

The menu features starters of aged pimento cheese with house flatbread, Gulf crab claws, bruschetta, a charcuterie board, and Fett Soux fries (smoked and fried pork belly, South Carolina barbecue sauce, and Chilton County peach chutney). Entrees include an 1895 Spencer Farms pork chop with onions, braised applies; Dijon herb demi and pierogis; Purple Magnolia short ribs with sundried tomato grits and a purple onion blossom; Angus beef filet; a 14-ounce veal chop; and a 7-ounce Scottish salmon. The dessert menu was equally appetizing, with options like Boston cream pie, dark chocolate cake, triple chocolate brownie, pecan pie, and apple crumble with ice cream and a bit of apple butter.

Central has a full bar and features specialty cocktails such as Pumpkin Fever—Absolut vanilla vodka, Baileys, pumpkin spiced syrup, and whipped cream.

The restaurant is open Mon through Thurs 11 a.m. to 2 p.m. (lunch) and 5:30 to 10 p.m. (dinner); Fri 11 a.m. to 2 p.m. (lunch) and 5:30 to 11 p.m.; Sat 5:30 to 10 p.m. Closed Sun. For more information, call (334) 517-1155 or check out the website at central129coosa.com.

Make the **Montgomery Area Visitor Center** (334-262-0013; visitingmontgomery.com) at 300 Water Street your first stop in the city. Housed in historic Union Station that dates to 1898, the center offers a handsome medley of exhibit panels on area attractions along with maps and information on accommodations, restaurants, festivals, and more. Take a virtual 13-minute city tour in the mini-theater and collect some souvenirs in the gift shop. Hours are Mon through Sat 8:30 a.m. to 5 p.m.

alabamatrivia

Nat King Cole was born at the Cole-Samford House on St. John Street in Montgomery.

On the city's southeast side, you'll find the **Alabama Shakespeare Festival (ASF)** (334-271-5353 or 800-841-4273). Just off East Boulevard on Woodmere Boulevard in the Wynton M. Blount Cultural Park, ASF presents works ranging from familiar classics to world-premiere Southern Writers' Project productions. You can take in a performance of works by such writers as Sir Noel Coward, Anton Chekhov, Eugene O'Neill, George Bernard Shaw, Tennessee Williams, and, of course, the Bard. The only American theater invited to fly the same flag as that used by England's Royal Shakespeare Company, ASF attracts more than 300,000 visitors annually from all fifty states and sixty foreign countries and is the world's fifth-largest Shakespeare festival.

Situated in a 250-acre, landscaped, English-style park, the $21.5 million performing arts complex houses two stages, rehearsal halls, and a snack bar along with costume, prop, and gift shops. The grounds, perfect for strolling or picnicking, feature a reflecting lake complete with gliding swans. Wend your way through Shakespeare Gardens, with a 325-seat amphitheater against a setting that brings to life the Bard's botanical references to flowers and herbs, such as rosemary "for remembrance" (and great as a garnish for most meat dishes, too). Linger awhile and enjoy the park's various colors, textures, and smells. For information, brochures, or tickets, call or write to Alabama Shakespeare Festival, One Festival Drive, Montgomery 36117-4605. You can visit asf.net to check on current productions.

alabamatrivia

The Wallace Foundation in Montgomery honors Lurleen Wallace, the third woman ever elected governor of a state.

Before leaving the park, take time to browse through the ***Montgomery Museum of Fine Arts*** (334-240-4333; mmfa.org). Located at One Museum Drive, this facility features the fine Blount Collection with works representing more than 200 years of American art. Also, you'll see Old Master prints, outstanding porcelain and glass collections, nineteenth- and twentieth-century American paintings and sculpture, and art of the American South. View mmfa.org for current exhibitions and more information on the museum's holdings. Admission is free. Except for major holidays, the museum's hours Tues through Sat 10 a.m. to 5 p.m. (Thurs hours extend to 9 p.m.); Sun noon to 5 p.m. Enjoy a lunch break in the museum at Cafe M, an artful bistro that serves Tues through Fri from 11 a.m. to 2 p.m., with a Sat brunch from 10 a.m. to 1 p.m. Sample the Mediterranean chicken salad and flourless fudge cake. Rates are economical to moderate.

When breakfast and lunch call, try a new restaurant in downtown Montgomery at 31 South Court Street. Wanting to bring historical Southern flavor with a new twist to diners, a brother and sister took the big step of opening their own restaurant. ***Cahawba House*** (334-356-1877, cahawbahouse.com) not only serves delicious cuisine, it also tells you the farm from which the ingredients were sourced. Curious? Check out the handwritten list on the blackboard in the restaurant's hallway.

As for that name, owners Tim and Tara Essary chose to name their restaurant after the first official state capital of Alabama. Cahawba House opened

Sad Story of F. Scott and Zelda Fitzgerald

Once the home of F. Scott and Zelda Fitzgerald, the rambling old house at 919 Felder Avenue, now *The F. Scott and Zelda Fitzgerald Museum* showcases memorabilia that speaks volumes of their unusual personalities and strange life together. It is the only place left in Montgomery where the Fitzgeralds lived together, and it is the only museum in the world dedicated to the famous couple.

Did he stare out this window, searching for the right words for his novel? Did she pace this living room floor, worrying about the darkness that was closing in on her mind? The museum houses an extensive collection of photographs, original correspondence between Zelda and Scott, prints of Zelda's paintings, furniture from Zelda's childhood home, newspaper clippings, and other artifacts.

Copies of Scott's novels, including original editions and foreign language translations fill shelves and table tops, including *This Side of Paradise*, *The Great Gatsby*, *Babylon Revisited*, *Tender is the Night*, *The Beautiful and the Damned*, and The *Last Tycoon*.

Francis Scott Key Fitzgerald was born in St. Paul, Minnesota, on Sept. 24, 1896. He spent four years at Princeton but left before graduating to join the army during World War I. Zelda Sayre was born July 24, 1900, in Montgomery. The daughter of the conservative, Episcopalian family of Alabama State Supreme Court Justice Anthony Sayre, Zelda was known as a rebel, a "flapper" and the belle of society.

In the summer of 1918, the two met at a country club dance while Scott was stationed in Montgomery. Instantly smitten, Scott wooed Zelda ardently to persuade the debutante darling to be his bride.

Zelda broke their first engagement in 1919, but the pair finally married April 3, 1920, after Scott's first novel, *This Side of Paradise*, made him temporarily rich and famous. Their only child, Scottie, was born in October of 1921.

A glamorous and witty couple, they lived an extravagant life. Always on the move, the Fitzgeralds personified the Jazz Age and partook in all its excesses, wandering aimlessly from coast to coast but always returning to Montgomery.

Between 1920 and 1927, Zelda published numerous essays and short stories. She took up ballet and painting and was talented in both. Over the years, the Fitzgeralds' continuing social round deteriorated into debts and alcoholism. In 1930, Zelda's suffered her first mental breakdown.

After a year in a Swiss sanitarium diagnosed as schizophrenic, Zelda returned to Montgomery with her husband and daughter and rented the house on Felder Avenue in October 1931. Here, Scott worked on his novel, *Tender is the Night*, and Zelda began her novel, *Save Me the Waltz*.

In April 1936, Zelda entered Highland Mental Hospital in Asheville, North Carolina. She lived there, intermittently between visits to her mother's home in Montgomery, for the rest of her life.

In 1940, Fitzgerald suffered a fatal heart attack in California. Eight years later, Zelda perished in a fire that partially destroyed Highland Hospital. She was buried alongside her husband in Rockville, Maryland.

The house opened as a museum in 1989. A video of Scott and Zelda's sad story, told through interviews of surviving relatives and friends, is shown on the enclosed side porch of the house.

The F. Scott and Zelda Fitzgerald Museum is open Tues through Sun 10 a.m. to 3 p.m. Donation $10 per person. For more information, call (334) 264-4222 or visit the website at thefitzgeraldmuseum.org.

in October 2016. One menu favorite is Alabama's famous Conecuh Sausage made in the county of the same name. "Conecuh" is a Creek Indian word for "Land of Sugar Cane." The sausage makes a yummy combo with homemade fluffy biscuits at Cahawba House. Other popular breakfast items are fresh-baked beignets and cheese grits. Local coffee connoisseurs say that Cahawba coffee is smooth and rich.

Add to that a tray with four jams and jellies. Cahawba House also notes on its menu where those sweets came from—strawberry jam and bramble jam from Handey's Farm, peach jam and blackberry jam from Hornsby Farms, apple butter from Cahawba House, and honey from Urban Hives. Cahawba House serves breakfast and lunch Mon through Fri from 6:30 a.m. to 2 p.m.; Sun 9 a.m. to 2 p.m.

Afterward head downtown to **Montgomery's capitol complex**, where you can easily spend a full day. If you enjoy digging into the past, you'll find this area fascinating to explore. From here *Jefferson Davis* telegraphed his "Fire on Fort Sumter" order, and the country suddenly found itself embroiled in the Civil War. Rising impressively above its surroundings on Dexter Avenue, the 1851 capitol reflects the period's prevailing architecture—Greek revival. In this building Jefferson Davis took his presidential oath for the Confederacy, and a six-pointed brass star now marks the spot.

At 644 Washington Avenue, just across the street from the capitol, stands the *First White House of the Confederacy* (334-242-1861; firstwhitehouse. org). Occupied by Jefferson Davis's family during the early days of the War Between the States, this Italianate-style home built by William Sayre dates to the early 1830s. Elegant downstairs parlors and second-floor bedrooms (including a charming nursery) contain Davis family possessions and period antiques. Other displays include Civil War relics, letters, and glass-cased documents. Hours are Mon through Fri 8 a.m. to 4:30 p.m.; Sat 9 a.m. to 4 p.m. Admission is free.

New Museum and Memorial Honor Lynching Victims

When her husband was lynched by a rampaging white mob, Mary Turner swore she would seek legal justice. Instead, the 8-months pregnant woman was captured by the mob and murdered on May 19, 1918, in Lowndes County, Georgia.

Turner is just one of more than 4,400 African Americans who were murdered by white mobs between 1877 and 1950. Their lives are honored at the Equal Justice Initiative's new *National Memorial for Peace and Justice*, the nation's first to recognize these atrocities.

Located in downtown Montgomery, the National Memorial for Peace and Justice and its companion *Legacy Museum: From Enslavement to Mass Incarceration* were opened in April 2018. Just a 16-minute walk apart, both the museum and the memorial were created to explore America's history of racial injustice and its legacy.

The Equal Justice Initiative raised more than $20 million from private donations for the project, Many of the donations were small amounts from people who supported the messages behind the museum and memorial.

Near the entrance to the hilltop memorial is a concrete sculpture by artist Kwame Akoto-Bamfo depicting six slaves in chains, including a woman carrying a baby and reaching out to a man bound near her.

The memorial features 800 steel columns representing the 800 counties throughout America where lynchings occurred. Names of lynching victims are engraved on the columns. Walking inside the plaza, visitors see that the steel monuments are suspended and dangle from beams much like the men, women, and children who were lynched and left hanging from trees. The final section of the memorial features brief information about the lynchings.

Built on a site where enslaved black people were once warehoused for slave auctions, the Legacy Museum is a block from one of the most prominent slave markets in America.

Upon entering, visitors are confronted with slave pen replicas that depict what it was like to be awaiting sale at the nearby auction block. There is also a collection of more than 800 jars of soil from lynching sites across the country.

One of those jars contains soil from a site in Salisbury, Maryland, where Matthew Williams was tortured and hanged on December 4, 1931, by a white mob who accused him of killing a white man he worked for after a pay dispute. Williams denied the allegation.

The National Memorial for Peace and Justice at 417 Caroline Street is open Mon and Wed through Sunday from 9 a.m. to 5 p.m. Tickets are $5 per person, children (ages 6 and under) free.The Legacy Museum at 115 Coosa Street is open Mon and Wed through Sat from 9 a.m. to 7:30 p.m.; Sun 9 a.m. to 5 p.m. Tickets are $8 adults, $5 students and seniors, children (ages 6 and under) free.

Combination tickets for both the memorial and the museum are $10 adults, $7 students and seniors, children (6 years and under) free. Timed entry tickets are required for the museum and it is suggested that visitors purchase tickets online in advance of a visit. A small number of same-day tickets are available at the ticket office on a first-come, first-served basis.

Next door to the Davis home, you'll find a treasure-filled museum, the **Alabama Department of Archives and History** (archives.state.al.us). This building houses an enormous manuscript collection and exhibits spanning the gap from the Stone Age to the Space Age. The Museum of Alabama is located within the Department of Archives and History. On February 15, 2014, the Museum of Alabama opened with its new centerpiece exhibit on "Alabama Voices." The permanent Smithsonian-quality exhibit covers nearly 11,000 square feet on the museum's second floor and details Alabama history from the dawn of the 1700s to the present. The museum and department of archives are open Mon through Sat from 8:30 a.m. to 4:30 p.m.

A short jaunt takes you to the **Dexter Avenue King Memorial Baptist Church** (334-263-3970; dexterkingmemorial.org). Located at 454 Dexter Avenue, the church became a National Historical Landmark in 1974. It was at this church, pastored by Dr. Martin Luther King Jr. that the Montgomery bus boycott was organized on December 2, 1955, launching the American Civil Rights Movement.

An hour-long tour covers the church's early history as well as the more recent role it played as a rallying place for civil rights activists. On the ground floor, a six-section folk mural illustrates major events from Dr. King's life. Tours are given Tues through Fri from 10 a.m. to 3 p.m., and on Sat from 10 a.m. to 1 p.m. Hours are Tues through Fri 10 a.m. to 4 p.m., and Sat 10 a.m. to 2 p.m. Admission.

To learn more about Dr. King's life and family, visit the Dexter Parsonage Museum, where Dr. King and his family lived between 1954 and 1960. Built in 1912, the nine-room clapboard parsonage at 309 Jackson Street has been restored to its appearance when Dr. King and his family lived there. Much of the furniture was used by Dr. King and his family. Adjacent to the parsonage is an interpretive center with photos of the twelve pastors who lived there, plus a wall of Pastoral Wisdom with inspirational quotes from pastors. Tours of the parsonage are offered on Tues through Fri from 10 a.m. to 3 p.m., and on Sat from 10 a.m. to 1 p.m. The parsonage is closed for lunch from noon to 1 p.m. on Tues through Fri. Admission.

Civil Rights Memorial Uses Theme of Water to Honor Martyrs

Tiny drops of water flow down her fingers and fall to the basin below. At the same time, an almost unnoticeable tear rolls down her cheek and slips into the water. It's as though she has become part of the slowly moving stream.

The *Civil Rights Memorial* has a way of doing that.

Dedicated in the Fall of 1989, the monument is a striking black granite memorial commissioned by the Southern Poverty Law Center. It sits outside the center in downtown Montgomery at 400 Washington Avenue.

Montgomery is, of course, the inevitable site for the memorial. This town is both the capital of the Confederacy and the birthplace of civil rights.

But there was no one specific memorial to the civil rights movement and the era it was about. In the Spring of 1988, the Southern Poverty Law Center contacted architect Maya Lin about such a memorial for civil rights martyrs. Lin also was the designer of the Vietnam Veterans Memorial in Washington, D.C.

Lin spent months doing research and thinking about the civil rights movement, an era she said she had learned little about in school. Lin later wrote that she was unaware that so many people had given their lives for civil rights.

"I was also horrified to realize that many of these murders had taken place during my lifetime and that I didn't know about them," she recalled.

The inspiration for the memorial came during a plane trip to Montgomery in 1988. Reading through research material, Lin came upon words King had used in his "I Have a Dream" speech and at the start of the Montgomery bus boycott. Paraphrasing a verse in the Bible, King said, "We will not be satisfied 'until justice rolls down like waters and righteousness like a mighty stream.'"

Water, Lin decided, would be her carrier of truth.

A curved black granite wall is engraved with the Biblical quote used by King. Water spills down the wall at waterfall speed, reflecting the people in front of it. The second part of the memorial is a 12-inch-diameter circular tabletop resting on an asymmetrical pedestal. Etched around the table's perimeter are fifty-three entries, radiating like a sundial. Twenty-one of the entries report landmark events in the civil rights movement. Forty entries describe individual deaths. Between the first and last entries is a space to represent civil rights heroes who died before or after this period and others whose stories were not known when the memorial was created.

Visitors to the memorial can touch the names of the civil rights dead and see themselves in the water flowing over it. The water rises from a hole in the tabletop and flows over it evenly. The table is only thirty-one inches high, deliberately accessible to children.

As an outdoor monument, the Civil Rights Memorial never closes. Some visitors are playful children, while others are adults and older folks who spend a long time reading the inscriptions. Almost all visitors touch the moving water. Their hands create ripples which seem to transform the memorial, perhaps in the same way those names inscribed have helped change our nation.

Don't miss the *Rosa Parks Library and Museum and Children's Wing and Children's Wing* (334-241-8615), a state-of-the-art facility at 252 Montgomery Street. Opened on Dec. 1, 2000—forty-five years after Parks' historic bus ride, the museum site marks the spot where Mrs. Parks was arrested in 1955 and offers an in-depth look at the event that started the Montgomery bus boycott. A project of Troy State University Montgomery, the interpretive museum features original exhibits, including historical papers from that era and a replica of the public bus, complete with a unique treatment of the scene in which Rosa Parks played her significant role in shaping history to become "Mother of the Civil Rights Movement." Visitors can look in the bus windows and watch a video that re-creates the famous conversation between Parks and the bus driver. The 42-year-old woman was on her way home from work at a downtown department store. Bespectacled, her hair pulled tightly in back, Parks didn't look like someone wanting to cause trouble. But when trouble came her way that day, Parks didn't flinch. She was arrested, fingerprinted, and put behind bars. But that was the beginning of the end of Jim Crow.

Parks' quiet courage helped bring to the forefront a young Montgomery preacher, the Rev. Martin Luther King Jr., who would go on to galvanize the nation. And the boycott of the busy bus system in the days that followed her arrest showed how nonviolence could be effective against oppression. The Montgomery Bus Boycott began December 5, 1955, and lasted 381 days until the U.S. Supreme Court struck down segregation laws. Through interviews, photographs, and words spoken by people who were there in the 1950s and 1960s, museum visitors hear what segregated Montgomery was like more than half a century ago was like.

One of the more compelling exhibits is a hand-crafted model of King sitting in a replica of his kitchen, praying for guidance in the days ahead. The exhibit is about "The Epiphany"—midnight at his kitchen table when Dr. Martin Luther King Jr. was questioning whether he should endanger his young family by continuing the civil rights movement. He heard the voice of Jesus telling him to fight on.

The Children's Wing features the Cleveland Avenue Time Machine, which takes riders on a unique trip to the past with an overview of events that led to the modern day civil rights movement. On the second floor visitors will find extensive historical information with kiosk, panel, and computer presentations detailing events before and during the Montgomery Bus Boycott. For more background on this pivotal event in the city's (and nation's) civil rights heritage, visit troy.edu/rosaparks. Museum open Mon through Fri from 9 a.m. to 5 p.m.; Sat 9 a.m. to 3 p.m. Admission: adults $7.50, children (age 12 and under) $5.50.

Also downtown, at 301 Columbus Street, you can step back into the nineteenth century at **Old Alabama Town** (334-240-4500 or 888-240-1850). This fascinating concentration of historically restored buildings provides glimpses of city and country living in the nineteenth and early-twentieth centuries. Start your tour at the **Loeb Center**, where you can also visit the museum store. Continue your excursion into the past at **Lucas Tavern** and other buildings in this history-filled complex. You'll see a 1850s dogtrot house (a dogtrot is a form of Southern architecture that features an open central hall connecting two rooms, sometimes called pens). Other stops include such buildings as a carriage house, grocery store, church, country doctor's office, and a one-room schoolhouse—complete with *McGuffey's Readers* and slates.

You'll also see the nearby Rose-Morris House, where you can enjoy music on the dogtrot, and the **Ordeman House**, a handsome townhouse with elegant furnishings and backyard dependencies. Except for major holidays, the center's hours Mon through Sat 9 a.m. to 4 p.m. Check out oldalabamatown .com to learn more. Admission: adults $10, children (ages 5 to 18) $5, children (age 4 and under) free.

"Your Cheatin' Heart" immediately brings **Hank Williams** to mind for all country music lovers, and fans from throughout the world travel to Montgomery to pay tribute at his grave site. Set in **Oakwood Cemetery**, the marble memorial is sculpted in the shape of two large music notes and a cowboy hat. You can also see a life-size bronze statue of the musician in Lister Hill plaza, across from City Hall.

Stop by 118 Commerce Street for an in-depth look at the legacy of Alabama-born Hank Williams. Paying tribute to the memory of this country music legend, the **Hank Williams Museum** (334-262-3600) contains recordings, albums, musical instruments, clothing, a saddle with silver trim, family photos, and other personal items. The museum's focal point is the baby-blue 1952 Cadillac convertible in which the singer/songwriter died while being driven to his scheduled performance in Canton, Ohio, on January 1, 1953. Eight rooms and thirty-five showcases feature memorabilia of family members and associates. A carved Kowliga, like the wooden Indian that inspired Williams's

Hank Williams's Funeral

Shortly after celebrating the New Year of 1953, mourners began flocking to Montgomery. They lined the streets and congregated outside a boardinghouse where a silver casket sat. So many people came to pay tribute that the funeral couldn't be held in a church. The service had to be moved to the biggest facility in town, the Municipal Auditorium.

Ironically, that was the very auditorium where the fallen star had performed so many times. Now it was where Hank Williams, the Drifting Cowboy, would be bade farewell for his last journey. On Sunday afternoon, January 4, 1953, an estimated 25,000 came to Montgomery for the funeral of Hank Williams.

Grand Ole Opry stars arrived in a special chartered plane. Among the Opry entertainers were Jimmy Dickens, Carl Smith, Webb Pierce, Bill Monroe, Ray Price, and June Carter. Loads of flowers were delivered, including two guitar-shaped floral arrangements that stood on each side of the coffin.

At 1 p.m. the casket was brought in and opened at 1:15. Dressed in a white cowboy stage outfit, Williams clutched a tiny white Bible in his hand. His band, the Drifting Cowboys, stood by as a guard of honor. Hundreds filed by to pay their respects.

At 2:30 p.m. the auditorium doors were closed and the service started with Ernest Tubb singing "Beyond the Sunset." A gospel quartet, the Statesmen, who would later sing at Elvis Presley's funeral, sang "Precious Memories." Possibly the only black quartet to perform at a prominent white funeral in Alabama prior to the civil rights era, the Southwind Singers sang "My Record Will Be There."

Roy Acuff performed Hank's popular song, "I Saw the Light." Red Foley's voice wavered and tears flowed down his face as he sang "Peace in the Valley." Foley and Williams had made a promise that whoever died first, the other would sing at his friend's funeral.

Hank Williams was only twenty-nine years old when he died. Slumped in the backseat of a baby-blue Cadillac speeding through a dark night, Hank Williams drew his last breath. The country music legend was on his way to a concert in Canton, Ohio. Somewhere in West Virginia, Williams's young driver became worried about the lifeless body draped in a navy blue overcoat in the backseat. By then it was too late. Carried into an emergency room, Williams was pronounced dead on January 1, 1953. His heart had given out after years of alcohol and prescription drug abuse. Hank is buried in Oakwood Cemetery in Montgomery

song, "Kowaliga" and created by the Wood Chippers (with a time investment of 559 hours), looms 8.5 feet tall. Museum open Mon through Fri 9 a.m. to 4:30 p.m.; Sat 10 a.m. to 4 p.m.; Sun 1 to 4 p.m. Admission: $10 for adults (ages 15 and up), $3 for children (ages 3 to 14). Visit thehankwilliamsmuseum. net for more details.

For a high-flying time, stop by the *Aviator Bar* at 166 Commerce Street. A popular spot with servicemen and women from nearby Maxwell Air Force Base, the unusual bar has a proud military theme. Model airplanes hang from the ceiling. There's a World War II London Blitz room and walls are decorated with historic aviation photos and portraits of local military heroes. Behind the bar is a patch board where visiting military men and women can donate a memento from their squadron.

A near-life-size replica of the Wright Flyer hangs overhead. Only makes sense since Montgomery was home to the nation's first civilian flying school. In the spring of 1910, aviation pioneers Wilbur and Orville Wright opened the *Wrights Brothers Flying School* at an old cotton plantation on the outskirts of Montgomery.

Aviator Bar (334-387-3333) is open Mon and Wed through Sat from 5 p.m. to 2 a.m.; Tues 5 p.m. to midnight.

At 551 Clay Street, you'll find a warm welcome at *Red Bluff Cottage Bed and Breakfast* (334-264-0056 or 888-551-2529), a perfect place to head-quarter in Alabama's capital city. In fact, the upstairs porch of this raised cottage offers fine views of the state capitol and the Alabama River. Bonnie and Barry Ponstein, who purchased the inn from previous owners Anne and Mark Waldo, share the cooking and dispense Southern hospitality—Alabama style. "We have a good time down here," says Barry, quoting his three rules: No smoking, no pets, and no grumpy people. The Red Bluff offers four rooms with private baths and a full breakfast, perhaps Bonnie's famed wild rice waffles with fresh berries. Pampering their guests, the Ponsteins offer extra amenities, such as complimentary soft drinks, snacks, fresh ground coffee, and a large selection of teas. Visit redbluffcottage.com and check for special packages. Moderate rates.

The courageous story of Eugene Bullard, the first African-American military pilot, and other enlisted personnel is told in an out-of-the-way museum in Montgomery. Located in a former mess hall, the *Air Force Enlisted Heritage Hall* (334-416-3202), holds a wealth of unexpected information.

However, it is not one of those places you're likely to find unless you had heard about it. Situated at Maxwell Air Force Base-Gunter Annex at 550 McDonald Street, the museum is well organized and tells the story of military aviation from the beginning balloons of the Civil War to the sleek technology of today.

Arranged in chronological order, the museum starts off with the history and development of ballooning. Balloons rapidly gave way to airplanes, of course, and in August 1912, Corporal Vernon Burge was certified as the Army's first enlisted airplane pilot. Other exhibits deal with aviation during the Korean War, Vietnam War, Desert Shield, and Desert Storm. A display of aircraft gun

Eugene Bullard: The Black Swallow of Death

Born in Columbus, Georgia, in 1895, Eugene Bullard faced racial discrimination from an early age due to his black Carribean and Creek Indian ancestry. He immigrated to Europe as a teenager, where he settled in France prior to WWI. When the war began, he enlisted in the French Foreign Legion. He then transferred to a regular unit in the French army and was wounded twice before being declared disabled. He was known as "The Black Swallow of Death." But that was only the beginning of his heroic exploits.

Against all odds, Ballard applied for pilot training with the French air service. He was accepted and became the first African-American fighter pilot. And that is where he really soared.

He flew twenty missions against the Germans, downed at least two German planes and was wounded three times before being honorable discharged. That still wasn't the end.

After his heroism in the French air service during World War I, Bullard volunteered his services to his homeland when America entered the war in 1917. At that time, the United States barred African Americans from flying. So the US Army denied Bullard the opportunity to fly for his country.

Instead, Bullard remained in France where he was proclaimed a French national hero. He married a French countess, served as a bandleader, and operated several successful businesses, including a popular nightclub.

When Hitler began to make plain his intentions toward France, Bullard joined the French underground as an agent against the Nazis. After being wounded fighting the Nazis with French underground resistance forces in Orleans, he returned to the United States to avoid capture. The Germans seized his property in France and Bullard never returned to his adopted country. He was forty years old and lived in New York City until his death in 1961.

stations operated by enlisted gunners is enough to make anyone cringe. How in the world human beings could be crammed into those tiny spaces, speeding through the sky, and firing aircraft guns is beyond me.

Featured on a Wall of Achievers are former enlisted air personnel who achieved fame in civilian careers or attained star ranks in the military service. Of note are Johnny Cash, Chuck Norris, Gene Autry, Flip Wilson, Charlton Heston, and Chuck Yeager. There is also a tribute to Glenn Miller and his band of enlisted men. The museum is open Mon through Fri 7 a.m. to 4 p.m. Free admission.

After exploring the capital of the
Old South, head north to **Wetumpka**,
a charming town with a unique setting.
Not only situated on the Coosa River's
banks, Wetumpka also sits in the bowl
of a 4-mile-wide crater created by the
impact of a meteorite about 83 million
years ago. Head first to the Wetumpka
Area Chamber of Commerce (334-567-4811; wetumpkachamber.com), located
at 116 East Bridge Street in the heart of downtown. While collecting travel
information at the chamber office, housed in a former bank building that dates
to 1905, notice the original brass chandelier with a Greek key design that
repeats the ceiling motif. Wetumpka comes from an Indian word that means
"tumbling waters."

Spanning the Coosa River, you'll see the town's focal point, a picturesque arched bridge built in 1937. Named for a former governor, the **Bibb
Graves Bridge** allegedly is the only one south of the Mason-Dixon Line suspended by reinforced concrete. After crossing the bridge, notice the historic
First Presbyterian Church, organized in 1834. It was here that soldiers in the
Wetumpka Light Guard gathered on April 16, 1861, before leaving to confront
their destinies in the Civil War.

If you saw the movie *Big Fish*, filmed in and around Montgomery and starring Jessica Lange, Albert Finney, Ewan McGregor, and Danny DeVito, then the
town might look vaguely familiar although the film crew made several exterior
changes.

Before leaving town, be sure to visit **Our Place Cafe** (334-567-8778) for
a delectable dinner. Located at 809 Company Street, the restaurant occupies a
brick building once owned by the Graham family. Back in the 1930s, the structure housed a grocery store with an apartment above and later served as an
office for the family's wholesale gasoline business.

Owners David and Mona Funderburk offer casual elegance in dining and
an ambience-filled restaurant with seating on two levels. Try the signature crab
cakes, served with a special dill sauce, or the evening special. David describes
his cuisine as "more Creole than Cajun," and his menu features six seafood
selections nightly as well as steaks. The restaurant opens Tues through Sat at
4:30 p.m. Prices are moderate.

Save time to explore nearby **Fort Toulouse–Jackson Park** (334-567-
3002; fttoulousejackson.org). To reach the park, the site of two forts from
different centuries, take US 231 North and watch for the turnoff sign to 2521
West Fort Toulouse Road. Continue 2.4 miles down this road to the main gate.

After entering the park you'll see the visitor center on the left. Inside, displays of artifacts unearthed in archaeological digs, from brass uniform buttons and silver earrings to French wine bottles and cannonballs, provide background on the site's history.

The original 1717 French fortress, named for Count Toulouse (son of Louis XIV), served as a trading post where Native Americans exchanged furs and deerskins for European goods. This French outpost also helped keep the British at bay. General Andrew Jackson's forces later built a larger nineteenth-century counterpart while fighting the Creek Indians. From here Old Hickory plotted his campaign against the British and Spanish that ended with the Battle of New Orleans.

Fort Toulouse and Fort Jackson living-history programs, staged monthly on the park's grounds, permit visitors to dip a bit deeper into the forts' earlier days. The park usually has something going on three out of four weekends.

This 164-acre park also offers a picnic area, campground, and launching ramp. Another attraction is the 30-acre arboretum with walkway, footbridges, and study decks. Nearby, the Coosa and Tallapoosa Rivers—with their cache of bass, bream, catfish, and crappie—beckon anglers. (A state fishing license is required.) Admission $2 for adults and $1 for students. Except for major holidays, park grounds are open daily from 8 a.m. to 5 p.m. and the visitor center hours run Mon through Sat from 9 a.m. to 4 p.m. For more information visit fttoulousejackson.org.

After your park outing follow State Route 14 west to *Prattville*. Daniel Pratt, for whom the town was named, came here from New Hampshire in the 1830s and established an industrial center—still the site for the manufacture of cotton gins. A drive through *Old Prattvillage* takes you past a section of restored nineteenth-century buildings. For a driving tour map which highlights about forty homes in the historic district along with area churches and industrial sites, stop by the Prattville Chamber of Commerce (131 North Court Street; 334-365-7392; prattvillechamber.com) or City Hall at 101 West Main Street.

Better yet, set off on a walking tour of the village. At *Prattvillage Gardens* you'll see a small 1800s plantation chapel surrounded by a profusion of plants and a butterfly walk. Open the gate and stroll past theme gardens devoted to herbs, perennials, and old-fashioned favorites like hollyhocks, dianthus, and oak-leaf hydrangeas.

Stop by the *Prattaugan Museum* (334-361-0961; autaugahistory.org), which houses the Heritage Center. Located at 102 East Main Street, this circa 1848 home showcases antiques, exhibits on area history, Indian artifacts, and genealogical records. In the backyard, notice the artesian well with a dipper hanging nearby. Prattville acquired its "Fountain City" title because it boasts a number of artesian wells. Except for city holidays, hours are Tues through Fri from 10 a.m. to 4 p.m. and Sat 10 a.m. to 2 p.m. Admission is free, and donations are accepted.

Heritage Park, which features a three-tiered fountain, overlooks the town's focal point, Daniel Pratt's big brick gin factory. From this scenic spot, you can watch water spilling over the dam into Autauga Creek. Wander along historic West Main Street past *Red Arrow Hardware* at 172 West Main Street (334-365-5988) with its nostalgic inventory. Across the street at 137 First Street, you can see all sorts of timepieces awaiting repair at *The Village Clocksmith* (334-491-8463).

Nature lovers will enjoy trekking through *Wilderness Park* on Upper Kingston Road. Located inside the city limits, the park could be a world away—in central China by the looks of it. Instead of a typical Southern forest's foliage, the paved half-mile path leads through a thick stand of towering bamboo.

Search out nearby *Buena Vista* (334-365-3690 or 334-361-0961; autaugahistory.org/Buena-vista), an early plantation home, located on Autauga County Road 4 between US 31 and State Route 14 at 641 County Road 4 East. Fronted by four Ionic columns and constructed of heart pine, the Greek revival–style structure stands on a sweeping lawn studded with camellias and magnolias. A striking circular staircase spirals from the large entrance hall to the third-floor banquet room. Originally built in the federal style and known as Montgomery House, the home is listed on the National Register of Historic Places. Some historians claim the house dates to 1822, but other sources say circa 1830 would be more accurate. You'll see some period furnishings and memorabilia. Owned by a local corporation and operated by the Autauga County Heritage Association, Buena Vista is open to the public for tours on Tues between 10 a.m. and 2 p.m. or by appointment. Admission is $5.

alabamatrivia

Alabama's forest acreage ranks as third largest in the nation and second largest in the South.

Want to visit the best little town in Alabama? Then head about forty miles (or minutes) south of Montgomery, take the Greenville exit 130 off I-65, and turn left. Ditto if you're looking for the best small town in America.

It's true—*Greenville*, with a population of some 8,000—outscored every other US city with fewer than 100,000 residents in a national home towns index that measures the power of place using statistical data compiled by academic researchers.

Known as "Camellia City," Greenville promises plenty for flower lovers, history buffs, and golfers. Founded in 1820, the town boasts lovely homes, churches, and public buildings, many on the Register of Historic Places. Cambrian Ridge, one of the award-winning courses on the Robert Trent Jones Golf Trail, beckons only minutes away, with the more famed RTJ course, Capitol Hill, in easy driving distance.

Stop by the **Greenville Area Chamber of Commerce** (334-382-3251; greenvillealchamber.com), housed in the old CSX depot on Bolling Street to pick up a brochure called *Historic Main Street Greenville*, which details a self-guided tour of the town's interesting sites. Shady streets, brick paving, and gas lights make Commerce Street an attractive place to stroll.

A jaunt takes you past a local landmark, the **Ritz Theatre**. Dating to 1935, the former movie house built in the then-popular Art Deco style later fell into disrepair. Now rescued and restored, the Ritz serves as the venue for a variety of productions from theater to music and dance. Other sites of interest include Greenville's circa-1936 City Hall, a WPA project and the city's best example of colonial revival civic architecture. Continue your stroll through Confederate Park, established in 1897. With a fountain as its centerpiece, this block-size space is sometimes the setting for evening concerts.

You'll see several handsome churches such as First Presbyterian, Greenville's oldest brick church. Search out the Pioneer Cemetery with its ornate cast-iron fence and elaborate monuments. Unusual cast-iron covers, an invention patented in 1874 by Greenville native Joseph R. Abrams, top several graves, and others are covered with giant cockleshells, a Victorian custom. Many of the area's early settlers, including Capt. William Butler for whom the county is named, are buried here.

Spend some time browsing through some of Greenville's one-of-a-kind boutiques and gift shops such as **The Pineapple** (334-382-7240) at 132 West Commerce Street, which offers unusual flags and banners, photo frames, hand-decorated clothing, and collectibles. In a beautifully restored building at 112 West Commerce, **Karen Rainey Interiors** (334-382-9486 or 334-382-0936; karenraineyinteriors.com) showcases antiques and accessories and provides decorator services for interiors from Gulf Coast condos to Atlanta townhouses. With a wooded recreation area plus playgrounds and pavilions for picnickers, **Sherling Lake** (334-382-3638 or 800-810-5253; sherlinglake.com), about four miles west of Greenville via exit 130 off I-65 at 4397 Braggs Road, offers plenty of recreation options, including camping and fishing. August visitors can take in the annual Watermelon Jubilee with arts, crafts, food, and fun.

From Greenville, a short drive south takes you to Georgiana and the **Hank Williams, Sr., Boyhood Home and Museum** (334-376-2396; hankmuseum. com). Located at 127 Rose Street, the home contains six rooms filled with walls of family photos, original posters, albums, 78 rpm recordings, a church pew, piano, and 1923 Victrola. Also, visitors will see one of the singer's Stetson hats and two suits. Fans from all over the world donated many of the items on display. Draperies, custom made for the musician's Nashville home, feature an overall design of lyrics and music from "Your Cheatin' Heart." Hours are Mon through Sat 10 a.m. to 4 p.m. Admission: adults $5, students $3, children (ages 6 and under) free. Each June, Georgiana hosts an annual Hank Williams Festival with country music concerts, food concessions, and street dances.

Travel Hank's Lost Highway

Hank Williams's home state has created a trail to honor the country legend and make it easier for fans to travel the "Lost Highway" where Williams was born and buried.

"People come from all over to see these sites," said Lee Sentell, Alabama tourism director. "For them, it's a pilgrimage and we thought this would be an opportunity for them to stop and learn about Hank Williams's life."

Created by the Alabama Department of Tourism, the **Hank Williams Trail** goes from Andalusia to Birmingham. "Andalusia is where he married Audrey and Birmingham is where he spent his last night alive," Sentell said.

Historic markers are two sided with display information about Williams and how the site relates to his life on the front. The back has information on other nearby historic attractions.

"I'm amazed at how many people are fascinated by Hank Williams," Sentell said. "It's people of all ages and they come from all over. They want more information about other places in his life and career."

Born near Georgiana on September 17, 1923, Hiriam (as spelled on his birth certificate) "Hank" Williams was the second child of Lon and Lillie Williams. His father was a World War I veteran who was hospitalized for war stress most of the boy's early life.

A small child afflicted with spina bifida, Williams seemed drawn to music from the beginning. He sang in the choir at Mont Olive West Baptist Church where his mother played the organ. His early youth is documented at the **Hank Williams Sr. Boyhood Home & Museum** in Georgiana.

Williams attended school in Greenville, where he also shined shoes and became friends with Rufus Payne, a black street musician known as "Tee-Tot." Williams later credited Payne with giving him "all the music training I ever had."

Hank and his mother moved to Montgomery in 1937. He was fourteen when he entered an amateur talent contest at the Empire Theater and won the first place prize of $15 for singing his original "WPA Blues." At sixteen, he quit school and turned to his music career. A regular on local radio shows, he played at almost every high school auditorium, honky tonk, and fair in the area, backed by his band, the Drifting Cowboys.

In 1944, Williams married Audrey Mae Sheppard, an Alabaman with a two-year-old daughter. They were married at a service station garage in Andalusia.

He became country music's first superstar, selling 10 million records from 1947 to 1953. On a warm night in June 1949, Williams's career reached the pinnacle—his debut at Ryman Auditorium for the Grand Old Opry.

But by mid-1952, his life was in a downward spiral prompted by his divorce and drug and alcohol addiction. Hank Williams died of cardiac arrest on January 1, 1953. He was twenty-nine years old. Oakwood Cemetery in Montgomery is his final resting place.

Williams recorded 225 songs, 128 he had written. Under the pseudonym "Luke the Drifter," he tried to work out his demons in gospel themes and recitations.

"I think that people today are looking for a more pure strain of country music and that is what Hank Williams wrote and sang," Sentell said. "Listening to Hank Williams' songs is like reading his diary."

For a PDF of the Hank Williams Trail, go to alabama.travel/trails/hank-williams-trail.

Places to Stay in Southeast Alabama

AUBURN/OPELIKA

Auburn Marriott Opelika Hotel & Conference Center at Grand National
3700 Robert Trent Jones Trail
(334) 741-9292 or
(866) 846-4655

The Hotel at Auburn University and Dixon Conference Center
241 South College St.
(334) 821-8200 or
(800) 228-2876
Auhcc.com

Chewacla State Park
124 Shell Toomer Pkwy.
(334) 887-5621 or
(800) 252-7275
alapark.com/
chewacla-state-park

Crenshaw Guest House
371 North College St.
(334) 821-1131 or
(800) 950-1131
crenshawguesthouse.com

Hilton Garden Inn
2555 Hilton Garden Dr.
(334) 502-3500

DOTHAN

Dothan Inn & Suites
3285 Montgomery Hwy.
(334) 793-4376

Courtyard by Marriott
3040 Ross Clark Circle
(334) 671-3000 or
(800) 321-2211

Hampton Inn & Suites
4684 Montgomery Hwy.
(334) 671-7672

Holiday Inn South
2195 Ross Clark Circle
(334) 699-6868 or
(800) 777-6611

ENTERPRISE

Best Western Plus Circle Inn
715 Boll Weevil Circle
(334) 393-5248

Hampton Inn Enterprise
8 West Pointe Court
(334) 347-5763

Marley House Bed & Breakfast
502 W. Lee St.
(334) 347-3796

EUFAULAB

Baker Street Bed and Breakfast
343 North Eufaula Ave.
(334) 695-6870
bakerstreetbnb.com

Lakepoint Resort
104 Old Hwy. 165
(334) 687-8011
alapark.com/
lakepoint-state-park

GREENVILLE

Baymont by Wyndham Greenville
71 Jameson Lane
(334) 382-6300 or
(800) 337-0300

MONTGOMERY

Drury Inn and Suites
1124 Eastern Blvd.
(334) 273-1101

Embassy Suites
300 Tallapoosa St.
(334) 269-5055 or
(800) 362-2779

Extended Stay America
5115 Carmichael Rd.
(334) 273-0075

Hillcrest Manor Bed and Breakfast
1632 South Court St.
(334) 264-8253
hillcrestmanorbedand
breakfast.com

Holiday Inn Express
6135 Carmichael Rd.
(334) 270-9199

Quality Inn & Suites
5035 Carmichael Rd.
(334) 396-6300

Red Bluff Cottage Bed and Breakfast
551 Clay St.
(334) 264-0056 or
(888) 551-2529
redbluffcottage.com

Renaissance Montgomery Hotel & Spa at the Convention Center
201 Tallapoosa St.
(334) 481-5000

The Lattice Inn
1414 South Hull St.
(334) 263-1414
thelatticeinn.com

Wingate Inn
2060 Eastern Blvd.
(334) 245-4684

PRATTVILLE

Montgomery Marriott Prattville Hotel and Conference Center
2500 Legends Circle
(888) 250-3767 or
(334) 290-1235

Smith-Byrd House Bed and Breakfast
137 N. Washington St.
(334) 365-1459
smithbyrdhouse.com

FOR MORE INFORMATION ABOUT SOUTHEAST ALABAMA

Auburn/Opelika Tourism Bureau
714 East Glenn Ave.
Auburn 36830
(334) 887-8747 or (866) 880-8747
aotourism.com info@aotourism.com

Dothan Area Convention & Visitors Bureau
3311 Ross Clark Circle
PO Box 8765 Dothan 36304
(334) 794-6622
visitdothan.com

Enterprise Chamber of Commerce
553 Glover Ave.
PO Box 310577
Enterprise 36331-0577
(334) 347-0581 or (800) 235-4730
enterprisealabama.com
chamber@enterprisealabama.com

Eufaula/Barbour County Chamber of Commerce
333 East Broad St.
Eufaula 36027
(334) 687-6664 or (800) 524-7529
eufaulachamber.com
info@eufalachamber.com

Historic Chattahoochee Commission
PO Box 33 Eufaula 36072-0033
(334) 687-9755 or
(877) 766-2443
hcc-al-ga.org

Montgomery Convention & Visitors Bureau
300 Water St.
PO Box 79 Montgomery 36101
(334) 261-1100 or
(800) 240-9452
visitingmontgomery.com
tourism@visitingmontgomery.com

Tuskegee Area Chamber of Commerce
121 South Main St.
PO Box 831034 Tuskegee 36083
(334) 727–6619
tuskegeeareachamber.org
info@tuskeegeeareachamber.org

Places to Eat in Southeast Alabama

AUBURN/OPELIKA

Acre Restaurant
210 East Glenn Ave.
(334) 246-3763
acreauburn.com

Ariccia Trattoria
241 South College St.
(334) 821-8200 or
(800) 228-2876
Auhcc.com

The Depot
124 Michigan Ave.
(334) 521-5177
allaboardauburn.com

The Hound
124 Tichenor Ave.
(334) 246-3300
thehound-auburn.com

The Lakeview Room
3700 Robert Trent
Jones Trail
(334) 741-9292

Niffer's Place
1151 Opelika Rd.
(334) 821-3118
niffersplace.com

Venditori's Italian Restaurant
2575 Hilton Garden Dr.
(334) 826-7360
venditoris-auburn.com

Warehouse Bistro
105 Rocket Ave.
(334) 745-6353
warehousebistro.com

DOTHAN

Hunt's Seafood Restaurant and Oyster Bar
177 Campbellton Hwy.
(334) 794-5193
seafoodsteakoystersdothan
.com

Old Mexico
2920 Ross Clark Circle
(334) 712-1434

The Old Mill Restaurant
2557 Murphy Mill Rd.
(334) 794-8530
oldmilldothan.com

ENTERPRISE

Annie's Café
212 Main St.
(334) 347-6622

Cutts Restaurant
417 East Lee (334)
347-1110
Cuttsrestaurant.com

Micks Dauphin Street Café
1442 Daupin St.
(334) 393-9072

Rawls Restaurant
116 South Main St.
(334) 308-9387
therawlsrestaurant.com

EUFAULA

Barb's Country Kitchen
114 West Broad St.
(334) 616-0035

Cajun Corner
114 North Eufaula Ave.
(334) 616-0816
thecajuncorner.com

Lakepoint Resort
104 Lake Point Dr.
(334) 687-8011
Alapark.com/
lakepoint-state-park

Old Mexico
1248 South Eufaula Ave.
(334) 687-7770

River City Grill
209 East Broad St.
(334) 616-6550

GREENVILLE

Bates House of Turkey
1001 Fort Dale Rd.
(334) 382-6123
bateshouseturkey.com

MILLBROOK

Catfish House
3011 Cobbs Ford Rd.
(334) 285-7225
catfishhouse.net

Fantail Restaurant
2060 Downing St.
(334) 285-7255
fantailrestaurant.com

Front Porch Grill
106 Deatsville Hwy.
(334) 285-7888

MONTGOMERY

Bonefish Grill
7020 East Chase Pkwy.
(334) 396-1770
bonefishgrill.com

**The House Restaurant
at Renaissance
Montgomery Hotel**
201 Tallapoosa St.
(334) 481-5166

Lek's Railroad Thai
Union Station,
300 B Water St.
(334) 269-0708

Martha's Place
7798 Atlanta Hwy.
(334) 356-7165
marthasplacebuffet.com

**The Tavern &
Porter Room**
12 West Jefferson St.
(334) 262-0080
tavernandporterroom.com

Sinclair's East
7847 Vaughn Rd.
(334) 271-7847
sinclairsrestaurants.com

**Vintage Year
Restaurant & Bar**
405 Cloverdale Rd.
(334) 239-0041
vymgm.com

PRATTVILLE

Oak Tavern Capitol Hill
2500 Legends Circle
(334) 290-1235 or
(888) 250-3767

TROY

**Mossy Grove School
House Restaurant**
1841 87 South Hwy.
(334) 566-4921

Sisters' Restaurant
13153 US 231
(334) 566-0064
sistersrestaurant.biz

WETUMPKA

**FIRE Steakhouse at
Wind Creek Wetumpka**
100 River Oaks Dr.
(866) 946-3360
firesteakhouse.com

Our Place Cafe
809 Company St.
(334) 567-8778

MAINSTREAM ATTRACTIONS WORTH SEEING IN SOUTHEAST ALABAMA

**Montgomery Zoo and Mann Wildlife
Learning Museum**
2301 Coliseum Pkwy. Montgomery
(334) 240-4900
montgomeryzoo.com

Observe more than 800 animals from
five continents in the zoo's naturalistic
settings and take a train ride around the
park. Relocated from its former home

in Opelika and housed next to the zoo,
the Mann Museum allows you to get
acquainted with bears, wolves, moose,
and more mounted specimens of North
American wildlife, all presented in realistic
settings. The natural history museum's
life-size exhibits numbered more than
300 at last count. The zoo is open daily
9 a.m. to 4 p.m. The Mann Wildlife
Learning Museum is open daily 9 a.m. to

5 p.m. (Dec hours are 9 a.m. to 4 p.m.) Admission: adults $15 for zoo and $7 for museum, or $20 for both; senior citizens $13 for zoo and $6 for museum, or $18 for both; children (ages 3 to 12) $11 for zoo and $5 museum, or $15 for both.

US Army Aviation Museum
6000 Novosel St.
Fort Rucker
(334) 255-3036, (334) 598-2508, or (888) 276-9286
armyaviationmuseum.org

This museum is in Fort Rucker, a training base for military helicopter pilots located five miles west of Ozark. Covering the complete history of Army Aviation, this complex contains one of the world's largest collections of helicopters. Exhibits include maps and photos of Army Aviation's role in the Louisiana Maneuvers through Operation Desert Storm, a full-scale model of the Wright B Flyer, and unusual pieces such as a Sopwith Camel and a Nieuport 28. You can even walk through a Chinook (CH-47-A) and view today's high-tech Apache combat helicopter. The Army Aviation Museum is free and open to the public Mon through Fri from 9 a.m. to 4 p.m.; Sat from 9 a.m. to 3 p.m.

Southwest Alabama

Black Belt

Alabama's Black Belt, so called because of a strip of dark, rich soil that stretches across part of the state's south-central section, covers 4,300 square miles. This fertile farmland became the setting for a host of plantations prior to the Civil War and you'll see many antebellum structures throughout the area. From **Selma**, which retains a lingering flavor of the Old South's cotton-rich aristocratic past, you can easily make a loop of several small Black Belt towns with their treasure troves of architecture. Situated on a bluff above the Alabama River, Selma served as a major munitions depot, making battleships as well as cannonballs, rifles, and ammunition for the Confederate cause.

US 80 west from Montgomery to Selma leads across the **Edmund Pettus Bridge**, a landmark that figured prominently in the civil rights struggle. In 1965 marchers followed Martin Luther King Jr. across this bridge on their trek to Montgomery during voting-rights demonstrations.

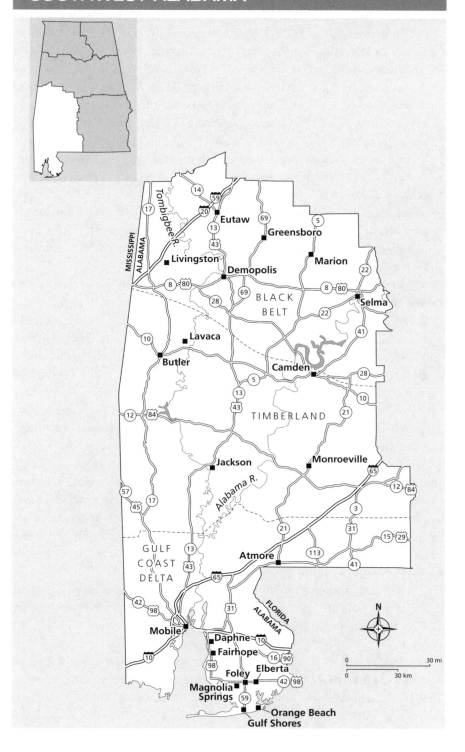

Located near the bridge, the **National Voting Rights Museum** (334-526-4340; nvrmi.com) at 6 US Highway 80 East presents a visual history of the Selma-to-Montgomery march and related events. Upon entering, viewers see themselves reflected in a mirrored "I Was There" wall with a display of cards recording firsthand observations by individuals. A series of rooms focus on reconstruction, suffrage, and other aspects of the voting-rights struggle. A large window, etched with the names Andrew Young, Martin Luther King Jr. Thurgood Marshall, Dick Gregory, and other museum Hall of Fame inductees, provides a fitting vantage point for viewing the historic Pettus Bridge. Hours are Mon through Thurs 10 a.m. to 4 p.m.; Fri through Sun by appointment only. Admission: adults $6.50; senior citizens and students $4.50.

Take time to stroll along historic Water Avenue, a restored nineteenth-century riverfront warehouse district with brick streets, arcades, and parks overlooking the river. Nearby, at 1124 Water Avenue, you'll find a mini-mall with an eatery and several interesting shops.

To dip into more of the city's interesting history, stop by the handsome **Old Depot Museum** (334-874-2197; olddepotmuseum.com), located on the corner of Martin Luther King Street and Water Avenue. Built in 1891 by the Louisville and Nashville Railroad, this arched and turreted two-story redbrick structure stands on the site of the Confederate Naval Foundry, which Union troops destroyed during the Battle of Selma in 1865. The museum houses everything from a 1908 portrait camera used by psychic Edgar Cayce (who once lived in Selma and operated a photography studio here) to Victorian hair combs, plantation records, quilts, Confederate bills, cannonballs, early medical equipment, and antique tools.

In the Black Heritage Wing, you'll see sculpture by Earl Hopkins, nationally recognized for his wood carvings and leather crafts. Hopkins, who uses exotic woods in his creations, worked at Colonial Williamsburg before retiring to his native Selma. A not-to-be-missed rare display of photographs, made between 1895 and 1905 by Selmian Mary Morgan Keipp, depicts daily life on a Black Belt plantation. The series is considered one of the finest and most complete collections of photos covering that period in history.

Behind the museum you'll see a Firefighters Museum plus a boxcar, caboose, and old farm equipment. The museum is open Mon through Fri from 10 a.m. to 4 p.m. or by appointment. Admission: adults $5, senior citizens $4, children $2.

Nearby at 410 Martin Luther King Street, stands **Brown Chapel African Methodist Episcopal Church**, another significant structure in Selma's history. This 1908 Byzantine-style building served as headquarters for the civil rights

BEST ATTRACTIONS IN SOUTHWEST ALABAMA

Battleship USS *Alabama*, Mobile Bay	Mobile Museum of Art, Mobile
Bellingrath Gardens and Home, Theodore	Old Cahawba Archaeological Park, Orrville
Dauphin Island	Town of Demopolis
Fort Morgan, Mobile Bay	Town of Fairhope
Gulf Coast beaches	Town of Marion
Mobile's historic districts	Town of Selma

activists who played a pivotal role in bringing about the passage of the National Voting Rights Act during the turbulent decade of the 1960s. Visitors may take a self-guided walking tour of the surrounding historic area.

Sometime during your local tour, be sure to stop at 109 Union Street to tour the white-columned, three-story, brick ***Vaughan-Smitherman Museum*** (334-874-2174), named for the local hospital (once housed here) and in honor of Selma's former mayor, who played an active role in historic preservation. Crowning Alabama Avenue, this impressive building opened its doors in 1848 as the Central Masonic Institute and later served as a hospital for wounded Confederates (escaping the fate of many Selma buildings when Union general John Harrison Wilson's raiders, disobeying orders, embarked on a wholesale campaign of wanton destruction in April 1865). The building later served as a courthouse, military school, and private hospital. Inside you'll see a large collection of Civil War relics, Confederate money, medical artifacts, and period furnishings from the mid-1800s. Open Tues through Sat 9 a.m. to 4 p.m. or by appointment. Modest admission.

On a drive through the Old Town Historic District, you'll see block after block of antebellum and Victorian architecture. On the third weekend in March, the ***Historic Selma Pilgrimage*** provides visitors with opportunities to tour many of the city's outstanding homes. See selmapilgrimage.com for more information. A reenactment of the Battle of Selma is another popular springtime event. On the second Saturday in October, the grand event is the Tall Tellin' Festival.

TOP ANNUAL EVENTS IN SOUTHWEST ALABAMA

Mardi Gras
Mobile, February
(800) 566-2453

Arts & Crafts Festival
Fairhope, March
(251) 229-1874
Fairhopeartsandcraftsfestival.com

Azalea Trail Run & Festival
Mobile, March
(800) 566-2453

Festival of Flowers
Mobile, March
(251) 639-2050 or (800) 566-2453
festivalofflowers.com

Historic Selma Pilgrimage
Selma, March
(800) 457-3562
selmapilgrimage.com

The Original German Sausage Festival
Elberta, last Saturday in
March and October
(251) 986-5805
Gulfshores.com

Crawfish Festival
Faunsdale, last weekend in April
(unless Easter)
(334) 628-3240

Blessing of the Fleet
Bayou La Batre, May
(251) 824-2415
fleetblessing.org

To Kill a Mockingbird
Monroeville, last weekend of
April and first three weekends in May
(251) 575-7433
monroecountymuseum.org

Alabama Deep Sea Fishing Rodeo
Dauphin Island, July
(251) 471-0025
adsfr.com

Alabama Tale Tellin' Festival
Selma, second weekend in October
(334) 878-2787
artsrevive.com

Selma Haunted History Tours
Selma/Dallas County locations, October
(800) 45-SELMA

Bayfest Music Festival
Mobile, first weekend in October
(251) 470-7730
bayfest.com

National Shrimp Festival
Gulf Shores, October
(251) 968-7200
myshrimpfest.com

Frank Brown International Songwriters Festival
Gulf Shores, November
(850) 492-7664
frankbrownsongwriters.com

Pow Wow
Atmore, November
(251) 368-9136

Magic Christmas in Lights
Bellingrath Gardens & Home
Late November through December
(251) 973-2217
bellingrath.org

Christmas on the River
Demopolis, December
(334) 289-0270
demopolischamber.com

For a memento of your visit, consider purchasing a cookbook called *Tastes of Olde Selma* available in several places throughout the city. Compiled by Selma's Olde Towne Association, the book contains line drawings and brief histories of many of the town's significant structures along with a selection of wonderful recipes. The front cover features a color illustration of **Sturdivant Hall** (334-872-5626), a neoclassical mansion located at 713 Mabry Street. Designed by Thomas Helm Lee (Robert E. Lee's cousin), this magnificent home that took three years to build boasts elaborate ceilings and decorative moldings with a motif of intertwined grape leaves and vines. You'll also see a spiral staircase, marble mantels, and servant pulls—each with a different tone. Other treasures include period furnishings, portraits, silver, crystal, china, and a rare French-made George Washington commemorative clock of ormolu and gold—one of only seven in existence.

Coral vines climb the home's back walls, and mock lemons perfume the air. You may be presented with a sprig or cutting of lavender, mint, or sage from the mansion's herb garden outside the backyard kitchen. The home's formal gardens, which feature a variety of native flowers, shrubs, and trees, serve as a lovely backdrop for the pilgrimage's annual grand ball. Sturdivant Hall is open Tues through Sat from 10 a.m. to 4 p.m., except for major holidays. Admission: adults $5, children $2.

By the way, some Selmians say the ghost of John McGee Parkman, one of Sturdivant Hall's former owners, roams the mansion. You may or may not see house ghosts here, but you can certainly find several in Sturdivant Hall's gift shop—sandwiched between the covers of some of Kathryn Tucker Windham's books, such as *13 Alabama Ghosts and Jeffrey* or *Jeffrey's Latest 13*. For a souvenir or gift, you might like to buy *Alabama—One Big Front Porch*, an engrossing collection of stories compiled by Alabama's famous storyteller Mrs. Windham, who died in 2011.

To hear other famous Southern storytellers, plan your visit to coincide with the **Alabama Tale Tellin' Festival**, an annual fall event staged in Selma.

Driving along Dallas Avenue (which becomes State Route 22), you'll pass the **Old Live Oak Cemetery**, filled with ancient trees festooned by Spanish moss. During spring, dogwoods and azaleas make this site even more spectacular. A number of Confederate graves and unique monuments may be seen here, including the mausoleum of William Rufus King, who named Selma and planned its layout. King, on the Democratic ticket with Franklin Pierce, died shortly after being elected vice president of the US.

For dinner strike out for the **Tally-Ho Restaurant** (334-872-1390), located at 509 Mangum Avenue, just off Summerfield Road in the northern section of town. Owner Bob Kelley's entrees run the gamut from seafood and chicken to prime rib au jus. A board features daily specials, which might include grilled pork chops with Thai sauce. Homemade zucchini muffins accompany entrees. For dessert try the chocolate cheesecake or amaretto soufflé. The restaurant's hours are Mon through Thurs 5 to 9 p.m.; Fri and Sat 5 to 10 p.m. Prices are moderate. Visit tallyhoselma.com.

During your Selma visit, swing southwest about nine miles on State Route 22 toward **Cahaba** ("Cahawba" is the historical spelling). Watch for a sign that says to cahaba, then turn left and travel 3.5 miles to 9518 Cahawba Road. When you reach a dead end, turn left again and continue three miles to **Old Cahawba Archaeological Park** (334-872-8058; cahawba.com), the site of Alabama's first permanent state capital. Here, near the place where the Cahaba and Alabama Rivers merge, once stood a thriving town. Today's visitors will have to use some imagination to visualize the remaining ruins as grand mansions that surrounded a copper-domed capitol, completed in 1820. A large stone monument and interpretive signs in conjunction with old street markers, brick columns, cemeteries, and domestic plants growing wild offer the few clues that this off-the-beaten-path spot once flourished as a political, commercial, and cultural center. You'll also see an artesian well (where watercress grows), the source of water for the elaborate gardens surrounding the Perine family mansion, which once stood nearby.

The visitor and education centers provide information on Cahaba's glory days. In 1825 legislators voted to move Alabama's capital to Tuscaloosa. While local lore holds that frequent flooding caused Cahaba to lose its position as the state's seat of government, evidence suggests that sectional politics probably played a larger role. Gradually Cahaba became a ghost town, and by 1900 most of its buildings had disappeared. The park offers a handicapped accessible nature trail. Except for major holidays, the park is open daily from 9 a.m. to 5 p.m., and the visitor center is open Thurs through Mon from noon to 5 p.m. Admission is free.

Afterward follow US 80 west from Selma until you reach Dallas County Road 45; then turn north to **Marion**, one of Alabama's oldest towns and a leading cultural center for planter society. The city is home to both **Judson College** and **Marion Military Institute**. The latter's chapel, Old South Hall, and Lovelace House on campus served as hospitals during the Civil War. The graves of more than 100 Southern and Union soldiers were later relocated from campus to **Confederate Rest**, a cemetery behind St. Wilfrid's Episcopal Church. The Old Marion City Hall (moved to MMI's campus from the downtown square) houses the **Alabama Military Hall of Honor**. For an appointment to see the exhibits, call (334) 683-2346.

Downtown you'll see several historical churches and the handsome Perry County Courthouse dating from the early 1850s. Be sure to drive down Green Street, the setting for a number of antebellum residences, including the **Lea-Griffith Home** (circa 1830), where Texas hero Sam Houston married Margaret Lea (their marriage license is recorded in the courthouse). With some 200 sites (in a wide variety of architectural styles) listed on the National Register of Historic Places, Marion promises plenty to see.

During your Marion excursion take a stroll across the Judson College campus and stop by the **Alabama Women's Hall of Fame**, which occupies the first floor of Bean Hall at 302 Bibb Street. Formerly the school's library, this Carnegie-built structure stands on the corner of Bibb and East Lafayette Streets. Bronze plaques pay tribute to Helen Keller, Julia Tutwiler, Lurleen Burns Wallace, Tallulah Bankhead, Zelda Sayre Fitzgerald, her daughter Frances Scott Fitzgerald Smith, and many other women of achievement with Alabama connections. Former first ladies Barbara Bush and Rosalynn Carter have spoken at past induction ceremonies. Except for major holidays, hours are Mon through Fri 8 a.m. to 5 p.m. For a tour call (334) 683-5100 or visit awhf .org. Admission is free.

After exploring Marion follow State Route 14 west to Alabama's Catfish Capital, **Greensboro**. Because this Black Belt town managed to escape the Civil War's ravages, a large number of its antebellum homes and churches have been preserved. In fact the entire downtown district, featuring some 150 nineteenth-century structures, is on the National Register of Historic Places. More than sixty of the town's homes predate the Civil War. Be sure to drive along Main, Tuscaloosa, and South Streets, all of which offer interesting architecture. At Market and South Streets, you'll see the **Noel-Ramsey House**. Built between 1819 and 1821, this is the only remaining residence of French settlers from nearby Demopolis's Vine and Olive Colony.

Don't miss **Magnolia Grove** (334-624-8618), a two-story Greek revival house built around 1840 by a wealthy cotton planter, Colonel Isaac Croom. Located at 1002 Hobson Street, the home stands among lovely magnolia trees and landscaped gardens on a 12-acre setting. Magnolia Grove was also the home of Croom's nephew, Rear Admiral Richmond Pearson Hobson, a Congressional Medal of Honor winner. A naval hero in the Spanish-American War, Hobson later served in Congress and introduced legislation (the Hobson

Amendment) that became the basis for the Constitution's prohibition amendment. The Museum Room contains memorabilia from Hobson's military and political careers.

The house also features family portraits, heirlooms, and furnishings from the 1830s to the early 1900s. You'll see an 1866 piano, a Persian rug from the late 1800s, a chaperon's bench, and antique quilts. Outbuildings include a kitchen, slave cottage, and a structure that probably served as Isaac Croom's office. Hours are Thurs through Sat 10 a.m. to 4 p.m. and by appointment. Admission: adults $7, college students and senior citizens $5, children (ages 6 to 18) $4, children (ages 6 and under) free.

From Greensboro head south on State Route 25 toward *Faunsdale*, population 92. Housed in a 1890s mercantile building on the town's main street, *Faunsdale Bar & Grill* (334-628-3240) serves great steaks and seafood, and owner John (Ca-John) Broussard, originally from Louisiana, offers a variety of crawfish specialties in season. The food speaks for itself, attracting diners from distant towns. Windows sport red-and-white checkered cafe curtains. A pot-bellied stove and fireplace add to the ambience. Saturday night patrons often can enjoy live music until the wee hours. Hours are Thurs and Fri 5 to 9:30 p.m.; Sat 11 a.m. to 9:30 p.m.; and Sun 11:30 a.m. to 2 p.m. Return to US 80 and head west toward Demopolis.

Sometime during your visit to the area, make an outing to *Prairieville*, the site of *St. Andrews Episcopal Church*. Located a short distance off US 80, this red Carpenter Gothic structure dates from 1853 and is a National Historic Landmark. Nearby you'll see a picturesque old cemetery, where many of this area's early settlers are buried.

Peter Lee and Joe Glasgow, master carpenters and slaves of Captain Henry A. Tayloe, supervised a crew of slaves belonging to church members in the construction of this edifice, built to serve settlers from the Atlantic seaboard.

alabamatrivia

An immense 1833 meteor shower inspired the song, "Stars Fell on Alabama."

Craftspeople created the mellowed appearance of interior wood walls by applying a brew made from the stems of tobacco plants. Pokeberry weeds provided color for some portions of the lovely stained-glass windows. Ragweed, chewed and molded, forms the decorative relief letters of a biblical quotation near the altar. Be sure to notice the pipe organ (which is still playable) and the choir gallery. Closed as a regular parish in 1927, the church hosts a special service the first Sunday in October followed by a picnic dinner on the grounds. Group tours can be arranged by appointment; call (334) 606-9612.

Traveling nine miles west on US 80 takes you to ***Gaineswood*** (334-289-4846), a gorgeous cream-colored mansion with white-columned porticos. Once the centerpiece of a huge plantation, the home now stands in the suburbs of the town of ***Demopolis*** at 805 South Cedar Avenue. Gen. Nathan Bryan Whitfield, a gifted inventor, musician, artist, and architect, started construction on the house in 1843. He spent almost two decades planning and building this elegant Greek revival home and continued to refine it until the Civil War's outbreak.

Stepping into the columned ballroom, you'll see yourself reflected thirteen times in the vis-à-vis mirrors. Be sure to notice the glass-ceiling domes and the elaborate friezes and medallions. The home contains its original furnishings, family portraits, and accessories. Don't miss the flutina (invented by Whitfield), a one-of-a-kind musical instrument that sounds something like a riverboat calliope.

Except for major holidays, Gaineswood is open Tues through Sat from 10 a.m. to 4 p.m. Special tours can be arranged by appointment. Admission: adults $7, children (ages 6 to 18) $3.

Continue to downtown Demopolis, "the City of the People," a town with an interesting origin that goes back to 1817 when 400 aristocrats, fleeing France after Napoleon's exile, landed here at the white limestone bluffs overlooking the Tombigbee River. They acquired a large tract of land along the river and set about establishing the ***Vine and Olive Colony***. The agricultural experiment, however, yielded little more than frustration for the colonists, who lacked essential farming skills and found the local climate and soil unsuitable for cultivating their imported grape vines and olive trees.

You'll see a display on this early colony in the French Room at ***Bluff Hall*** (334-289-9644; marengocountyhistoricalsociety.com). Located at 407 North Commissioners Avenue next to the Civic Center, this 1832 brick home takes its name from its position overlooking the Tombigbee River. Originally built in the federal style, the home took on a Greek revival appearance after later additions. Furnishings are Empire and mid-Victorian.

As you start upstairs notice the newel post's amity button, symbolizing a state of harmony between the owner and builder. In addition to documents, crystal, silver spoons, cannonballs, portraits, and other memorabilia of the Vine and Olive Colony, you'll see a room filled with period costumes, such as an 1831 wedding dress. Bluff Hall is noted for its extensive collection of vintage clothing.

The kitchen's interesting gadgets range from an egg tin, sausage stuffer, and fluting iron to the "humane" rat trap on the hearth. Adjacent to the home, the Canebrake Craft Corner offers a choice selection of items including posters depicting a European artist's imaginative conception of the early Vine and Olive Colony, handmade split-oak baskets, and eye-catching pottery by Susan Brown Freeman. Bluff Hall is owned and operated by the Marengo County Historical Society. (The county's name was inspired by Napoleon's victory at the Battle of Marengo in northern Italy.) Except for major holidays, Bluff Hall is open Tues through Sat 10 a.m. to 5 p.m., and Sun 2 to 5 p.m. Admission: adults $5, students $3.

Demopolis offers more than mansions and water recreation. You'll find plenty of interesting places to shop, too. Downtown, at 101 West Washington Street, *The Mustard Seed* (334-289-2878) offers fine gifts, china, crystal, housewares, collectibles, dolls, and toys. The Mustard Seed also has a coffee shop with gourmet casseroles to go as well as chicken salad, pimiento cheese spread, turtleback cookies, and much more. Local festivals include a July the Fourth celebration, Freedom on the River at City Landing, Rooster Day in April, and December's *Christmas on the River*. which features a weeklong festival of parades, tours, and events culminating in an extravaganza of decorated, lighted boats gliding down the Tombigbee River. For more information on these or other special events, including productions by the Canebrake Players (a local theater group) or on other area attractions, call the Demopolis Chamber of Commerce at (334) 289-0270 or visit Demopolischamber.com.

Traveling north takes you to *Eutaw*. a charming hamlet situated around a courthouse square that dates from 1838. The town boasts fifty-three antebellum structures, with many on the National Register of Historic Places. Head first to the Eutaw Area Chamber of Commerce at 110 Main Street (205-732-9002) on the courthouse square, where you'll find information on both Eutaw and Greene County.

Beside the historic Vaughn Morrow House on Main Street stands the First Presbyterian Church. Organized in 1824 as Mesopotamia Presbyterian Church, the congregation's current home dates from 1851. This white-steepled structure looks as if it belongs on a Christmas card (without the snow, of course—a rare commodity in most of Alabama). Original whale-oil lamps, stored for a time in the slave gallery, have been wired for electricity and again grace the church's interior. For a tour, inquire at the church office in the adjacent Educational Building.

Nearby, on the corner of Main Street and Eutaw Avenue, stands St. Stephen's Episcopal Church. The handsome brick structure features a hand-carved lectern, an elegant white marble baptismal font, and beautiful stained-glass windows. To see the lovely interior, check with the church office. For a tasty meal, locals flock to *Warrior Bar & Grill* at 802 Boligee Street (205)

346-2111. Open Thurs through Sat 4 to 9 p.m., Warrior specializes in steaks, fresh Gulf seafood, pit barbecue, and creative cocktails.

After exploring Eutaw head west to *Gainesville*, a delightful piece of the past populated by 307 people. Most places like this charming town have vanished from today's landscape. Here you'll see historic cemeteries and churches like the *First Presbyterian Church*, which dates from 1837 and has been rescued from flames on three occasions—once with a hand-to-hand bucket brigade. Interior features include whale-oil lamps, box pews, the altar's original chairs, and a bell with a tone enhanced by 500 melted silver dollars. Because several denominations share this church (one per Sunday), attendees label themselves "Metho-bap-terians." Other sites of interest include the *1872 Methodist Church*; *St. Alban's Episcopal Church*, founded in 1879; and the *Confederate Cemetery*. For more local information stop by one of the downtown stores.

Afterward continue south to nearby *Livingston*. The town was named for Edward Livingston, who served as Andrew Jackson's secretary of state.

On your way into town, stop by Sumter County's *Alamuchee Covered Bridge*, across from the Baptist Student Union on the campus of Livingston State University. Captain W. A. C. Jones of Livingston designed and built this 1861 structure, one of the South's oldest covered bridges. Made of hand-hewn heart pine held together by large wooden pegs, the bridge originally spanned the Sucarnochee River, south of town. In 1924 the bridge was taken down and reconstructed across a creek on the old Bellamy-Livingston Road, where it remained in use until 1958. The bridge was moved to its present location and restored in 1971. You might enjoy seeing more of the campus, which also boasts two lakes.

Downtown you'll see a lovely square surrounding the impressive domed *Sumter County Courthouse* (circa 1900). This area remained Choctaw country until 1830, when the US acquired it in the Treaty of Dancing Rabbit Creek.

Head to *York*, about eleven miles southwest of Livingston. In this small town near the Mississippi border, you'll find a wonderful art museum inside *The Coleman Center for the Arts* (205-392-2005 or 205-392-2004; colemanarts.org), at 630 Avenue A. The museum, a library, genealogical room, and a cultural center occupy an early-twentieth-century general store. On an exterior wall of the building, a repainted vintage ad shows silent film star Clara Bow promoting an early brand of gasoline. You'll enter The Coleman Center through a courtyard on the opposite side.

A staff member described the four-building complex as a community effort and the only facility of its kind in Sumter County. Local citizens contributed the land, building, services, and funds for the center. In addition to its permanent collection, which includes an original etching by Renoir, prints, paintings, pottery, and other items, the museum features traveling exhibits. Office hours are Mon through Fri 10 a.m. to 5 p.m. Gallery hours are Mon and Wed from 10 a.m. to noon and 1 to 4 p.m.; Tues and Thurs from noon to 6 p.m.; Fri and Sat from 10 a.m. to 1 p.m. Admission is free.

Timberland

Timber is big business in this part of the state, and hunting and fishing are popular pastimes. If you're in the mood for a feast, head for **Ezell's Fish Camp** (205-654-2205; ezellscamp.com) near **Lavaca** at 776 Ezell Road. This out-of-the-way restaurant is definitely worth adding some extra miles to your trip. In fact, some customers fly in, and an Ezell's staffer meets them at the airport. The restaurant also gets a lot of river traffic and often provides transportation into town for boating customers who need motel lodging.

To reach the restaurant from Lavaca, take State Route 10 east toward Nanafalia and turn left just before reaching the big bridge. Located on the west bank of the Tombigbee River, this family operation is the granddaddy of "catfish cabins" you might see while driving through the state. Following family precedent, each of the Ezells' three children went into the restaurant business.

As you arrive, you'll see a large rustic structure with a roof of wooden shingles. The restaurant started out as a Civil War–era dogtrot cabin, and the Ezells added more rooms for their brisk business. The rambling structure now seats 400 people. Mounted deer and moose heads line the walls. (Mr. Ezell, an avid angler, hunter, and trapper, used to ship his furs to New York's garment district.)

The back porch, a favorite spot for eating, overlooks the river. Start with an appetizer of onion rings, crab claws, or fried dill pickles. In addition to catfish, the restaurant serves seafood specialties such as shrimp and oysters. Entrees come with slaw, potatoes, and hush puppies. Open every day except Monday, Ezell's has flexible hours, but the typical schedule is Sun through Thurs 11 a.m. to 9 p.m., and Fri and Sat to 9:30 p.m. Moderate prices.

Traveling south from Lavaca takes you through large expanses of timberland. Forestry and related industries play major roles in the area's economy. Clarke County holds the title of Forestry Capital of Alabama, and Fulton, a small town south of Thomasville, pays tribute to this important industry by hosting a **Sawmill Days** celebration each fall.

Need Some **Mama Nems Pepper Jelly**? Then hurry to the **Alabama Rural Heritage Center** (334-627-3388; ruralheritagecenter.com) in Thomaston, a Black Belt hamlet northeast of Lavaca at 133 Sixth Avenue. Along with batches of the popular pepper jelly, you'll find a wide selection of Alabama art and handmade crafts in the gift shop. A jar of watermelon rind pickles just might make the perfect souvenir. That special Mama Nems Pepper Jelly is homemade at the center using a time-tested local recipe. The center even grows its own peppers for topnotch quality.

So how to eat the tasty jelly? It's a great glaze on ham and pork chops, a sweet barbecue sauce for ribs and chicken, and a delicious spread on warm corn bread.

The once-humble facility was renovated in 2006, thanks to the innovative efforts of two teams of fifth-year architecture students from Auburn University, who designed and worked on the project over a three-year period. Annual events include Evening under the Stars, utilizing the Heritage outdoor stage, on Friday and Saturday evenings during Mother's Day weekend, a Pepper Jelly Festival in April, and an annual Rural Fun Day with storytelling, spinning, weaving, quilting, and other crafts demonstrations the fourth Saturday in August. Hours are Thurs and Fri 10 a.m. to 4 p.m., and Sat 10 a.m. to 1 p.m.

If you head south from Jackson, you'll pass unusual geographical features known as salt domes. (A salt dome is the tip of a huge mountain of salt forced to the surface from deep within the earth.) According to a local historian, the salt domes in this area are as close as any to the earth's surface, but you probably won't recognize them as such because they're covered with foliage. After Union forces cut off supplies during the Civil War, the local salt mines became extremely important. Many people made their way here for this commodity, essential for curing and preserving meats.

Take your time while discovering the treasures and pleasures of the Black Belt, a region where history still resonates in its stories—the kind best savored on front porches. Kathryn Tucker Windham, Alabama's famous First Lady of Folk Tales and Ghost Stories grew up in Thomasville, located about an hour south of Demopolis on US 43. She died in 2011.

"We're not New York City, and we don't want to be," says tourism coordinator Linda Vice, who can direct you to plenty of interesting, off-the-beaten-path spots in this history-rich area. "We have developed a Black History/Heritage Trail, a Native American Trail, an overall History Heritage Trail, and a Foods Trail through this area." Call Linda at (334) 636-5506.

On the outskirts of Thomasville stands Alabama Southern Community College (334-637-3146), located at 30755 Highway 43. The college library houses the ***Kathryn Tucker Windham Museum***, which fans enjoy visiting. Hours are Mon through Thurs from 7:30 a.m. to 5 p.m., and Fri from 7:30 a.m. to 3:30 p.m. or by appointment. Free admission.

Continue to **Camden**, where you'll find the **Black Belt Treasures Cultural Arts Center** (334-682-9878) downtown at 209 Claiborne Street in a handsomely restored old car dealership. The gallery showcases arts, crafts, books, and food from more than 200 artists and craftsmen from this region. Hours are Tues through Fri 10 a.m. to 4 p.m.; Sat 10 a.m. to 2 p.m. Visit blackbelttreasures.com.

Before leaving town, stop by **Camden Jewelry and Gifts** (334-682-4057) on the 47 Camden Bypass. Besides jewelry, you'll find a selection of taste-tempting gourmet food items, a children's section, kitchen section, bath and body products, travel items, and more. The friendly staff will help you choose the perfect souvenir or gift for everyone on your list. Hours are Mon through Fri 10 a.m. to 5 p.m., and Sat 10 a.m. to 2 p.m. If you visit Camden during the Wilcox Historical Society's biennial (slated for odd-numbered years) Fall Tour of Homes, you can survey some of the area's antebellum structures. The stately **Wilcox Female Institute**, which dates from 1850, serves as tour headquarters. Located at 301 Broad Street, the former school (open by appointment) houses a small museum of local history.

No Black Belt ramble is complete without a visit to **St. Stephens Historical Park**. It was here, in 1799, the first US flag flew over what would become Alabama. Executive director Jim Long, sixth-generation grandson of John McGrew, who settled in St. Stephens during the 1770s, can share many anecdotes about the original site of Alabama's territorial capital, the now vanished but once-thriving Old St. Stephens.

Make your first stop the 1854 territorial courthouse, now called the Old Washington County Courthouse, on US 34 West to collect information. A trio of flags fronts this two-story white building, which houses a museum and serves as headquarters for the St. Stephens Historical Commission. Take the tiny grill-fronted elevator or the stairs to the second floor for a look at the exhibits, which include Indian artifacts, a dugout canoe made somewhere between 600 to 1,000 years ago, portraits of early settlers, and the Old Washington County courtroom with its original furnishings. Once a major fossil site, this area shipped fossils to museums in other parts of the country, and you'll see some interesting specimens.

Afterward, head to the 200-acre park, which offers camping, fishing, and other outdoor recreation. Exploring the park, you'll see an architectural site, old cemetery, and the unusual Indian Baths.

"They've been called the Indian Baths as far back as anyone knows, but their origin remains unknown," said a staff member, who came across a mention about mineral springs here in 1818 and also heard speculation that this feature might have been part of an early Spanish irrigation system.

For a modest park admission, which you pay at the camp store by the lake, you can spend a full day hiking, swimming, picnicking, and relaxing. Campers will find that the "view of the night sky is fabulous, and you can hear coyotes howling."

The facility opens at sunrise and closes at sunset, and the main gate is locked at 10 p.m. For more information on this intriguing site located on the west side of the Tombigbee River in Washington County near Jackson, call (251) 246-6790.

For a Southern taste treat, make reservations at the **Gaines Ridge Dinner Club** (334-682-9707; wilcozwebworks.com), located about two miles east of Camden at 933 Highway State Route 10. The restaurant, housed in Betty Gaines Kennedy's two-story circa-1830 family home, seats about 100 guests in five dining rooms. From shrimp bisque to spinach salad and steak or seafood, everything on the menu is well prepared and tasty. (Ask Betty about the home's ghosts.) Prices fall in the moderate range, and hours are Thurs through Sat 5:30 to 9 p.m.

Wilcox County, which promises good fishing, attracts out-of-state deer and turkey hunters, and many make their headquarters at nearby **Roland Cooper State Park** at 285 Deer Run Drive (334-682-4838; alapark.com/rolandcooper). Paved campsites with 30 amp electric hookups, plus water and sewer are available with bathrooms and showers nearby. The state park offers forty-seven campsites and thirteen primitive sites. The park also offers one dog-friendly cabin as well as five completely furnished two-bedroom cabins. A new addition is four two-bedroom "tiny house" cabins that are fully furnished. Smoking is not permitted in any of the cabins. For more information on Camden and the surrounding area, call the Wilcox Area Chamber of Commerce at (334) 682-4929, visit wilcoxareachamber.com, or stop by at 1001 Earl Hilliard Road.

Traveling south from Camden on State Route 265 takes you by **Rikard's Mill**, just north of Beatrice. Stop by to browse through the **Covered Bridge Gift Shop** and watch the old-fashioned water-powered gristmill in operation. You'll also find a restored blacksmith shop and hiking trails. Open Apr through mid-Dec on Sat from 9 a.m. to 5 p.m. Call (251) 789-2781 or (251) 575-7433. Modest admission.

Continue south to **Monroeville** where Alabama authors Truman Capote and Harper Lee played as children. Harper Lee thinly disguised Monroeville in her book as Scout's hometown "Maycomb" and the town welcomes Lee fans. The Monroe County Heritage Museum in the **Old Monroe County Courthouse** is often a first stop. This stately 1903 courthouse was the model for movie scenes where Scout's father, lawyer Atticus Finch (played by Gregory Peck in the film), fights valiantly to save a black man accused of rape.

Lee's Real Life Characters

The Old Monroe County Courthouse also has displays about Lee and her next door neighbor Truman Capote.

Born in New Orleans and shuttled among relatives, Capote lived with his aunts in Monroeville as a youngster. Capote was the inspiration for the *Mockingbird* character of Dill with his snow-white hair "that stuck to his head like duck fluff." Kids often picked on the young boy because he was small and a smart aleck. However, Capote wouldn't fight.

Lee, on the other hand, was a tomboy and not above punching boys or kicking their shins.

Townspeople claim the character of *Mockingbird*'s Boo Radley (played by Robert Duval in his movie debut) was based on a real Monroeville teen who spent his life locked up by his father.

The boy, Alfred "Son" Boulware, and two other boys stole cigarettes from a local market. When Son was sentenced to a year in reform school, his father implored the judge to release the teen into his care, promising the boy would never get in trouble again. To ensure that he didn't, the father kept his son imprisoned at home where the boy grew old and became a legendary ghostly figure. If a ball went into the Boulware yard, townspeople said, youngsters would draw straws for who had to go get it because a crazy man lived there.

The upstairs courtroom is where Lee's father, attorney Amasa Lee, tried his cases and where his young daughter watched spellbound from the balcony. Outside the courthouse is a sculpture of Scout, Jem, and Dill sitting on a park bench and reading a copy of *To Kill a Mockingbird*. Down the street is the assisted living facility where Lee spent the final years of her life before she died on February 19, 2016 at age 89.

During the last weekend in April and the first three weekends in May, visitors can watch the stage version of *To Kill a Mockingbird* in a bona fide courtroom setting. Produced by the Mockingbird Players, the local stage adaptation boasts the authenticity of the story's actual location plus cultural awareness and genuine Southern accents.

Don't miss this performance, whose first act takes place on the courthouse lawn when a historic automobile and a mule-drawn wagon arrive for the trial. The Mockingbird Players also draw the audience into the play by choosing members from the audience to fill seats of the all-white, all-male jury, which, of course, convicts defendant Tom Robinson. For more information, visit the website at monroecountymuseum.org.

alabamatrivia

More than half a century after Harper Lee's novel was released, a "newly discovered sequel" called *Go Set a Watchman* was published on July 14, 2015 from Lee's early drafts of *Mockingbird*. The book's release was highly controversial for fans of Lee's work.

Before leaving town, head to the **Ol' Curiosities & Book Shoppe** to pick up a copy of *To Kill a Mockingbird* or *Go Set a Watchman* as a souvenir.

Dip into the town's rich literary heritage at the **Old Courthouse Museum** (251-575-7433; monroecountymuseum. org), which also features changing exhibits related to Monroe County's past and a gift shop with works by area artists. Adjacent to the courtroom, you'll see an informative Harper Lee exhibit with archival photos, quotes, and a continuous video of local citizens sharing anecdotes from the 1930s. Museum folks can share plenty of firsthand information on the town, its celebrated authors, and the Monroe County Heritage Museums. The museum is located at 31 North Alabama Avenue; admission is $5 per person. Hours run Mon through Fri from 10 a.m. to 4 p.m., Sat 10 a.m. to 2 p.m.

The Quilters of Gee's Bend Create a Bridge to the World

To visit the home of the famed quilters whose works captured the imagination of people across the country, head to Camden and board the **Gee's Bend Ferry**. (Former Senator John McCain did this during his presidential campaign.) Created by four generations of African-American women whose quilts have been called bold, colorful, and unique, the *New York Times* described their designs and needlecraft as "some of the most miraculous works of modern art America has produced."

The quilters work at Boykin Nutrition Center, and a nearby building houses their current inventory of colorful quilts, which sell for prices ranging from $1,500 to $4,000. The Quilts of Gee's Bend exhibit has intrigued gallery goers to Boston's Museum of Fine Arts, Atlanta's High Museum, and others across the country. The women have also been featured in such publications as *House and Garden,* Oprah's *O* magazine, *Newsweek,* and *Country Home* and on National Public Radio and CBS's *Sunday Morning.*

The quilters struck a chord with people everywhere. To see some of the quilts, visit quiltsofgeesgbend.com or call the Gee's Bend Foundation at (256) 679-9423.

To reach Gee's Bend, located in a curve of the Alabama River about thirty miles southwest of Selma, forget the long way via Wilcox County Route 29 and take the ferry from Camden. For schedules, rates, and more information on the Gee's Bend Ferry, see geesbendferry.com.

Monroeville—Literary Capital of Alabama

In recognition of the exceptional literary heritage of Monroeville and Monroe County, the Alabama legislature designated this region the **Literary Capital of Alabama** in a 1997 joint resolution. Author of "A Christmas Memory," *In Cold Blood, Breakfast at Tiffany's,* and other classics, Truman Capote spent idyllic hours roaming the town as a youngster along with friend Harper Lee, who penned the Pulitzer Prize–winning novel *To Kill a Mockingbird.*

Other writers who have called Monroeville home include nationally syndicated columnist Cynthia Tucker and novelist Mark Childress. The small town of Monroeville, which packs a rich literary history, hosts an Alabama Writers Symposium the first weekend in April. For more information on this event, contact the Coastal Alabama Community College at 2800 South Alabama Avenue, Monroeville, AL 36430 or call (251) 575-3156 or visit coastalalabama.edu.

Afterward, take a walking tour around town, where several buildings feature murals illustrating scenes from *To Kill a Mockingbird.* While downtown, stop by **Finishing Touches** (251-575-2066) at 18 East Claiborne Street. You'll enjoy browsing through this shop with lovely handmade items, antiques, kitchen accessories, gifts, clothing for children and ladies, customized baskets, and books.

Before leaving the area, you might want to visit the **River Heritage Museum**, housed in the old Corps of Engineers building at the Claiborne Lock & Dam. The surrounding region is a great place for camping and fishing, too. Located about eighteen miles from the square in downtown Monroeville, the museum can be reached by taking State Route 41 to County Road 17 and then following the signs to the Claiborne Lock & Dam. The museum's exhibits feature fossils, Native American artifacts, and steamboat relics. The museum is open for special events or by appointment only. A great time to visit is the annual Alabama River Festival in March when reenactors and demonstrators create a frontier encampment from the late 1700s and early 1800s. Admission is free. For more information call (251) 575–7433.

Gulf Coast Delta

After your timberland excursion head south to Escambia County, where traveling pilgrims can spend an authentic Thanksgiving Day with the Poarch Band of Creek Indians at their annual Pow Wow. Tribal members welcome friends, relatives, and visitors to help them celebrate Thanksgiving Day on the **Poarch Creek Reservation**, eight miles northwest of Atmore at 5811 Jack

Springs Road. Festivities include exhibition dancing by tribes from throughout the country, a greased pig chase, turkey shoot, and much more. You can feast on roasted corn, Indian fry bread, ham, fried chicken, or traditional turkey and dressing. Booths feature beadwork, basketry, silver work, and other Native American crafts. Take a lawn chair, camera, and your appetite. Modest admission. For more information on this event, call (251) 368-9136 or visit pci-nsn.gov.

Continue southwest toward the Eastern Shore and stop by Malbis, twelve miles east of Mobile on US 90. On Baldwin County Road 27, you'll find the *Malbis Plantation Greek Orthodox Church*. This magnificent neo-Byzantine–style structure, built at a cost of more than $1 million, was dedicated to the memory of Jason Malbis. A former monk who emigrated from Greece in 1906, Malbis traveled through thirty-six states before selecting this Baldwin County site to establish Malbis Plantation (virtually a self-supporting colony that grew to cover 2,000 acres).

The marble in this edifice came from the same Greek quarries used to build Athens' ancient Parthenon. The majestic interior features a dark-blue 75-foot domed ceiling, stained glass windows, mosaics, and murals. Greek artists spent eight months completing the paintings that extend from the cathedral's entrance to its altar. Except for Christmas Day, the church is open daily, and admission is free. Hours run from 10 a.m. to 4 p.m. For tour information call (251) 626-3050.

Next swing westward to *Daphne*, perched on Mobile Bay's Eastern Shore where fishing is a popular pastime. If you want to stretch your legs and maybe get a glimpse of alligators or other wildlife, take a stroll along *Daphne's Gator Alley Boardwalk*. The half-mile boardwalk over D'Olive Creek opened in 2004 and recently underwent about $769,000 worth of renovations. Located at 29281 North Main Street, the free boardwalk is open dawn to dusk.

After exploring Daphne continue south to *Fairhope*, a charming flower-filled town founded about 1894 on the "single tax" concept of economist Henry George, who considered land the source of all wealth. The Fairhope Single Tax Colony still functions today, one of the country's few model communities operating on George's taxation theories. A percentage of the town's property is held by the Fairhope Single Tax Colony office, and a resident can lease his or her land for 99 years (or perpetuity). The resident pays a single annual tax on the land only—not on improvements—and this yearly payment covers school district, city, county, and state taxes as well as community services.

Whether or not you hear the cry of "Jubilee!" during your visit to the Eastern Shore of Mobile Bay, you can see this strange spectacle depicted in a photo display at *Manci's Antique Club* (251-626-9917; mancisantiqueclub

Weird But True: Fishing Jubilees

It sounds too far-fetched to be true. But local folks swear the phenomenon known as "Jubilee" actually happen.

It all starts with a phone call to a select few, usually in the middle of the night. Then the message is relayed with shouts of "Jubilee."

And the fishing is on.

Seems strange to call it fishing. It's more like gathering: Fish, shrimp, crabs, and other sea critters crawl, flop, or wobble up on the shore. All folks have to do is go around and pick them up.

Although jubilees have been reported in other areas, Mobile Bay is probably the only body of water in which this phenomenon occurs regularly, according to the Auburn University Marine Extension and Research Center in Mobile.

What causes them? The whole scientific explanation involves oxygen, salty water, fresh river water, wind, and too much plant matter. Fish and shellfish trapped by jubilee conditions behave very strangely. But their behavior is simply an attempt to get enough oxygen to survive, the research center says.

Since they cannot get the oxygen they need from the water as they normally do, they try to get it from the air. Jubilee-affected blue crabs can be seen blowing bubbles from their mouths while clinging to pilings. Flounder often lie at the water's edge gulping air and passing it over their gills. Eels leave the water and burrow tail-first into the moist sand, leaving their heads in the air with their mouths open.

Jubilees happen most often along the Bay's upper eastern shore from Great Point Clear to just north of Daphne. Jubilees also occasionally occur south of Point Clear to Mullet Point and on the western shore at Deer River and Dog River. Jubilees may affect the entire eastern shore from Daphne to Mullet Point, a distance of about fifteen miles. Or, they may be limited to only a few hundred feet of beach. The smaller, localized jubilees occur more often than the larger ones but are more difficult to locate. They occur only in the summer, between June and September, usually in the early morning before sunrise. You have to stumble on the happening yourself or be one of the lucky ones on a call list to participate. It's said that the weird event probably happens more often than people know. It's just that nobody is around to see it.

Sometimes it's primarily flounder that congregate. At other times, it might be a shrimp jubilee or crab jubilee. Most generally all three species plus a few other fish like shiners, anchovies, and small catfish, along with some eels, are involved.

Some lucky people have no trouble at all filling up buckets, sacks, and even wash tubs with the high-priced delicacies of the deep. When the sun comes up, all returns to normal. Then the affected fish and shellfish that haven't been hauled away for dinner tables then swim back to their bottom-water habitat—until the next jubilee.

.com) in downtown Daphne. Located at 1715 Main Street, this combination bar/museum (originally opened as a gas station in 1924 by Frank Manci, converted to its current status in 1947 by Arthur Manci, and now operated by a third-generation family member, Alex Manci) houses a rickshaw, oxen yokes, and Victrolas. You'll also see collections of antique tools, cowbells, political campaign buttons, and Native American artifacts. The club boasts the biggest assemblage of Jim Beam decanters outside the distillery's own collection. Claiming the title "Bloody Mary Capital of the Eastern Shore," the house serves its specialty garnished with a pickled string bean. A sign over the bar promises free beer tomorrow.

Those who visit the ladies' room at Manci's will see the wooden figure of a man—dressed only in a fig leaf. The observant will notice the fig leaf is hinged, and the curious might go even further. Unrestrained curiosity can soon turn to horror, however, because a blaring alarm alerts all within hearing distance that one possesses an inquisitive nature. One then must make the uncomfortable choice of exiting—red-faced—to the merriment of Manci's patrons or occupying the ladies' room till closing time. An off switch has been added so as not to interfere with Manci's live music. Manci's hours are Tues through Thurs 3:30 to 11 p.m.; Fri and Sat 11 a.m. to 11 p.m.; Sun 10 a.m. to 2 p.m. for brunch.

Save plenty of time for strolling through the pages of this storybook town with baskets of colorful blossoms cascading from every street corner and rose gardens galore in its bayfront park. Downtown art galleries, boutiques, and eateries beckon browsers. Indulge your whims as you pass restaurants featuring coastal cuisine fresh from the Gulf and shops offering everything from antiques, toys, and custom-designed clothing to nautical gear.

Wander to the **Eastern Shore Art Center** (251-928-2228) at 401 Oak Street and view its current exhibits. Top that off with individual galleries that call your name. At Fairhope's monthly First Friday Artwalk, you can hop a free trolley or stroll a 5-block area to visit galleries like Lyons Share and Summit. For a great local souvenir, stop by the **Christine Linson Gallery** (251-929-2015) at 386 Fairhope Avenue and pick up a pack of note cards depicting local scenes.

On a trip to Alabama in 1998, Christine painted the town (in watercolor) and fell in love with its charms. She promptly returned to her lifelong home in Cleveland, Ohio, packed her belongings, moved to Fairhope, and opened her gallery. In addition to her popular Fairhope and Eastern Shore prints and limited edition Christmas cards, you'll see original floral and figurative art work. Open Mon through Sat 10 a.m. to 5 p.m. Check out christinelinson.com for a peek at the artist's portfolio.

Hosts Becky and Bill Jones and Judy Smith also welcome visitors to **Bay Breeze Guest House** at 742 South Mobile Street on historic Mobile Bay, where they can watch the glorious sunsets, go beachcombing or fishing, and feed the resident ducks. Ask Becky, a former biology teacher, about the local jubilee phenomenon. From May through September, guests can enjoy breakfast served on Bay Breeze's pier. Moderate rates. For reservations at either property, call (866) 928-8976.

South of Fairhope at Point Clear (designated "Punta Clara" on sixteenth-century maps of Spanish explorers), you'll find the **Grand Hotel Resort, Golf Club & Spa** (251-928-9201 or 800-544-9933) on scenic US 98. This legendary resort on Mobile Bay offers facilities spreading over 550 lovely acres studded with moss-festooned oaks more than 300 years old. The locale has long attracted generations of wealthy Southern families—the site's first resort dates from the mid-1800s. Today's guests continue to enjoy "the Grand's" traditions, such as afternoon tea.

If hotels possess survival instincts, the Grand's got an instinct second to none. The Queen of Southern Resorts refused to accept Hurricane Katrina's ravages and soon regrouped, rebuilt, and refurbished. No stranger to adversity, the grande dame emerged from her own tsunami in the same manner she rebounded after Civil War shelling and fire during the past century and a half.

So settle in and set off on a stroll or Segway tour to see the glorious grounds. Look for the life-size bronze statue of local legend, **Bucky Miller**. Known for his incredible photographic memory, Bucky (as he was fondly known) called hotel guests by name even when years had lapsed between their visits. He greeted everyone warmly and personified the Grand's legendary hospitality during his 64-year tenure. Presiding over the Bird Cage Lounge, he delighted guests with his famous mint juleps. Though Bucky died in 2002, his spirit lives on at the Grand, and his statue was dedicated on Kentucky Derby Day in 2005.

The resort has consistently earned Four Diamond status each year since 1977 when AAA tourism editors started their awards for excellence. With so much to enjoy, from fine dining and a world-class spa to water recreation, tennis, and challenging golf courses, you'll want to check out grand1847.com and check in soon after. Call for current vacation packages and reservations at this family-friendly historical hotel. Deluxe.

Be sure to visit a candy shop called **Punta Clara Kitchen** (800-437-7868; puntaclara.com), located in an 1897 gingerbread house a mile south of the Grand Hotel at 17111 Scenic Highway 98. Here you can sample confections from pecan butter crunch and divinity to chocolate-covered bourbon balls and buckeyes (balls of creamy peanut-butter confections hand-dipped in chocolate). The shop also sells jellies, recipe books, pickles, and preserves. Before leaving, take a few minutes to look around this historic home, furnished as it was during the late 1800s. Hours are Mon through Sat 9 a.m. to 5 p.m., and Sun 12:30 to 5 p.m.

The Hut of the Poet of Tolstoy Park

Founded in 1894 by a group of utopian dreamers, Fairhope has a way of inviting folks to be themselves, to quietly look inside and see what makes them special. One of those unusual characters has left a strange sort of tourist attraction that still draws visitors today.

Henry Stuart moved to Fairhope from Idaho because he was told he was dying, that he only had a year to live. The doctor was wrong.

Diagnosed with consumption in the 1920s, Stuart lived another two decades after moving to Fairhope. Known as the Hermit of Montrose (a neighborhood in Fairhope), Stuart built himself a small round hurricane-proof hut out of concrete. He made all the bricks himself and put the date on each one.

An admirer of famed author Tolstoy, Stuart named his patch of ground Tolstoy Park. It took him over a year to build his hut, which was shaped somewhat like a beehive. He decided he wasn't going to wear shoes but then he found out he needed one shoe to use a shovel so he went to a store and tried to buy one shoe for his right foot. When they said they couldn't sell just one shoe, he bought the pair and told them to keep the left shoe for someone who needed it.

Stuart was said to have earned a living by weaving rugs. Stuart died in 1946 at 88 years old. His hut still stands, now surrounded by office buildings. It rests just off the parking lot of a real estate office. If you can't find it, ask townsfolks and they can probably point you in the right direction.

For a fascinating read, look for Sonny Brewer's 2006 novel, *The Poet of Tolstoy Park*. The hut is open to the public any time. Guests can visit and take a book or leave a book. Guests often leave a few coins as well.

Behind the Victorian home stands a weathered cedar and cypress structure that originally served as a laundry and wine cellar. It now houses **The Wash House Restaurant** (251-928-4838; washhouserestaurant.com) at 17111 Scenic Highway 98, a great place to savor Southern coastal cuisine. The restaurant features the original working fireplace and wash pot, nowadays in the softly lit bar. Behind the building, a large deck under ancient live oaks makes a romantic setting for dinner.

Owners Wade Selsor and Robert Yarbrough learned their way around the kitchen as kids growing up in Camden, a small town south of Selma. "Wade develops the recipes, but we both play around with them," said Robert, noting they also draw from a broad spectrum of family favorites.

Entree options include savory rack of lamb, seared tuna steak, and chateaubriand, a succulent cut from the heart of the tenderloin, served with potato casserole and blackened asparagus. Green Goddess dressing makes Wade's salads memorable, and his delicious key lime bread pudding offers a different twist. Open Sun through Thurs 5 to 9 p.m.; Fri and Sat 5 to 10 p.m. Reservations are encouraged. Moderate.

Ready for an anti-stress kind of place? Then head for nearby *Magnolia Springs*, where you can unwind in a serene setting of dappled sunlight and live oaks. In its heyday as a resort area during the early part of the 1900s, Magnolia Springs lured visitors with twice-a-day train service from Chicago, St. Louis, and Cincinnati. "Many a consumptive, rheumatic, nervous, worn-out and over-worked person whose case was thought hopeless by the physicians has found health and a new lease on life by spending a few months at Magnolia Springs," states an early promotional pamphlet.

Once known as the Sunnyside Hotel, the *Magnolia Springs Bed & Breakfast* (251-965-7321 or 800-965-7321; magnoliasprings.com) at 14469 Oak Street exudes a friendly aura with its welcoming wraparound porch accented by a swing, wicker furniture, rocking chairs, and ferns. One of the county's three re-maining hotels from the resort era, the historic structure is painted a buttery yellow with white trim. Committed to providing warm hospitality, innkeepers David Worthington and Eric Bigelow welcome guests to their 1867 home, nourish them with a delicious breakfast, and recommend local excursions. If you go cruising down the river, you'll see mailboxes at the water's edge. Magnolia Springs' first postmaster launched a mail service by water in 1915, and many residents still get their mail delivered by boat. "It's one of only a few places in the country with a water mail route," says David. Moderate to deluxe rates.

Magnolia Spring B&B Salsa Scramble

Magnolia Springs Bed & Breakfast is known for its delicious cuisine. A popular dish is the Salsa Scramble which the hosts say is easy to prepare and serve. Try it and see.

1 can Mexicorn, drained

2 cans black beans, drained

2 bunches green onions, chopped

2 cans Rotel tomatoes

2 tomatoes, chopped

1 bunch fresh cilantro, chopped

salt and pepper to taste

Mix all ingredients and let sit overnight. The next morning, add as little or as much as preferred to raw scrambled eggs. Cook until eggs are done. The mixture also could be spooned on the side of the scrambled eggs if diners would prefer not to have it cooked in the eggs. Some people like more mixture than others so this is an easy way to let them do it themselves.

A short stroll down tree-lined Oak Street takes you to *Jesse's Restaurant* at 14770 Oak Street. The restaurant is named in honor of the beloved shop-keeper at Moore's Store, which is now closed. Jesse King reportedly never missed a day of work for more than sixty years at the store. You can enjoy lunch Mon through Sat from 11 a.m. to 4 p.m. Dinner hours: Mon through Thurs 5 to 9 p.m.; Fri and Sat 5 to 10 p.m. Evening specials might mean prime rib, shrimp scampi, or whiskey steak. Other popular entrees include crab cakes, Cajun fettuccine, stuffed flounder, and chicken Pontalba. Moderate prices.

Across the road from Jesse's stands *Magnolia Springs Park*, which showcases one of the town's springs and makes an inviting shady retreat.

After basking in Magnolia Springs' serenity, head for *Foley*, situated around the intersection of US 98 and State Route 59. The town offers not only factory-outlet shopping but a host of attractions such as antiques malls, arts centers, and charming eateries.

Start your tour at 111 West Laurel Avenue with the *Baldwin Museum of Art* and the *Holmes Medical Museum* (251-970-1818), housed in a building that dates to the early 1900s. After viewing the current downstairs art exhibits, climb to the second floor for a close-up look at instruments and memorabilia from medicine's earlier years. Once a hospital for Baldwin County residents, the rooms contain an operating suite complete with table, bone-breaking appar-atus, Kelly pad, ether container, and attendant tubes. Also on display are X-ray equipment and medical cabinets filled with delivery forceps, tonsil guillotine and snare, and other instruments. In addition to patient quarters, you can inspect a room devoted to quackery paraphernalia—a color spectrum device for treating everything from headaches to kidney infections, barber bowl for bleeding patients, and diagrammed phrenology skull. Hours are Mon through Sat 10 a.m. to 2 p.m. Admission is free.

Take a break next door at *Stacey Olde Tyme Soda Fountain* (251-943-7191), with its sweet drinks from the past. In this delightful pharmacy at 121 West Laurel Avenue, you can savor a banana split, slurp on an ice-cream soda, cherry Coke, or chocolate milk shake, and listen to old favorites from the jukebox or player piano while watching a toy train make its rounds above the soda fountain. A penny scale reveals your weight and fate. Hours run Mon through Fri from 8 a.m. to 6 p.m., and Sat 9 a.m. to 5 p.m. Economical rates.

Continuing to the next block, you'll find *The Gift Horse* (251-943-3663; thegifthorserestaurantandantiques.com), located at 209 West Laurel Avenue. Beyond the restaurant's leaded-glass doors, you'll see a grand banquet table with a buffet of salads, vegetables, meats, breads, and desserts. House special-ties include fried biscuits, spinach soufflé, mystery crab-shrimp salad, and the restaurant's famous apple cheese—all prepared from owner Jackie O. McLeod's recipes. Hours are 11 a.m. to 8:30 p.m. daily. Rates are moderate. Jackie's cookbook, available in the gift shop, makes a great souvenir and divulges some of her culinary secrets. While in Foley you may want to visit the *Gift Horse Antique Centre*, too.

To see the work of artists and craftspeople who live throughout the Southeast, stop at the *Foley Art Center* at 211 North McKenzie Street. Classes also are offered. Open Tues through Fri 10 a.m. to 4 p.m., Sat 10 a.m. to 2 p.m. The *Graham Creek Nature Preserve* (251-923-4267; grahamcreekpreserve. org) offers almost 500 acres of forests, tidal marshes, wetlands and pine savannas. Located at 23004 Wolf Bay Drive, the nature preserve features a 5-mile hiking trail, canoe and kayak launch, 7.5-mile bicycling trail, two disc golf courses, picnic areas, and more. Opened in 2016, the *Graham Creek Nature Center* at 23030 Wolf Bay Drive is home to live native reptile exhibits and other educational displays. The area is known for its bird watching. The nature preserve is open daily from dawn to dusk. The Nature Center is open Mon through Sat from 10 a.m. to 4 p.m.

Follow US 98 east to *Elberta*. During the first half of the century, this fertile area attracted families from central, northern, and southern Europe, as well as Quebec. At Elberta's *German Sausage Festivals*, staged on the last Saturday of March and October, descendants of early settlers dress in native attire to perform Old World dances. Spearheaded by Elberta's Volunteer Fire Department in 1978, the two festivals are used to make improvement for the fire department and the town. The tasty sausage recipe has changed over the years but the original recipe is credited to Alfred Stucki, manager of Elberta's Locker Plant from 1953 until his death in 1973. Call (251) 986-5805 or visit elbertafire.com for more information.

To learn more about the ethnic diversity and lifestyles of the county's early settlers, stop by the *Baldwin County Heritage Museum* (251-986-8375), a half-mile east of Elberta at 25521 US 98. In front of the five-acre wooded setting called "Frieden Im Wald," you'll see a working windmill and several outdoor agricultural exhibits.

Displays inside the museum feature the Kee tool collection and vintage farm equipment, a printing press, and an interior section of a post office from Josephine, Alabama. Household items include an Edison phonograph, antique sewing machines, stoves, cooking utensils, and washing machines. Also on display are old-fashioned school desks, folk sculpture, and a moonshine still. You'll also find a blacksmith shop and a church that dates to 1908. The museum is staffed entirely by volunteers, many of them snowbirds from Minnesota, Wisconsin, Michigan, New York, and other northern states, as well as Canada, who contribute their time and skills to restoring artifacts and putting old machinery in running order again. Admission is free. Hours are Wed through Sat 10 a.m. to 3 p.m. Weekday tours can be arranged by appointment.

At 12695 County Road 95 in Elberta, you can study carnivorous plants like Venus flytrap, pitcher plants, and other unusual botanical specimens native to the area at **Biophilia Nature Center**. Biophilia is the human love for living things.

"Different kinds of wildlife can be seen in season," said Carol Lovell-Saas, who promotes environmental education and takes you on a walk through her "open book of nature" that spreads across twenty acres. Tours offer a mini-course in butterfly gardening for the South or the Midwest and include free pamphlets on each plus literature on eco-gardening.

From spring through early winter, several kinds of showy native butterflies are raised indoors and outdoors, allowing visitors to observe all stages from egg to adult. You'll see forest wildflower meadows and swamp, now being restored with 300 native species, and can stop by a plant nursery and bookstore on the premises. Contact (251) 987-1200 for specific directions. Tours are offered by appointment only. Check out biophilia.net.

Afterward make your way back to Foley, then follow State Route 59 south to the glistening white sands of **Gulf Shores**. Although a Diners' Club publication once conferred highest honors on the stretch of shoreline along the Florida panhandle between Destin and Panama City, calling it "the world's most perfect beach," fewer people know about the other end of the Southern Riviera—Alabama's toehold on the Gulf of Mexico. In fact, the relatively new town of Gulf Shores did not appear on Alabama's official highway map until the 1960s. But a retreat offering sugar-sand beaches and a balmy climate cannot remain a secret forever, and this 32-mile crescent known as Pleasure Island (once a peninsula) now attracts vacationers from across the country.

Each year, *Southern Living* magazine gives some 16 million readers the chance to vote for their favorite places in the Best of the South Readers' Choice Awards. And Gulf Shores always ranks among the favorites in the Beach Town/ Resort category. Renourishment programs have made the white-sand playground even wider and just as enticing as before the hurricane visitations. You can check out the new Alabama Gulf Coast for yourself at gulfshores.com.

Although some people still picture Alabama as being land locked, it has a marvelous Gulf Coast. With its toehold on the Gulf of Mexico, Alabama's Gulf Coast is bordered on the north by the Intracoastal Waterway, on the west by Mobile Bay, on the south by the Gulf of Mexico and on the east by Perdido Bay. The 30,000-acre island is home to Alabama's deep sea fishing charter fleet with a wealth of boats available, each equipped with electronic fish-finding and navigation devices and operated by a licensed captain.

Inland seas are framed by the shade of century-old live oaks and pines. Freshwater lakes, river and bayous and coves add nearly 400,000 acres of protected waterfront to the area.

With thirty-two miles of sugar white beaches, windswept dunes, balmy ocean breezes, evening stargazing so incredible you can almost dance on the Milky Way, the Alabama Gulf Coast has proven a magical place for many people.

Mother Nature's Water Miracles

In Orange Beach, the 53-foot pontoon boat *Miss Janet* has just left the dock for another excursion cruise. Beneath a sunny sky, the emerald waters stretch to the horizon. Dolphin leap alongside the boat, seagulls follow in its wake.

One of the best ways to enjoy Orange Beach waterways is to take a cruise with Captain Skip Beebe on his **Sailaway Charters** aboard the *Miss Janet* or the 48-foot ketch *Windy Ways*.

Since starting his business in 1996, Skip has educated thousands of visitors about the diverse wildlife of his Orange Beach home. "It's never the same," he said. "But it is always interesting."

On this two-hour cruise, everyone moves to the front of the boat for a "tonging" demonstration. Using what looks like two giant forks joined together, Skip reaches into an oyster bed to pluck some oysters.

The forks are the only way to take oysters from Alabama public oyster reefs besides using your hands, Skip said. American Indians used the same tonging method to dig oysters when the first European settlers arrived. The Indians would stand in hollowed out trees and twirl sticks around to harvest oysters. Indians knew that oysters were down there because they saw them at low tide.

Bottle-nosed dolphins are a common sight around these parts, darting and splashing around the pontoon boat. Have your camera ready!

As the boat pulls into deeper water, a crewmember drops a net overboard for a few minutes of trawling, Skip hauls it back in and dumps its contents into a seawater aquarium on the boat. Digging his hands into the tank, Skip pulls out one treasure after another—a tiny jellyfish, anchovy, stingrays, ocean gar, squid, shrimp, eels, small speckled trout and a puffer fish.

One by one, Skip separates the contents of the tank. He explains what each critter is and how it lives, then gently slips it back into the water. Boat passengers have a chance to touch many of the creatures and ask as many questions as they like.

Sailaway Charters is located at 24231 Gulf Bay Road in Orange Beach. Open daily from 8 a.m. to 6 p.m. Rates are $29 per person. Sailaway Charters also offers other cruises and beach walks with Captain Skip. For more information, call (251) 974-5055 or visit sailorskip.com.

Situated on the shores of the Intracoastal Waterway at **Orange Beach, The Wharf** is a 200-acre resort and entertainment center less than two miles from the area's beckoning beaches. Here, in a holiday atmosphere, you can stroll along the boardwalk and browse through boutiques, local shops, and major retail stores. You can take in an exciting concert at the amphitheater or take a spin on the Southeast's largest Ferris wheel. The complex offers restaurants, upscale accommodations, a much-acclaimed destination spa, an outfitter's center, and a marina with public and private boat slips. Condominiums at Levin's Bend stretch for half a mile. **The Wharf** lures locals and visitors alike with something for everyone. Visit alwharf.com for a look at what's happening this season on Alabama's Gulf Coast.

Some 100 charter boats dock at nearby Orange Beach marinas, offering outings from sunset cruises to fishing excursions. Surrounding waters feature world-class fishing throughout the year. (For information about state fishing licenses, call 334-242-3829 or 888-848-6887, or check out outdooralabama.com.)

While in Orange Beach, consider signing up for a cruise aboard the **Blue Dolphin** at Alabama Point to view this stretch of the Gulf Coast's spectacular inland waterways. You'll view other native wildlife and pass beautiful Ono Island, where several celebrities own luxury homes. Call (251) 981-2774 for reservations on this 51-foot, 45-passenger air-conditioned pontoon boat with inside and outside seating. Passengers board at 29603 Perdido Beach Boulevard just across the road from the Flora-Bama. Passengers see dolphins almost every time they go out. And because the boat sits so low in the water, passengers feel like they can almost reach out and touch the dolphins. Check out bluedolphincruises.com for more information. Normal business hours are daily 8 a.m. to 8 p.m.

To see some secluded portions of the area, sign up for a barefoot cruise aboard the **Daedalus**. Based at 5749 Bay La Launch, you'll find the 50-foot sailboat at Bear Point Marina in Orange Beach. Because the big vessel performs in shallow water, passengers can visit hidden bayous and bays and even venture onto an uninhabited beach. Also, you'll enjoy watching cavorting dolphins, ospreys, blue herons, and other wildlife. To book your passage call (251) 987-1228 or click on sailthedaedalus.com for more information.

You'll find good eating at **King Neptune's Seafood Restaurant** (251-968-5464; kingneptuneseafoodrestaurant.com) at 1137 Gulf Shores Parkway. Al Sawyer, known as the King of Crustaceans and the Prince of Prawns, owns the popular dining spot. Because Sawyer knows his seafood, visitors and locals alike flock to his places for oysters, Royal Red shrimp, and crab claws. The restaurateur, who has appeared on the Travel Channel's *Lonely Planet* and Bobby Flay's *Food Nation* on the Food Channel, serves only oysters from Bon

Flora-Bama: Home of the Annual Mullet Toss

Jimmy Buffett used to come here and jam. John Grisham wrote about it in a novel. It's the area's hottest hangout—the **Flora-Bama**, boasting an identity all its own. Located ten minutes from Gulf Shores on the Alabama/Florida line, the place bills itself as "one of the nation's last great roadhouse watering holes."

"You never know what'll be going on here," says a local. The crowd is mixed, and so is the music—everything from country to rock and roll—and mostly original music. Flora-Bama offers entertainment every day of the year and attracts throngs including now-and-future-famous musicians and songwriters.

The party heats up after 5 p.m., and the parking lot gets full fast. Though success often invites duplication, Flora-Bama's idiosyncratic style and haphazard floor plan make cloning a remote possibility. A No Tears in the Beer demolition and rebuilding party took place after Hurricane Ivan dealt the place a big blow. Then, in 2005, along came Katrina dumping sand. In spite of it all, they have continued to function, and have had music every day.

You can also take in the annual Interstate Mullet Toss, held the last full weekend in April. (What's a mullet toss? An event on the beach where people vie for the dubious distinction of pitching a dead fish the greatest distance—from Florida to Alabama.)

If your April calendar is too full to fit in the Mullet Toss, there's always next January 1 and the Polar Bear Dip. After testing the Gulf of Mexico's cold waters, you can warm up with a serving of black-eyed peas—the traditional Southern dish declared to bring good luck throughout the year. (The luck intensifies if you consume collards or other greens, and adding hog jowl almost guarantees more luck than you can stand.)

Otherwise you can meander around, buy souvenirs, consume beverages, visit the **Beach Oyster Bar**, eat crab claws or Royal Reds (the very best of steamed shrimp), purchase lottery tickets, or converse with other patrons. The person standing next to you might have a total of five dollars in his jeans pocket or five million on his net worth statement.

Located at 17401 Perdido Key Drive, with a Pensacola zip, Flora-Bama (850-492-0611 in Florida or 251-980-5118 in Alabama) opens daily at 9 a.m. and shuts down in the wee hours. Check florabama.com for more information.

Secour Fisheries and Alabama wild shrimp. King Neptune's is open daily from 11 a.m. to 9 p.m.

During the second weekend of October, more than 300,000 seafood lovers flock to **Gulf Shores' National Shrimp Festival** to eat shrimp, enjoy music, and look at arts and crafts, as well as fine art, created and presented by more than 200 artists. The Alabama Gulf Coast Area Chamber of Commerce produces this festival. Visit myshrimpfest.com for information. Speaking of shrimp, this

Birders Flock to Alabama Gulf Coast

An osprey wings her way to a nest of hungry hatchlings. An elusive snowy plover makes a surprise appearance. Fun-loving loons show off their surfing skills. Migrating hawks move west over a picturesque old fort. And terns skitter on secluded sand dunes where patches of sea oats dance to the gulf breezes.

The Alabama Gulf Coast is a birder's paradise. Grab some binoculars, slip on comfortable walking shoes, and bring along a "life list" of birds to see. Whether an expert or a novice at bird watching, visitors are awed at the wealth of feathered friends that can be spotted on the beautiful Gulf Coast.

Birding is a rapidly growing hobby in Orange Beach and Gulf Shores. It's easy to see why. Located in the Mississippi Flyway—a major route for migratory birds—the coast is a prime destination for a wide variety of birds. At any season, birders are likely to spot a bevy of birds in the best possible surroundings. Many species are permanent residents, while others may spend only the summer or winter on the coast. Possibly the most exciting group is the transients, passing through during fall and spring migration. The fall migration of the Monarch butterflies is an added bonus.

Public areas with easy access for birders make excellent observation points. And the amenities offered by Gulf Shores and Orange Beach let bird watchers know that pursuing their beloved hobby doesn't mean they have to "rough it" or forego such pleasantries as comfortable accommodations, delicious cuisine, spectacular scenery and activities galore.

Uniquely surrounded by the alluring emerald waters of the Gulf of Mexico, sugar-white beaches, sleepy lagoons, secluded marshes, meandering rivers, century-old forests and wind-swept dunes, the Gulf Coast showcases the wonders of nature by land and by sea. Thousands of acres of reserves and preserves protect the abundant wildlife, marine life, and wildflowers. Opportunities abound to view them all in their natural habitats—up close and personal.

Now birders from all over the world can easily find some of the best bird-viewing locations thanks to the *Alabama Coastal Birding Trail*. A map introduces the trail that leads visitors from Orange Beach up through the Mobile-Tensaw Delta and down to Dauphin Island.

Arranged as a series of eight loops, the trail has 270 stops with directional and interpretive signs that are easy for birding enthusiasts to use. The loops are in close proximity to one another, so that several birding expeditions can be enjoyed in a short time.

Each loop is distinctive. The Fort Morgan Loop, for example, travels along the coast and provides opportunities to see herons, egrets, loons, gulls, and other shore birds. The Civil War-era fort is an excellent location for spring and fall neotropical migrants as well. One of the largest annual hummingbird banding events and other bird studies are conducted by the Hummer-Bird Study Group during the spring and fall migrations at Fort Morgan. This group welcomes the public to visit their site and observe the birds as they are given their free physicals and then released to continue their journey.

The Alabama Gulf coast is naturally beautiful but it has not stayed that way by accident. People from all walks of life have volunteered to keep their community among the most appealing in the world for residents, visitors, and wildlife alike. Annual beach cleanups, environmental water monitoring and just plain hard work and civic pride have helped preserve the treasures of the Gulf Coast.

The Alabama Coastal Birding Trail map can be downloaded at fws.gov/southeast/pdf/brochure/the-alabama-coastal-birding-trail.pdf

is the place to walk into a seafood outlet, just after the fleet has docked, and buy your dinner fresh from coastal waters. Many area fish markets will ice-pack local seafood for travel.

The tiny fishing village of **Bon Secour**, located west of State Route 59 between Foley and Gulf Shores, is home to several shrimp-packing operations. At some of these, you can crunch your way through oyster shells to watch the unloading process and buy the day's freshest catch directly off the boat. Look for signs along Baldwin County Road 10 that lead to several of these markets with their colorful shrimp boats on the Bon Secour River.

During the late 1700s French settlers staked a claim here, naming the area Bon Secour for "Safe Harbour." While driving around, notice the lovely little church, Our Lady of Bon Secour, framed with Spanish moss in its tree-shaded setting.

After dipping into the Gulf of Mexico's foaming waves and basking in the sunshine, you may want to sally forth to other points of interest, such as historic **Fort Morgan** (251-540-7127; fort-morgan.org). Located at the end of a scenic drive twenty-two miles west of Gulf Shores on State Route 180, the fort—built to guard Mobile Bay—played a major role during the Civil War. At the Battle of Mobile Bay on August 5, 1864, "torpedoes" (underwater mines) were strung across the channel to stop the Union fleet from entering. This strategy failed when Adm. David Farragut issued his famous command: "Damn the torpedoes—full speed ahead!"

Today's visitors can explore vaulted corridors and peer into dark rooms of this historic fort, named in honor of Revolutionary War hero Gen. Daniel Morgan. Designed by Simon Bernard, a French engineer and former aide-de-camp to Napoléon, the five-pointed-star structure pays tribute to the craftsmanship of men who labored from 1819 to 1834. As technology changed, the original fort continued to be modified and upgraded, said the curator. In the museum, exhibits cover military history from the fort's early days through World War II. Take one of the guided tours with a costumed guide to make history come alive. Be sure to put your fingers in your ears for the cannon-firing

Freakish Accident at Fort Morgan

If the walls of Fort Morgan could talk, imagine the tales they would tell. The old fort guarding Mobile Bay was the site of a freakish accident that visitors can learn about in the fort museum. It involves Charles S. Stewart, who died April 30, 1863.

Born in New York in 1828, Stewart moved to Alabama and became a successful merchant in Mobile and married Julia Brown. When Alabama seceded from the Union in 1861, Stewart cast his lot with his adopted state and joined the Mobile Cadets No. 2 of the Confederate army, proving to be a daring leader in the battles of Shiloh and Corinth.

Promoted to lieutenant colonel in May 1862, Stewart was placed in command of Fort Morgan. He regularly wrote long letters home to his wife, some of which are displayed at the fort museum. Amid rumors of a powerful Union ironclad fleet preparing to attack Fort Morgan, Stewart decided to ready the fort, testing its 33-pounder cannons.

On April 30, 1863, Stewart was standing by with other officers and his gun crew when one of the cannons was fired. Somehow by accident, the gun had been loaded with two powder charges instead of one. When the order to fire was given, the cannon exploded, spewing large pieces of metal.

Five soldiers were killed, including Stewart, who died instantly when a 200-pound fragment struck him in the head. Years later, Stewart's granddaughter placed a marker on the steps of Fort Morgan, at the exact spot where Stewart was killed. Tradition says that stains from Stewart's blood are still visible on the steps.

alabamatrivia

Isabella de Soto planted America's first fig trees, which came over from Spain, at Fort Morgan.

demonstration. Loud! Except for major holidays, the museum is open daily from 9 a.m. to 5 p.m., and the museum and fort are open from 8 a.m. to 5 p.m. Admission: adults $7, college students and senior citizens $5, military plus guest free, children $4 (ages 6 to 12).

After seeing Fort Morgan you may want to board the Mobile Bay Ferry for a visit to *Fort Gaines* on Dauphin Island. The ferry transports passengers and vehicles between the two forts at 90-minute intervals. Call (251) 861-3000 for specific times and current rates.

History buffs will get a charge out of exploring the *Fort Gaines Historic Site* (251-861-6992) at the eastern end of Bienville Boulevard. To learn more about this Renaissance-style fort that dates to 1821 or Dauphin Island's public parks, beaches, and campgrounds, check out dauphinisland.org. By the way, this barrier island is a birder's paradise.

Memorable Battle Order Given at Fort Gaines

As the first light of dawn streaks the sky, a fleet of ships steams slowly toward the coast of Alabama. It's August 5, 1864, and the eighteen Union ships led by Rear Admiral David Glasgow Farragut aim to get past Fort Gaines into Mobile Bay.

But Confederate defenders of the fort have other ideas.

At 7:30 a.m., as cannon fire reaches a crescendo, the leading Union monitor, the USS *Tecumseh*, strikes a mine—known as a torpedo during the Civil War. The *Tecumseh* sinks within a minute, taking most of the 100 crewmembers with her.

The sudden disaster throws the Union fleet into confusion, causing it to hesitate under the guns of Fort Gaines. At this critical moment, Farragut gives his famous order, "Damn the torpedoes, full speed ahead!"

The rallying cry pushes the remaining vessels past the fort, through the minefield and into Mobile Bay.

"Fort Gaines and Fort Morgan were very important because Mobile was the last supply port for the Confederacy," said park ranger Mark Lyman.

Fort Gaines withstood the Union army and navy bombardment for three days. "But on August 8, 1864, the Confederates at Fort Gaines surrendered," Lyman said. "And the rest is history."

Located on the east end of Dauphin Island, the fort was named for General Edmund Pendleton Gaines, who died in 1849. Gaines won fame for his tenacious defense of Fort Erie on the Niagara River during the War of 1812.

Opened to the public in 1995, Fort Gaines is one of two mirror-image fortifications in the shape of stars in Mobile Bay. Fort Gaines is on Dauphin Island; Fort Morgan is on the peninsula. The two brick structures were the sentries that once protected Mobile and its bay from the enemy-laden seas of the Gulf of Mexico.

Today, visitors can see the actual cannons used in the Battle of Mobile Bay, as well as the huge anchor of Admiral Farragut's flagship, the USS *Hartford*.

"That is all that's left of the *Hartford*," Lyman said. "We're lucky to have it. They waited too long to try and salvage the rest of the ship."

Rooms in the fort are excellent examples of brick mason skills. Accessed by long tunnels from the courtyard or spiral stone staircases to the cannons above, the vaulted brick ceilings are impressive. Even more striking are the small munitions rooms at the end with brick walls lacking straight angles and appearing more like the flowing hull of a ship.

Visitors can see the original kitchen, bakery, and blacksmith shop. A blacksmith often is at work, and some of the items created are for sale in the gift shop—iron triangle dinner bells, candleholders, nails and copper flowers.

Preparing to give a rifle demonstration, Lyman explained that the bayonet on a rifle was an important tool. The goal of an experienced soldier was to wound his enemy, Lyman said, not to kill him.

"All in all," Lyman concluded, "more men were killed from disease and infection in the Civil War than from bullets."

You can also reach **Dauphin Island** via State Route 193 South, which peels off I-10 south of Mobile. So set your GPS and go.

At the **Estuarium at the Dauphin Island Sea Lab** (102 Bienville Boulevard on Dauphin Island; 251-861-7500; disl.org), visitors are invited to get up close with the denizens of the deep. At the Touch Table, treasures from the sea are spread out to touch while a guide explains about the preserved specimens. A magnifying camera projects enlarged images of minute details of the estuary life on an overhead screen.

Nestled on the waters of Mobile Bay on Dauphin Island, the Estuarium has been educating and entertaining guests since March 1998. The Mobile Bay Estuary is the fourth largest estuary system by volume in North America. A visit to the Estuarium is an in-depth journey through the native ecosystems of Mobile Bay and its surroundings waters. You can amble along the Living Marsh Boardwalk and watch pelicans drift lazily by or herons stalking their prey. You can meet "Mr. Sand" on the Boardwalk. A cartoon character, he explains the process of coastal erosion and the impact of hurricanes and what we can do to save the dunes.

A film called "A World of Water" is a good way to start a visit. Then you can enter the exhibit hall and journey the same path that water travels through the rivers—starting at the swamps of the Delta, to the waters of Mobile Bay, to the sands of the Barrier Islands, and finally, go the depths of the Gulf of Mexico.

Using thirty-one aquariums, the Estuarium offers a fascinating glimpse of an underwater world. Drawing plenty of oohs and aahs, the Gulf of Mexico exhibit features a 16,000-gallon Gulf tank showcasing the hard bottom community discovered off Alabama's coast in the mid-1980s. The largest Delta tank is an above- and below-water representation of the habitat. You can see turtles basking on logs and ancient gar peeking through the cypress roots. Children are mesmerized by the carnivorous bog tank and baby alligator habitat.

The Gulf produces almost half of all the seafood in the nation. Its ports are among the largest in the United States. Up to 95 percent of the commercial seafood of the Gulf depend upon the estuaries for food and protection during some part of their life cycle. Sharks, rays, snapper, grouper, jacks, and many more fish glide through the waters of the Gulf. Other Gulf aquariums feature octopus, lobster, and schooling fish.

The Mobile Bay area exhibit features the 9,000-gallon Bay tank with rock jetties, oyster reefs, and replica of the legs of the Middle Bay Lighthouse, a historic landmark in Mobile Bay since 1887. Other tanks represent salt marshes, tidal pools and submerged grass beds found in Mobile Bay.

Learn about the destructive force of hurricanes in the Barrier Islands Gallery or duck into the Billy Goat Hole Room to play on the computer or guess what's aboard the Discovery Ship, an interactive hideaway. For the latest weather, check out the up-to-date monitoring station. And save time for the Estuarium Gift Shop, one of the best in the area with everything from a pewter serving dish to a colorful book on marine life.

The sea lab is open Mon through Sat from 9 a.m. to 5 p.m., and Sun 1 to 5 p.m. (Sept through Feb). From March 1 through August, Mon through Sat hours are 9 a.m. to 6 p.m.; Sun noon to 6 p.m. Admission is adults $11, $9 seniors, $6 children (ages 5 to 18).

Don't miss nearby **Bellingrath Gardens and Home** (251-973-2217 or 800-247-8420), located at Theodore about twenty miles southwest of Mobile at 12401 Bellingrath Gardens Road. Once a simple fishing camp, the 65-acre wonderland lures visitors year-round. Because of south Alabama's climate, you can expect gorgeous displays of blossoms here, whatever the season. Upon arrival you'll receive a map illustrating the layout of the six gardens linked by bridges, walkways, streams, lakes, and lily-filled ponds. (Be sure to wear your walking shoes.)

alabamatrivia

Mobile is Alabama's oldest city.

After exploring the gardens you may want to tour the former home of Bessie and Walter Bellingrath (he was an early Coca-Cola executive). The house contains outstanding collections of Dresden china, Meissen figurines, and antique furnishings. The world's largest public exhibit of porcelain sculptures by Edward Marshall Boehm is on display in the visitors lounge. Separate admission fees for gardens and home: adults $21 for both or $13 for gardens only; children (ages 5 to 12) $13 for both or $7.50 for gardens only. The gardens are open daily from 8 a.m. to 5 p.m. Home tours are from 9 a.m. to 3:30 p.m. Visit Bellingrath.org to see what's in bloom.

Enjoy a sightseeing tour down the Fowl River or opt for a weekend dinner cruise. For more information call **Alabama Cruises** (251) 973-1244 or check out alabamacruises.com.

Save plenty of time for **Mobile** (cityofmobile.org), a city famous for its magnificent live oaks, some reputed to be more than 400 years old. Trimmed in silvery Spanish moss, the enormous trees spread their branching canopies over city streets. Always magical, Mobile is especially so during spring in late March and early April, when masses of azaleas explode into vibrant pinks, reds, and magentas, making the Church Street area, DeTonti Square, Oakleigh Garden, Spring Hill, and other historic districts more beautiful than ever. March is the month to view the azaleas at their vibrant peak. During the annual **Azalea Trail Festival**, you can follow the signs along a 56-mile route that winds past lovely homes ranging in style from Greek revival and Italianate to Southern Creole. (Mobile's own "Creole cottage," adapted for the local climate, evolved from the French colonial form.)

Be sure to stop by **The Fort of Colonial Mobile** (251-208-7304; colonialmobile.com) also known as Fort Conde at 150 Royal Street, for some background on Alabama's oldest city. Mobile has been governed by France, England, Spain, the Republic of Alabama, the Confederate States of America, and the US. Built in 1711, Fort Condé was once home base for the sprawling French Louisiana territory, and a re-created version now serves as a living-history museum. Soldiers in period French uniforms greet visitors, guiding them through the complex with its thick walls and low-slung doors.

On special occasions, costumed guides set the early scene for visitors and may even fire a cannon in the courtyard. Displays and dioramas tell the city's story. You'll see military furnishings typical of the times, a barracks room, jail cell, photography exhibits, and artifacts such as china and pottery shards, brass buckles, buttons, porcelain and bisque doll parts, dice, and gun barrels. Hours are 10 a.m. to 5 p.m. daily. Admission fees are $8 for adults and $5 for children.

For a breakfast you won't forget, stop by **Spot of Tea** (251-433-9009; spotoftea.com) at 310 Dauphin Street, across from Cathedral Square. Now celebrating more than a decade of business, the restaurant offers much more than breakfast and tea. The property features an inviting sidewalk cafe, lovely gift shop, Victorian dining room, private Victorian Tea Room, and New Orleans–style carriageway. Spot of Tea also offers Segway tours, a guided tour that runs about a 2-mile loop around downtown Mobile.

Quench your thirst with the award-winning strawberry iced tea. Breakfast/lunch, served seven days a week, offers items such as bananas Foster French toast and banana waffles, as well as the signature breakfast choice, eggs cathedral (an English muffin topped with a crab cake, eggs, and seafood sauce). Omelets, pancakes, eggs Benedict, soups, sandwiches, and salads are all included on the extensive menu. Hours are Mon through Fri 7 a.m. to 2 p.m.; Sat and Sun 7 a.m. to 3 p.m. Economical to moderate.

Phoenix Fire Department Protected Historic Mobile

The threat of fire hung over the young city like the Spanish moss that drapes her live oaks. Three times Mobile burned almost to the ground. Historic photos showcase areas where there was nothing left but chimneys and steps.

It's no wonder then that Mobile has one of the nation's oldest volunteer fire departments. And it shares the history of those firefighters in the *Phoenix Fire Museum*.

Built in 1859, the old home of Phoenix Volunteer Fire Company No. 6 was standing in the road of progress when Mobile's civic center was built. Instead of demolishing the beautiful brick building, however, the city moved it several blocks away to its new location at 203 South Claiborne Street.

The building was taken down board by board, brick by brick and moved to its new home as a museum. The free museum opened its doors to the public in 1964 and has welcomed visitors from around the world.

The building houses an interesting collection of authentic turn-of-the-century steam engines as well as other firefighting equipment and mementos. One of the most unusual items is two steamers bought in 1900 with consecutive serial numbers. The steamers are in very good condition and the fire museum may be the only place in the nation that has two like that.

From 1819 to 1888, Mobile firefighters were organized into all volunteer companies, whose service was a badge of honor. The first volunteer fire department of Mobile was a loosely formed group of volunteers. In 1818, five years after Mobile became part of the United States, it had only one piece of equipment—a small hand pumper imported from Boston.

When another pumper was brought to town in 1819, a decision was made to formally organize two fire companies. One of these was Creole No. 1. The other was Neptune No. 2. Together, these companies fought a large fire in August 1820 that destroyed thirty houses and many stores. They also fought a major fire in October 1827 that destroyed 169 structures.

In 1965, Mobile was hit hard again when a Civil War ammunition dump blew up and burned most of the north end of town. Buildings in early Mobile were composed primarily of wood with wooden shingle roofs so fire spread easily.

Mobile's first firefighters were volunteers from all walks of life. Membership in the companies was a special privilege and an important civic duty. Election to member-ship brought honor and respect from the community and a special social standing. It also demanded considerable sacrifice—volunteers had to be available at all times, every day to respond to a fire.

Their duties were combined with an active social life that included competitions, parades, and festive balls. The fireman's ball was the big social event of the year. The firemen parades were even bigger than the Mardi Gras.

In 1888, the companies were municipalized into a professional department, the seventh oldest in the country. Mobile now has nineteen fire companies with almost 500 paid firefighters.

At the museum, visitors can see the rich history of Mobile firefighting. On display are steam engines, hand pumpers, photos, journals, news clipping, extinguisher grenades, fire poles, helmets, belts, uniforms, and much more.

The Phoenix Fire Museum is open Mon through Thurs 9 a.m. to 5 p.m.; Fri 9 a.m. to noon. Admission is free. For more information, call (251) 208-7508 or visit historymuseumofmobile.com/phoenix-fire-department.

Take a tour of the Lower Dauphin Street Area (LoDa) and follow your nose to the **A&M Peanut Shop** at 209 Dauphin Street (251-438-9374; ampeanuts.com) with its freshly roasted nuts, served warm from a 90-year-old roaster. The shop is open Mon through Thurs 9 a.m. to 6 p.m.; Fri and Sat 9 a.m. to 8:30 pm.; Sun 11 a.m. to 5 p.m.

Then saunter into **Three Georges Candy & The Nuthouse** (251-433-1689; 3georges.com) at 226 Dauphin Street, a spot that has lured locals and visitors since 1917. Marble-based cases and original glass candy jars hold hand-dipped chocolates, pralines, divinity, and many varieties of fudge plus a rainbow assortment of jelly beans and rock candy. Hours are Mon through Sat 9:30 a.m. to 6 p.m.; Sun noon to 4 p.m.

When hunger pangs hit again, head for **Wintzell's Oyster House** (251-432-4605), which dates to 1938 at its historic downtown address, 605 Dauphin Street. Wintzell's also offers its fried, stewed, and nude delicacies at other nearby locations as well as in Guntersville in the state's northeastern section.

"He was a bold man that first ate an oyster," wrote Jonathan Swift, the eighteenth-century satirist. If you're bold and enjoy oysters enough to attempt breaking the current consumption record—280 for women and 421 for men—declare your intentions at any of Wintzell's locations. The staff will then alert the restaurant's suppliers if you look like a serious contender. You have one hour, while seated at the bar, to consume oysters on the half shell. If you set a new record, your feast is free, and you receive a check for $25. Otherwise, well, you would have had to pay anyway.

If you prefer your oysters not nude, then order them steamed, fried, or in stew. Other delectable versions include oysters Rockefeller, Bienville, Buffalo, Monterey, Alfredo, and Parmesan. Try the yummy gumbo while reading Wintzell's signs (on life in general) as you dine. Hours at all locations are Sun through Thurs 11 a.m. to 10 p.m.; Fri and Sat 11 a.m. to 11 p.m. Slither to wintzellsoysterhouse.com for more pearls of wisdom on these bivalves.

At the William and Emily Hearin *Mobile Carnival Museum* (251-432-3324; mobilecarnivalmuseum.com), you can dip into the magical world of Mardi Gras. You can't miss it. Look for an 1870 Italianate townhouse at 355 Government Street with two colorful 10-foot-tall jesters on the front porch.

Mobilians celebrated America's first Mardi Gras in 1703, and you'll get a great overview here, surrounded by a glittering array of memorabilia. You'll encounter a fire-breathing dragon float in the den (former carriage house) and can climb aboard the rocking float to enjoy a rollicking good time.

Volunteer guides, some affiliated with Mobile's mystic societies, share fascinating anecdotes with visitors. Exhibits showcase elaborate gowns with their flowing trains. These creations reflect intricate workmanship, and countless hours go into their construction. According to *National Geographic*, Mobile's coronations rival those of real coronations in Europe. Today's Mardi Gras festivities, which extend over a two-month period (with preparations going on around the calendar), feature many spectacular parades and magnificent balls. At last count thirty-two parading organizations and fifty-five non-parading organizations staged balls during the Mardi Gras season. Museum open Mon, Wed, Fri, and Sat from 9 a.m. to 4 p.m. Open every other Thurs 9 a.m. to 4 p. Admission: adults $8, military, students and seniors $6, children (age 12 and under) $3.

Look for the *Malaga Inn* (251-438-4701 or 800-235-1586; malagainn.com) at 359 Church Street. A charming place to make your base, this quaint hotel started out as twin townhouses in 1862—the families of sisters shared a patio between their mirror-image houses. In 1967 the historic structures were joined by a connector and converted into a hotel with thirty-nine inns and suites, each individually decorated.

Individually decorated rooms and suites are furnished with antiques or nostalgic reproductions. You'll enjoy relaxing in the inn's garden courtyard with its flowing fountain, umbrella-topped tables, and surrounding galleries of ornamental ironwork. The inn serves a deluxe continental breakfast. Guests also are served spiced tea and cookies. Rates range from standard to moderate.

Several mansions, including the *Richards-DAR House Museum* (251-208-7320; richardsdarhouse.com), open their doors to the public not only during spring tours but throughout the year. Located at 256 North Joachim Street in DeTonti Square, this 1860 Italianate antebellum home is noted for its "frozen lace" ironwork that decorates the facade in an elaborate pattern. Be sure to notice the etched ruby Bohemian glass framing the entrance. Other fine features include a suspended staircase, Carrara marble mantels, and striking brass and crystal chandeliers signed by Cornelius. In the rear wing you'll find a gift shop. Except for major holidays, the home, operated by the Daughters

America's First Mardi Gras

After surviving a deadly scourge of yellow fever, a colony of French soldiers in Mobile decided to celebrate life. Painting their faces red, they feasted and drank. There is no historical record that they paraded. But this festive gathering has gone down in history as the first Mardi Gras celebration in America, a century before Alabama became a state. Today, it remains an important part of Alabama Gulf Coast culture.

It was not until years later, in 1830, that the parade part became popular in Mobile. On New Year's Day, a cotton broker named Michael Krafft and some of his friends gathered up some cowbells, rakes, and hoes in a local hardware store. They then proceeded to march through the streets of Mobile and called themselves the Cowbellion de Rakin Society.

They liked it so much that the Cowbellions decided to have an annual event tied into Mardi Gras. Some of this partying group carried their customs to New Orleans. In 1857 the Cowbellion de Rakins assisted the Big Easy in setting up a mystic society of its own, the Mystic Krewe of Comus, to this day New Orleans's most prestigious Mardi Gras society.

Mobile festivities grew until the Civil War, when celebrations were put aside. Even after the war, Mobile was under Union occupation and no one felt like partying. That's when Joseph Stillwell Cain decided that people needed to be happy and he was going to do something about it. On Shrove Tuesday in 1866, town clerk Cain dressed up in Indian regalia, called himself "Chief Slacabormorinico," and climbed aboard a coal wagon he had decorated. The defiant Cain rode his mule-powered one-float parade through the streets of Mobile, and single-handedly brought about the rebirth of Mardi Gras festivities to the depressed city.

By the time Cain died at age 72, he had founded a number of mystic societies, including the well-known Order of Myths. In Mobile's historic Church Street Cemetery, Cain's tombstone notes: "Here lies Joe Cain, the heart and soul of Mardi Gras in Mobile."

Every year on the Sunday before Mardi Gras, the Joe Cain Parade pays honor to the rebel. A "people's parade," the Joe Cain Parade is not filled with big floats. Instead, it is a time to decorate a jalopy, wagon, wheelbarrow, or bicycle and join the parade. Of course, there are always plenty of "Cain's widows" in the processional, weeping and wailing for their man.

of the American Revolution, is open Mon and Wed through Fri from 11 a.m. to 3:30 p.m.; Sat 10 a.m. to 4 p.m.; Sun 1 to 4 p.m. Admission: adults $10, children (ages 5 to 11) $5.

You may also want to tour the *Oakleigh Historic Complex* (251-432-1281; historicoakleigh.com) in its serene oak-shaded setting at 300 Oakleigh Place. President James Garfield sipped his first mint julep at Oakleigh, the

Oakleigh's Ghost

But the antebellum mansion has still another claim to fame—a ghost is said to walk its halls, the spirit of former resident Miss Daisy. Southern tradition is alive with good-spirited ghost tales. And Oakleigh is no exception.

"Rumor has it that lights occasionally come on at night in the house and furniture is moved about," our tour guide said. "While I cannot substantiate that these things happen without human action, I do know that there are those among our guides and visitors who are convinced ghosts inhabit Oakleigh. When things go bump without explanation," she added, "We like to say Miss Daisy is responsible."

But the spookiest incident happened several decades ago when plans were being made for the annual candlelight Christmas celebration at Oakleigh. A photographer for the local newspaper came to take photos of two chairmen talking about the event. The two were seated in front of a big window at Oakleigh. When the picture appeared in the paper, there was an image of a lady in a long white dress in the window. The image looked very much like a photograph of Miss Daisy.

Miss Daisy Irwin Clisby was the last member of the Irwin family to reside in Oakleigh around the turn of the century. Daisy loved her Alabama home. "If her ghost really is here, I think it's because she was happiest at Oakleigh," the guide said. "She doesn't want to hurt anyone. She just wants to keep an eye on the home she loved."

historic home that has long been referred to as "the most photographed house in Mobile." The guides dress in authentic costumes of the 1830s to conduct tours through an 1833 antebellum house/museum filled with early Victorian, Empire, and Regency furnishings. Open Mon, Tues and Thurs through Sat from 10 a.m. to 4 p.m. Admission: adults $10.

The mansion was built in the 1830s by James W. Roper, a Mobile merchant who had come to the city from South Carolina. The Oakleigh mansion was intended to be the home of Roper and wife, but Mrs. Roper did not live to see the mansion completed. She died in childbirth in April 1832. Her infant daughter died six months and six days later. However, the great loss did not deter Roper from completing the dream home. He was a gifted man with a sufficient knowledge of architecture and construction to plan and supervise the building himself. Work began in 1833 and was completed sometime in 1838.

In 1838, Roper brought his second wife to share his beautiful Oakleigh. He chose that name for his home because of the grove of large oaks that surrounded it. But Roper and his bride did not get to enjoy their happiness for long. Roper was caught in a great financial panic that lasted for several years. He had borrowed $20,000 on a mortgage, using Oakleigh and nine acres of land as security. In 1840, Roper had to let the bank claim his property because he could not pay. He and his wife left Mobile to try and start anew somewhere else.

Alfred Irwin became the next owner of Oakleigh for the sum of $4,525. The mansion remained in the Irwin family for over sixty-five years. Oakleigh changed hands four more times before it was sold to the city of Mobile in 1955. Listed on the National Register of Historic Places, Oakleigh has been named Mobile's Official Period House Museum and is managed by the Historic Mobile Preservation Society.

Nestled under a canopy of luxurious oaks in the heart of an historic garden district, the Oakleigh Historic Complex features costumed guides who lead visitors on tours just as gracious hostesses did when cotton was king and Oakleigh was the center of social activity. Oakleigh is beautifully furnished with antiques, arts collections, and personal items such as jewelry, china, sculpture, toys, fans, books, eyeglasses, and even a humidor that once belonged to Father Abram Ryan, the "Poet-Priest of the South." Kitchen exhibits include a corn mortar with wooden pestle used by local cooks to grind corn, a cypress cupboard, pie safe, beaten biscuit assembly, and collection of primitive flat irons.

Historic Oakleigh is open 10 a.m. to 4 p.m. daily except Wed and Sun. Admission is $10 for adults.

To dip into more of the city's past, make reservations at the ***The Kate Shepard House Bed & Breakfast*** (251-479-7048) in the heart of historic Dauphin Way. Located at 1552 Monterey Place, this handsome Queen Anne Victorian home is listed on the National Register of Historic Places. Built by C. M. Shepard in 1897, it was designed by well-known architect George Franklin Barber.

Shepard's daughters, Kate and Isabel, operated a private boarding and day school here during the early 1900s. Wendy, who continues to research the home's history, filled several glass-front cases with school memorabilia and framed several photos from that era. Moderate to deluxe rates. For more information, visit kateshepherdhouse.com.

"Guests can pull into the driveway and park under the porte cochere," says Wendy James, who with her husband, Bill, owns the home. "We have a dog that will bark loudly when you arrive, but will be your best friend in minutes." The couple, who lived in Hawaii for almost fifteen years, searched the southeast for the perfect historic house and setting to establish their long-planned bed-and-breakfast. Captivating Mobile and this lovely home, surrounded by century-old magnolia trees, won their hearts. Along with eleven fireplaces, four original stained glass windows, and beautiful woodwork, the home came with a surprise—an attic full of treasures. Wendy shares stories regarding this lagniappe (something extra) with her guests.

To launch a kayak or canoe outing through the country's second largest river delta, head to Spanish Fort, about five miles from downtown Mobile. *Five Rivers Delta Resource Center* (251-625-0814) marks the spot where the Mobile, Spanish, Tensaw, Apalachee, and Blakeley Rivers converge in Mobile Bay. Here, you can immerse yourself in the area's natural beauty, learn about its history, and set off on an adventure through scenic waterways, woods, and wetlands.

Swing by the *Nature Center Complex*, a trio of pilesupported buildings with wraparound porches and decks, overlooking the Delta. A favorite with visitors, the exhibit hall showcases some of the state's wildlife. You'll also find information on other nature-based attractions in this coastal area: Blakeley State Park, Dauphin Island Estuarium, Gulf State Park, and Weeks Bay Reserve.

Special Saturday programs offer canoe and kayak lessons, wilderness survival training, cooking demonstrations, and more. Located across from Meaher State Park on the Mobile Bay Causeway (US 90/98) at 30945 Five Rivers Boulevard, the center is open daily from 8 a.m. to 5 p.m.

No visit to the Port City would be complete without scaling the decks of the *Battleship USS* **Alabama** (251-433-2703), moored in Mobile Bay. This

Mobile's Changing Skyline

Mobile's downtown renaissance continues with a skyline that looks very different—just as it did when construction on Alabama's first skyscraper started here a century ago. Looming above its neighbors, the impressive *RSA Battle House Tower* can be seen for thirty miles—all the way up Mobile Bay. So again this city on the move boasts the state's tallest structure—a 40-story tower that stretches skyward. Companion to the historic, rejuvenated *Battle House Renaissance Mobile Hotel & Spa*, the pair represents a fusion of past and present.

Once again, the Battle House dispenses classic Southern hospitality, which translates to plenty of pampering. Don't pass up a chance to unwind in the spa. Then dine on divine regional and continental specialties in the *Trellis Room*. The historic hotel is connected to the new RSA Battle House Tower by the 9,628-square-foot Moonlight Ballroom.

With its grand staircase (plus the whispering arches that heard goodness knows how many secrets), the Battle House served as the setting for countless debutante balls. Besides presiding over the social scene in downtown Mobile for a century, this iconic hotel played host to such American statesmen as Woodrow Wilson and Confederate president Jefferson Davis. The hotel's historic roots date back to 1852. For more information on the Battle House, a Renaissance Hotel & Spa, at 26 North Royal Street in downtown Mobile, call (251) 338-2000 or (866) 316-5957.

renowned vessel played the role of the USS *Missouri* in the movie *Under Siege*, starring Steven Seagal. Now the focal point of the 155-acre park on Battleship Parkway just off the I-10 causeway, the USS *Alabama* rode out hurricanes Camille, Frederick, and Ivan, but Katrina slammed in with a 12-foot storm surge and triple-digit winds, tilting the ship by eight degrees.

Setting a structure of this magnitude—half the length of the Empire State Building's height—upright presented quite a challenge. Waves swept over the ship's bow, 30 feet above sea level. As for the park's Aircraft Exhibit Pavilion, hurricane winds lifted and dropped military tanks and artillery exhibits, scattering parts across the grounds and severely damaging fourteen planes. After $6 million in restoration costs, the iconic USS *Alabama*, the submarine **USS Drum** (which received no storm damage), and a new pavilion reopened to the public. Anchored beside the battleship, the USS *Drum* gives visitors a chance to thread their way through a submarine and marvel at how a crew of seventy-two men could live, run their ship, and fire torpedoes while confined to such tight quarters.

Open every day except Christmas, the park can be visited Apr through Sept from 8 a.m. to 6 p.m.; Oct through Mar from 8 a.m. to 5 p.m. Admission: adults $15, senior citizens $13, active or retired military free, children (ages 6 to 11) $6. For more information, check out ussalabama.com.

USS *Alabama* Saved From Scrapheap to Honor Veterans

For more than three and a half years, Bob Feller called the narrow metal bunk his home. With scarcely enough room to move his lanky frame, Feller probably spent countless nights dreaming of his family and the Iowa farm where he was born.

A record-breaking baseball pitcher for the Cleveland Indians, Feller also might have pondered what his future could have held if not for World War II. Two days after Japan attacked Pearl Harbor, Feller joined the Navy. Upon his enlistment at age twenty-two, Feller was at the peak of his career—he had 109 Major League victories, by far the most-ever record in Major League history by a pitcher at age 22.

During the forty-four months he was in the Navy, Feller spent most of that time stationed on the USS *Alabama* in the gunnery department. He gained eight battle stars. Stories such as Feller's are brought home with sudden impact to visitors aboard the USS *Alabama*, now moored at Mobile.

The battleship, like so many others, is almost tangibly serene. A warm sun shines and the bay has scarcely a ripple on this cloudless day. Visitors walk the decks and cabins in respectful silence, as if entering a church. They read the historic papers and scan the old photographs and try to imagine what it was like.

But it's impossible to envision the roaring thunder and smoke, the ear-shattering shouting and scrambling, the unspeakable horror and death that happened on the USS *Alabama*, not once but throughout thirty-seven months of active duty.

She earned not only nine battle stars but also the nickname "Lucky A" from her crew of 2,500 because she emerged unscathed from the heat of each battle. The *Alabama* saw action in the Atlantic for a year before joining the Pacific Fleet in mid-1943. There she fought at such key locations as Leyte, the Gilbert Islands, and Okinawa. The *Alabama* served in every major engagement in the Pacific during World War II.

After the signing of the war-ending surrender documents in September 1945, the "Mighty A" led the American Fleet into Tokyo Bay. Less than twenty years later, the beloved battleship was headed for the scrap heap. A small group of Alabama people were dismayed to read a short Associated Press report on May 1, 1962, that four battleships were to be destroyed—the *Alabama*, the *South Dakota BB57*, the *Indiana BB58*, and the *Massachusetts BB59*.

The group sprang into action. In a matter of months, they had raised $1 million, including over $100,000 that came from Alabama school children. The USS *Alabama* was saved, as was the USS *Massachusetts*, which now rests in Fall River, Massachusetts. The other two battleships were scrapped.

It took three months for the *Alabama* to travel from Bremerton, Washington, to Mobile Bay. It is the longest ton/mile tow in history. The 35,000-ton *Alabama* was towed 5,600 miles, barely squeaking through the Panama Canal. The ship is 108 feet and 2-inches wide. The Panama Canal is 110 feet wide in some places. It was only by a razor's edge that the *Alabama* made it.

The *Alabama* rounded the bay into Mobile in the summer of '64. She was opened to the public on January 9, 1965—eighteen years to the day after she was decommissioned—as a non-tax-supported project. Since then, the *Alabama* and the surrounding 100-acre Battleship Memorial Park have attracted millions of visitors.

Visitors can explore below and upper decks and roam through the captain's cabins, officers' staterooms, messing and berthing space, and crew's galley. Authentic touches include calendar girl pinups and background music, with such singers as Bing Crosby and Frank Sinatra crooning songs popular during the 1940s.

Visitors can see museum displays and hear first-hand the remembrances of crew members who served aboard the *Alabama*. A continuous running film showcases the recollections—some humorous, many poignant and painful—of the crew. The interviews are interspersed with startling footage of aircraft attacks.

A tiny bunk is designated with a plaque, "Bob Feller Slept Here." After the war ended, "Bullet Bob" Feller returned to the Cleveland Indians, became an All-State pitcher again and is honored in the Baseball Hall of Fame. Fellow players said the war veteran never complained about enlisting and giving so many years of his life to protect his beloved country instead of staying home and having more chances to win more Major League games.

Places to Stay in Southwest Alabama

CAMDEN

Liberty Hall Bed & Breakfast
627 Highway 221
(334) 412-3513
libertyhallbandb.com

Roland Cooper State Park
285 Deer Run Dr.
(334) 682-4838
alapark.com/
roland-cooper-state-park

EUTAW

Everhope Plantation
11334 Alabama Hwy. 14
(205) 500-0780
everhopeplantation.com

FAIRHOPE

Bay Breeze Guest House
742 South Mobile St.
(866) 928-8976

Emma's Bay House
202 South Mobile St.
(251) 990-0187
emmasbayhouse.com

GULF SHORES/ ORANGE BEACH

The Beach Club
925 Beach Club Trail
(866) 627-1259
Thebeachclub.
spectrumresorts.com

Island House Hotel
26650 Perdido Beach Blvd.
(251) 981-6100 or
(800) 264-2642

Meyer Real Estate
(for resort rentals)
1585 Gulf Shores Pkwy.
(251) 968-7516 or
(800) 487-5959

Original Romar House Bed & Breakfast Inn
23500 Perdido Beach Blvd.
(251) 974-1625
theoriginalromarhouse.com

Perdido Beach Resort
27200 Perdido Beach Blvd.
(251) 981-9811 or
(800) 634-8001
perdidobeachresort.com

MAGNOLIA SPRINGS

Magnolia Springs Bed & Breakfast
14469 Oak St.
(251) 965-7321 or
(800) 965-7321
magnoliasprings.com

MARION

The Gateway Inn
1615 State Rte. 5 South
(334) 683-9166

MOBILE

The Battle House, a Renaissance Hotel & Spa
26 North Royal St.
(251) 338-2000

Holiday Inn
301 Government St.
(251) 694-0100 or
(800) 692-6662

The Kate Shepard House Bed & Breakfast
1552 Monterey Place
(251) 479-7048
kateshephardhouse.com

Malaga Inn 359 Church St.
(251) 438-4701 or
(800) 235-1586
malagainn.com

Mauvila Mansion
1306 Dauphin St.
(251) 408-9478

Renaissance Riverview Plaza Hotel
64 South Water St.
(251) 438-4000 or
(866) 749-6069

MONROEVILLE

Best Western Inn
4419 South Alabama Ave.
(251) 575-9999

Country Inn & Suites
120 Hwy. 21 South
(251) 743-3333

Mockingbird Inn
4389 South Alabama Ave.
(251) 743-3297
mockingbirdinn.com

POINT CLEAR

Grand Hotel Marriott Resort, Golf Club & Spa
One Grand Blvd.
(251) 928-9201 or
(800) 544-9933

SELMA

Hampton Inn
2200 West Highland Ave.
(334) 876-9995 or
(800) HAMPTON

Holiday Inn Express Hotel & Suites
2000 Lincoln Way
(334) 874-1000

Quality Inn
2420 North Broad St.
(334) 874-8600

FOR MORE INFORMATION ABOUT
SOUTHWEST ALABAMA

**Alabama Gulf Coast
Convention & Visitors Bureau**
23685 Perdido Beach Blvd.
Orange Beach 36561 or
PO Drawer 457
Gulf Shores 36547
(251) 974-1510 or (800) 982-8562
gulfshores.com info@gulfshores.com

Alabama's Front Porches
Official website of Rural Southwest
Alabama
alabamasfrontporches.org

**Demopolis Area Chamber of
Commerce**
102 East Washington St.
PO Box 667 Demopolis 36732
(334) 289-0270
demopolischamber.com

Eastern Shore Chamber of Commerce
327 Fairhope Ave. Fairhope 36532
(251) 928-6387
eschamber.com

Foley Welcome Center
104 N. McKenzie St. Foley 36535
(251) 943-1300
visitfoley.com

Gulf Shores Welcome Center
3459 Gulf Shores Pkwy.
(Alabama Highway 59 South)
Gulf Shores 36542
(251) 968-7511 or (800) 745-7263
gulfshores.com

**Mobile Bay Convention &
Visitors Bureau**
1 S. Water St.
PO Box 204 Mobile 36602
(251) 208-2000 or (800) 566-2453
mobile.org info@mobile.org

**Monroeville Area Chamber
of Commerce**
86 North Alabama Ave.
Monroeville 35460
(251) 743-2879
monroecountyal.com
info@monroecountyal.com

**Selma/Dallas County Chamber
of Commerce**
912 Selma Ave.
PO Box 467 Selma 36701
(334) 875-7241 or (800) 457-3562
SelmaAlabama.com
info@SelmaAlabama.com

MAINSTREAM ATTRACTIONS WORTH SEEING
IN SOUTHWEST ALABAMA

**Gulf Coast Exploreum, Science
Center, and IMAX Theater**
65 Government St. (at exit 26B off I-10),
Mobile
(251) 208-6873 or
(877) 625-4FUN
exploreum.com

Features fascinating exhibits from the
world of science, and that's not all.
Throngs of visitors find the permanent
galleries exciting with more than 150
hands-on science adventures—Healthy
Life Science Lab, Hands On Hall, the
Wharf of Wonder, and MyBodyWorks.
The center also hosts traveling exhibits.

History Museum of Mobile
111 South Royal St.
(251) 208-7569
historymuseumofmobile.com

This museum offers a treasure trove in a National Historic Landmark building that dates to 1857 and occupies a portion of the Southern Market/Old City Hall. From the entry's 1936 WPA murals depicting the history of Mobile to the hands-on Discovery Room and Special Collections Gallery, this museum offers something for all ages and interests. You'll see a dugout canoe from the fourteenth century, relive the atrocious passage on an African slave ship, hear stories of Civil War soldiers, and learn about disasters like hurricanes, yellow fever, and fires that have impacted the area. The Themes Gallery puts the spotlight on Hank Aaron, Satchel Paige, and other sports figures from this city, known as a "baseball mecca."

Mobile Museum of Art
4850 Museum Dr., Langan Park
(251) 208-5200
mobilemuseumofart.com

Established in 1964, the museum moved in 2002 from its former quarters on Civic Center Drive to its present setting at. The grand lobby's commanding glass entrance hall overlooks a lake and makes the outdoors seem part of a sweeping landscape. The handsome building is home to a permanent collection of more than 6,000 works of art, which span 2,000 years of cultural history, and is particularly strong in American paintings of the 1930s and 1940s plus works by Southern artists, art of the French Barbizon School, and contemporary American crafts.

Places to Eat in Southwest Alabama

CAMDEN

Gaines Ridge Dinner Club
933 State Rte. 10 East
(334) 682-9707

Hunters Run
40 Camden Bypass
(334) 682-5037

DAPHNE

Cousin Vinnie's/Guido's Italian Restaurant
1709 Main St.
(251) 626-6082

Pigeon Hole
1716 Main St., Ste. C
(251) 222-4120
pigeonholedaphne.com

DEMOPOLIS

The Red Barn
901 US 80 East
(334) 289-0595

FAIRHOPE

Sunset Pointe
831 N. Section St.
(251) 990-7766
sunsetpointefairhope.com

FAUNSDALE

Faunsdale Bar & Grill
35558 State Rte. 25
(334) 628-3240

FOLEY

The Gift Horse
209 West Laurel Ave.
(251) 943-3663

GULF SHORES/ ORANGE BEACH

Fish River Grill
1545 Gulf Shores Pkwy
(251) 948-1110
fishrivergrill.com

King Neptune's Seafood Restaurant
1137 Gulf Shores Pkwy
(251) 968-5464
kingneptunesseafood restaurant.com

Lulu's Gulf Shores
200 East 25th Ave.
(251) 967-5858
lulubuffett.com

Villaggio Grille
4790 Main St., F108
(251) 224-6510
villaggiogrille.com

LAVACA

Ezell's Fish Camp
776 Ezell Road
(205) 654-2205
Ezellsfishcamp.com

MAGNOLIA SPRINGS

Jesse's Restaurant
14770 Oak St.
(251) 965-3827
Jessesrestaurant.com

MOBILE

Noja
8 North Jackson St.
(251) 433-0377
nojamobile.com

Royal Scam
72 Royal St.
(251) 432-7226
royalscammobile.com

Spot of Tea
310 Dauphin St.
(251) 433-9009
spotoftea.com

The Trellis Room Battle House Hotel
26 North Royal St.
(251) 338-5493

Wintzell's Oyster House
605 Dauphin St.
(251) 432-4605
wintzellsoysterhouse.com

POINT CLEAR

The Wash House Restaurant
17111 Scenic Hwy. 98
(251) 928-4838
washhouserestaurant.com

SELMA

Lannie's Bar-B-Q Spot
2115 Minter Ave.
(334) 874-4478

Tally-Ho Restaurant
509 Mangum Ave.
(334) 872-1390
tallyhoselma.com

Index

About the Author

An award-winning journalist and photographer, **Jackie Sheckler Finch** has covered a wide array of topics—from birth to death, with all the joy and sorrow in between. She has written for numerous publications and is the editor of a nationally award-winning regional magazine. She is also the author of more than a dozen books and has been named the Mark Twain Travel Writer of the Year by the Midwest Travel Writers Association a record five times, in 1998, 2001, 2003, 2007, and 2012. She also belongs to the Society of American Travel Writers and the Midwest Travel Journalists Association. She shares her home with resident guard and entertainer, a rescued pooch named Pepper. One of her greatest joys is taking to the road to find the fascinating people and places that wait over the hill and around the next bend.